Stephen King

McFarland Literary Companions

Stephen King

A Literary Companion

ROCKY WOOD

McFarland Literary Companions, 11

McFarland & Company, Inc., Publishers
Jefferson, North Carolina, and London

ALSO OF INTEREST

Horrors: Great Stories of Fear and Their Creators,
written by Rocky Wood; illustrated by Glenn Chadbourne
(a graphic novel; McFarland, 2010)

LIBRARY OF CONGRESS CATALOGUING-IN-PUBLICATION DATA

Wood, Rocky.
Stephen King : a literary companion / Rocky Wood.
p.   cm. — (McFarland literary companions, 11)
Includes bibliographical references and index.

ISBN 978-0-7864-5850-9
(softcover : 50# alkaline paper) ∞

1. King, Stephen, 1947– — Criticism and interpretation.   I. Title.
PS3561.I483Z954   2011   813'.54 — dc22   2011005814

British Library cataloguing data are available

Front cover: Stephen King (ABC/Photofest);
background © 2011 Shutterstock

Manufactured in the United States of America

McFarland & Company, Inc., Publishers
Box 611, Jefferson, North Carolina 28640
www.mcfarlandpub.com

Table of Contents

Preface

Stephen King is one of the most famous and well read authors of all time. He has created tales we know well, such as *The Shining, 'Salem's Lot, The Stand, It* and *The Dead Zone*; some of the best-known fictional characters, such as Jack Torrance, Annie Wilkes, Carrie White and Cujo; and his works have been translated into some of the best-loved movies of all time — *The Shawshank Redemption, The Shining, Carrie,* and *Stand by Me*, to name a few. His readers are numbered in the tens of millions, and hundreds of millions more have seen movies based on his tales.

This is a companion to all things King, designed to help fans read and access Stephen King in many different ways. It's written by an unabashed fan (King lovingly calls us his "constant readers"), and written for movie-goers who queue for his latest offering; for comic book fans with standing orders for his adaptations; and for all those who wish they knew just a little bit more about what's behind each scary tale, each mythic character, each obscure small Maine town. King fans are a breed apart and this is their own private, secret, window into the King-dom. Hopefully there will be something in the pages that follow to surprise or inform even the most ardent Stephen King fan, from information about King's more obscure tales to little-known details about his books and characters.

The material is presented in two parts. An introduction to the works covers the broad sweep of Stephen King, his world and his work; the literary companion that follows allows the reader to delve into stories, characters, his many imaginary worlds and universes, themes, genres and adaptations. One note — this is not a biography, although many of the autobiographical aspects of King's work are included. This is a book about the stories, the characters and the worlds King has created and how they impact readers.

The Introduction also deals with some approaches to reading King and particularly considers the parts of King's body of work readers may have neglected to date, as well as ways to introduce others, such as young adults, to his tales. Next is a look at the linked worlds and stories King continues to deliberately create — his version of Maine, particularly Castle Rock and Derry; the peculiarly parallel world of *The Dark Tower*; and post-apocalyptic worlds, such as America after the super flu epidemic of *The Stand*.

Then follows a look at the silver screen and television adaptations of King's stories— many a King fan has never read his books but love the visual telling of the tale as much as hard-core readers love the written version. We'll explore their impact upon moviegoers and mainstream culture, and offer some advice on what movies to see, when to see them and why they merit one's attention.

While critical acceptance has been hard for King to garner in some circles, due to a judgmental predisposition to dismiss his work as "popular" writing and a bias against horror writing in general, in recent years King's work has been viewed in a more positive light by many critics and scholars. Some rate King along with such greats as Shakespeare, Dickens, Twain, Stevenson, Poe and Lovecraft, and a review of the importance of these seminal writers in relation to King will place his body of work in some context when considered alongside the fiction of past masters. The introductory section concludes with a look at what King himself describes as his magnum opus, his *Dark Tower* series of novels and short stories, as well as obscure references to the series in other tales.

The literary lompanion provides easy access to a myriad of interesting King material; presented in an encyclopedic, alphabetical arrangement. Included is an entry for each of King's fictional works, from novels to short stories and poetry. As an example, the entry for *Carrie* gives background about the novel's inspiration, when and how it was published, and sets the tale up for the reader to enjoy more thoroughly. What it does not do is spoil the story, yet it provides plenty of interesting background to ensure the reader is privy to more than a few secrets.

Other entries cover King's unpublished or uncollected fiction, outlining the stories and giving advice on how to find them; major characters, such as Carrie White (*Carrie*), John Coffey (*The Green Mile*), Roland Deschain (*The Dark Tower*), and even the infamous St. Bernard, Cujo; the key locations in King's universe, which have detailed entries, as do towns such as Jerusalem's Lot. Also included are entries on film, comic book and stage adaptations, with information specific to each while of interest relative to the whole of King's work.

The literary companion also features an abundance of fascinating facts and tidbits. Readers can focus on their particular interest, or use the information within to better understand a book or character, before, during or even after reading the relevant story or seeing the film. And that's really the purpose of the present work — to make the experience of exploring Stephen King's work, whatever the format, that much more enjoyable and interesting. Who inspired the character Carrie White? Where was the original Marsten House (of *'Salem's Lot* infamy)? On what famous book does King base *Bag of Bones*? What happened to *The Cannibals*, a book King wrote in the 1980s? Why does King bring back characters decades after their original appearances? And of course, what exactly is the secret to King's constant connection with his fans? All of this and more will be discussed within. With that, let's dive in the deep end of Runaround Pond (if you don't know it, see the entry) and the worlds and works of Stephen King.

Introduction to the Works

I don't believe any novelist, even one who's written forty-plus books, has too many thematic concerns; I have many interests, but only a few that are deep enough to power novels. These deep interests (I won't quite call them obsessions) include how difficult it is—perhaps impossible!—to close Pandora's technobox once it's open (*The Stand*, *The Tommyknockers*, *Firestarter*); the question of why, if there is a God, such terrible things happen (*The Stand*, *Desperation*, *The Green Mile*); the thin line between reality and fantasy (*The Dark Half*, *Bag of Bones*, *The Drawing of the Three*); and most of all, the terrible attraction violence sometimes has for fundamentally good people (*The Shining*, *The Dark Half*). I've also written again and again about the fundamental differences between children and adults, and about the healing power of the human imagination.

—Stephen King, *On Writing*

Reading Stephen King

Let's get this up front—Stephen King is not a horror writer. He writes of horror, the supernatural is often an overlay to his tale, but usually the horror King exposes is what we as individual humans will do to our fellows, if given the chance, or if put under certain pressures. Jack Torrance and the violence he visits upon his family under the influence of alcohol (perhaps combined with a haunting entity at the Overlook Hotel). Paul Edgecombe, trapped by the law and John Coffey's own nature. Annie Wilkes, insane and in control of her favorite author. Roland LeBay and Ace Merrill, petty thugs. Joe St. George and Norman Daniels, wife-beaters. John Rainbird, a psychopath with a license to kill. The list is endless but demonstrative of one fact—the deepest horror in King's fiction is that we all know people who act like these characters and others who would, given circumstance, opportunity or pressure.

If King is not a horror writer per se, then those who do not read him because they look down on the horror genre (or are genuinely scared by it) have many alternative ways to access his superb storytelling. A few of these alternate approaches are canvassed below.

Mainstream

It is often not well understood that King writes a lot of mainstream (i.e., non-genre) fiction. Apart from horror, some science fiction, fantasy, crime and mystery, he has, more

3

and more often in recent years, strayed into this area of storytelling, particularly with his short stories.

Some of this mainstream fiction is so powerful that it has been published in significant venues such as *The New Yorker* magazine. For those who dismiss King's genre offerings, the following tales will serve as excellent introduction to this corner of his fiction: "The Last Rung on the Ladder," "The Woman in the Room," "The Body," "Rita Hayworth and Shawshank Redemption," "My Pretty Pony," "Blind Willie," "Hearts in Atlantis," "All That You Love Will Be Carried Away," "Harvey's Dream," "The Death of Jack Hamilton," "Rest Stop," "Morality" and "Premium Harmony." A number of King's novels are close to mainstream (with some genre overlay), for instance *Dolores Claiborne*, *Gerald's Game* and *Rose Madder*.

Fantasy

Are you a fantasy fan? Do you love *The Lord of the Rings* or perhaps J.K. Rowling's Harry Potter novels; or did you, as a child, enjoy *The Chronicles of Narnia*? The fantasy genre is alive and well today through such authors as Terry Pratchett (the *Discworld* series), Robert Jordan (*The Wheel of Time* series), and Ursula K. Le Guin (the *Earthsea* novels).

King has made a major contribution to the fantasy genre with his Dark Tower cycle. Originally conceived partly as a riff on Tolkien's *The Lord of The Rings*, the Dark Tower cycle of seven novels, a novella and many connected works has the same epic quality as the best fantasy and, like many, is also a quest tale (in this case Roland Deschain searching for the physical Dark Tower, and possible redemption). In King's case he has merged significant components of the western, science fiction and horror genres with fantasy to create a unique blend.

So, for those who are strong fans of fantasy but don't consider themselves horror readers, the best place to start with King is definitely the Dark Tower universe. As many readers find the first book in the cycle—*The Dark Tower: The Gunslinger*—a dense and difficult read, two good starting places present themselves. One is the second book in the cycle—*The Dark Tower: The Drawing of the Three* (read through the fourth, *The Dark Tower: Wizard and Glass* before reverting to *The Gunslinger* and then complete the series from volume five, *The Dark Tower: Wolves of the Calla*). A second choice is to begin with a novella, "The Little of Sisters of Eluria." There readers discover the hero of the saga, Roland Deschain, and should become interested enough to want to learn more about him and his quest.

Another significant fantasy tale (and another quest) is *The Talisman* (written with Peter Straub). Like many fantasy sagas it does have a touch of the supernatural, but young Jack Sawyer's ability to flip into the Territories (where magic replaces science) and his adventures there will thrill most fantasy fans. Younger fantasy readers will enjoy *The Eyes of the Dragon*, a mythic tale set in the land of Delain.

Delving into King through fantasy should create a demand in the reader's mind for his broader work, although it is established there is a whole group of King readers who are Dark Tower fanatics and could care less if he ever wrote another horror or mainstream tale.

Horror Buffs Widening Their Horizons

Interestingly enough, some horror buffs have not read King's work. How could that be? There are many sub-genres of horror (particularly in recent years, zombies and vampires) and lately many readers (particularly young adults) have been attracted to such series fiction as Stephanie Meyer's *Twilight*, Charlaine Harris' Sookie Stackhouse books (filmed as *True Blood*), even J. K. Rowling's Harry Potter novels. Yet others have simply viewed King as too commercial and gained their love of the genre through H. P. Lovecraft's work, classic horror writers such as Edgar Allan Poe, or through a specific sub-genre such as splatterpunk or gay-oriented horror. There has also been a huge upsurge in so-called supernatural romance (by authors such as Heather Graham)—a sub-genre layering supernatural components over the standard romance formula—in recent years.

Equally, many horror buffs came to the genre via movies (*Saw*, *Hostel*, Romero's "Dead" zombie movies, or any of the slasher franchises, such as *I Know What You Did Last Summer* and *Halloween*, for instance), television (*Charmed*, *Buffy the Vampire Slayer* or even *Dexter*) and even gaming. Any of or all of these horror fans (although they may shy away from the label) have a veritable cornucopia of fiction to devour in King's output.

There are many channels into King's fiction, including his short stories (an underrated form of storytelling). Those who enjoy gothic novels or supernatural romance may wish to begin with *Bag of Bones* or *Rose Madder*. Zombie fans could begin with *Cell* or "Home Delivery." Vampire fans have the classic *'Salem's Lot*. Slasher fans will find plenty of mayhem in King tales such as *Cell*, *Under the Dome* or *Needful Things*. Fans of *Twilight* might enjoy "The Body," *The Talisman* or *The Girl Who Loved Tom Gordon*. Harry Potter fans might try *Eyes of the Dragon* or *The Dark Tower* cycle of novels and stories. King has written Lovecraftian works (for instance "Crouch End") and an homage to Poe ("The Old Dude's Ticker").

Young Adult

Stephen King does not believe in censorship. As a result many of his novels contain traps for young readers (sexual politics, violence, outright horror) and many parents will want to guide their children through an introduction to King's work. This will depend on the reader's maturity and reading ability.

King caters to young readers with some very specific tales, and these may also serve as a life-long springboard to a love of reading in general. The following stories are highly recommended for introducing young and young adult readers.

Eyes of the Dragon is set in the mythic land of Delain. King Roland is not the best or the worst king who had ever ruled there, and the problem in Delain is not the king, but rather his advisor, Flagg. Flagg realizes the king's elder son and heir to the throne, Peter, will not be easy to influence and that his younger brother, Thomas, is likely to do everything Flagg advises. Flagg poisons King Roland and frames Peter for the murder. Peter is sentenced to spend the remainder of his life in two small rooms at the top of a high tower. Determined to prove his innocence, the young prince plots his escape. King originally wrote this book for his daughter, at a time when she was a young adult who did not enjoy horror.

In *The Talisman*, Jack Sawyer is not yet 13 when his mother is struck low with cancer. His father is long dead, and he befriends Speedy Parker, a retired blues musician, who teaches him how to "flip" between our world and an alternate reality, the Territories, a land where magic serves in place of science. Speedy also tells him about the Talisman, which can save his mother's life. Flipping between the two worlds, Jack begins an epic journey to find the Talisman.

In *The Girl Who Loved Tom Gordon*, nine-year-old Trisha McFarland becomes lost while trekking part of the Appalachian Trail with her mother and brother. Disoriented, she walks away from civilization and any hope of rescue, deep into the uninhabited Maine woods. She has very little food and each night listens to baseball games on her Sony Walkman in the hope of picking up a Boston Red Sox game, in which perhaps her hero Tom Gordon will be pitching. As she slowly becomes delirious, "Tom Gordon" becomes her traveling companion, helping her overcome her fears. Despite this, Trisha is not out of the woods and realizes she is being followed by something, something she begins to think of as "The God of the Lost." King wrote this book with young readers in mind and it will particularly appeal to young girls.

Cycle of the Werewolf features a wheelchair-bound boy who confronts a supernatural creature in his town and is written in a style easily accessed by younger readers. "The Body" (filmed as *Stand By Me*) is another story that appeals to young males.

One interesting channel is to introduce the younger reader to *The Dark Tower*, *The Talisman* and *The Stand* graphic novel collections. As these are highly visual, they may be an easier access point for certain younger readers. Certainly, *The Dark Tower* graphic novels begin with late teenage characters and the storyline is not unusually difficult or confronting and is compelling.

Older and more sophisticated teenagers may enjoy *It*, which features a group of youngsters standing up to Pennywise and his evil, but parents should note there is one particularly confrontational sexual scene. The American Library Association Best Books for Young Adults includes both *'Salem's Lot* and *Firestarter*.

Library Access

All libraries will carry King, although a very small number have actually banned certain titles (*Rage* for instance, or even less likely titles such as *'Salem's Lot*). Depending on the reader's age, most titles will be available either at a branch, or perhaps through interlibrary loan. As King is particularly popular, readers may have to reserve a title and wait for it to come back into circulation (this is especially the case for King's new titles as they are published).

The Stephen and Tabitha King Foundation has given very large sums of money to libraries throughout America to assist in building facilities and to fund literacy programs and book purchases. Books are a relatively cheap form of entertainment, and borrowing a book from a library is cheaper than purchasing one. Armed with a list of King's titles, a reader can get years of reading pleasure for literally nothing.

Those Who've Read It All (But Actually Haven't)

Many King readers believe they have read all he has ever published, with this misconception based on having purchased every mainstream book from *Carrie* to *Full Dark, No Stars*. However, this may not include a couple of obscure stand-alone titles—*Blockade Billy* and *The Colorado Kid*, or the Bachman books.

They may not have read stories King has published but not collected—from "The Glass Floor" and "Night of the Tiger" right through to tales published since 2009, which have yet to be collected. A diligent search through the pages of this work, and on the internet, will reveal a list of these stories for compulsive King readers to track down and enjoy. Separate entries in this volume advise readers how best to find these obscure pieces.

Another Method (or Two)

Another way to approach King is to find one novel or collection you think might draw you in — for instance *Bag of Bones*, and use that to determine if King's style, pace and storytelling are to your liking. If it is, then broaden out to similar or adjacent themes. Some readers fall in love with King's Maine novels (particularly those that feature Castle Rock); others enjoy his more modern writing style (since around 1999); while others much prefer the style of his early writing ("the original King") but almost all readers will move from one style or period to another without much fuss.

Long-term fans, of course, discovered King book by book, as they were released — they had to wait a year or so between the early books, six months or so between later collections, and agonized for years between installments of the Dark Tower cycle. A brand new reader could replicate the feel of growing with King by starting with *Carrie* and reading each book in chronological order of publication and, considering his body of work, that would provide years of reading enjoyment.

The Top Characters in King's Fiction

One certainty about King's fiction is how attached his readers become to many of the characters. Each "constant reader" (as King calls his fans who buy every book) has their own favorites, some reflecting their own image of themselves, others, those they may wish to be like, those of the sex they are attracted to, or those villains they love to hate.

Another thing is clear — King's characters are as multi-dimensional as any in modern fiction. It is this life-like quality that most endears his readers and builds empathy so strong that it is not unusual to hear that a reader cried over the death of a character, or for their circumstance.

This book's author has defined what he believes is the "Top 10" characters in King's fiction. While such a list will always be subject to debate, the point here is very much whether these characters will still resonate in English literature in fifty or one hundred years. On that basis, there is little doubt about any of these. Randall Flagg is King's ultimate villain, Roland Deschain his ultimate flawed hero, John Coffey and Jake Chambers the sacrificed innocents, Johnny Smith the everyman in all of us, Jack Torrance and Carrie White the tortured souls, Stu Redman and Jack Sawyer the clean American heroes, and Annie Wilkes the insane evil lurking in dark pockets of our society.

Some popular characters did not make this top ten, which is inevitable when considering a body of work through which King has created over 30,000 characters. So, the top characters in all King's fiction (again, in this author's opinion) are listed below. They include Pennywise, perhaps the most dreaded creature in all of King's fiction; Greg Stillson, the most dangerous politician; Dolores Claiborne, Rose McClendon, Sara Tidwell, Abagail Freemantle and Fran Goldsmith, women who refuse to break; Cujo, the good dog who loses his mind; Oy, the most courageous animal in the universe; the patient Andy Dufresne; Tom Cullen and "Duddits" Cavell, two men who won't let their disabilities undermine their true loyalties; Andre Linoge and Leland Gaunt with their traveling evil; and Eddie and Susannah Dean with their everlasting love. It's almost impossible to draw a line, but as one must, read on.

All Top Characters

"All That You Love Will Be Carried Away"—Alfie Zimmer
"Apt Pupil"—Kurt Dussander/Arthur Denker; Todd Bowden
Bag of Bones—Michael Noonan; Mattie Devore; Sara Tidwell
Black House/The Talisman—Jack Sawyer; Henry Leyden; Wolf
Blaze—Claiborne Blaisdell, Jr. ("Blaze")
"Blind Willie"—Bill Shearman/"Blind Willie" Garfield
"The Body"—Gordie Lachance; Ace Merrill
Carrie—Carrie White; Margaret White
"Children of the Corn"—Isaac
Christine—Arnie Cunningham; Roland LeBay
Cujo—Tad Trenton; Cujo
Cycle of the Werewolf—Marty Coslaw
The Dark Half—Thad Beaumont; George Stark
The Dark Tower cycle—Roland Deschain; Walter/The Man in Black/Randall Flagg; Eddie Dean;
    Susannah Dean; Jake Chambers; Oy; Sheemie Ruiz
The Dead Zone—Johnny Smith; Greg Stillson
Dolores Claiborne—Dolores St. George/Claiborne
Dreamcatcher—Gary Jones; "Duddits" Cavell
Duma Key—Edgar Freemantle
"Everything's Eventual"—Dink Earnshaw
Firestarter—Charlie McGee; John Rainbird
Gerald's Game—Jessie Mahout/Burlingame
The Girl Who Loved Tom Gordon—Trisha McFarland
The Green Mile—John Coffey; Paul Edgecombe; William Wharton
"Hearts in Atlantis"—Peter Riley; Stokely Jones
"Home Delivery"—Maddie Pace
Insomnia—Ralph Roberts
It—It/Pennywise; Bill Denbrough; Beverly Marsh/Rogan
"It Grows On You"—Gary Paulson
Kingdom Hospital—Earl Candleton
"The Library Policeman"—Dave Duncan
Lisey's Story—Scott Landon
The Long Walk—Raymond Garraty
"Low Men in Yellow Coats"—Bobby Garfield; Ted Brautigan; Carol Gerber; John Sullivan
"The Man in the Black Suit"—Gary
Misery—Annie Wilkes; Paul Sheldon
The Mist—Mrs. Carmody
"Mrs. Todd's Shortcut"—Ophelia Todd
Needful Things—Leland Gaunt; Alan Pangborn
"The Night Flier"—Richard Dees
"Nona"—The Prisoner
Pet Sematary—Louis Creed; Jud Crandall; Gage Creed
Rage—Charles Decker
"The Reach"/"Do the Dead Sing?"—Stella Flanders
The Regulators—Seth Garin
"Riding the Bullet"—George Staub
"Rita Hayworth and Shawshank Redemption"—Andy Dufresne; Red
"The Road Virus Heads North"—Richard Kinnell
Rose Madder—Rose McClendon/Daniels/Steiner; Norman Daniels
Rose Red—Annie Wheaton; Sukeena
The Running Man—Ben Richards

'Salem's Lot — Ben Mears; Kurt Barlow; Mark Petrie
"Secret Window, Secret Garden" — John Shooter
The Shining — Jack Torrance; Danny Torrance; Dick Hallorann
The Stand — Stu Redman; Fran Goldsmith; Randall Flagg; Abagail Freemantle; Nick Andros; Glen
    Bateman; Larry Underwood; Harold Lauder; "The Trashcan Man"; Tom Cullen
Storm of the Century — Andre Linoge
"The Sun Dog" — Pop Merrill
"Sword in the Darkness" — Edie Rowsmith
Thinner — Billy Halleck
The Tommyknockers — Bobbi Anderson; Jim Gardener
"Weeds" — Jordy Verrill
"The Woman in the Room" — John

    Reading Stephen King is easy in that his works are very readable, very accessible and offer many approaches. In short, his body of work should offer something that will fit the tastes of any reader.

The Worlds of Stephen King

> "Go then. There are other worlds than these."
> — Jake Chambers to Roland Deschain,
> in *The Dark Tower: The Gunslinger*

    Even casual readers quickly realize King tends to link his stories to each other using place and character. More dedicated readers look forward with glee to each new book and some subtle reference to a previous event. While some mentions are obscure (and some can only be inferred) others are quite blatant and probably intended to reward King's massive loyal readership.

    As years and thousands of pages of fiction passed, it became obvious that King was deliberately creating a number of "worlds" or "realities" — Roland's All-World in the Dark Tower cycle for instance, or the Territories of *The Talisman* and *Black House*. And King's passion for his home state meant that an almost totally fictional Maine also developed around towns such as Castle Rock, Derry and Jerusalem's Lot.

The "Realities" of King's Fiction

    From the earliest of his writings Stephen King began establishing these "realities" within his works and developing stories and story lines within each. It is most unlikely this was intentional in the early days — after all, like most young, ambitious writers, King was simply writing for himself and hoping to sell some of his output. However, it quickly became clear that King had decided to focus much of writing on the region he knew best — Maine. At the age of only 22, in 1970 King began to write the tale he now considers his magnum opus — the Dark Tower series, an altogether separate setting or "reality" from the charms of the Pine Tree State.

    Any of King's dedicated readers will have quickly noted virtually all his fiction can be grouped into one of a number of these realities. *The Complete Guide to the Works of Stephen King*, which I co-authored in 2002, determined five sweeping realities and placed all his works of fiction into them: Maine Street Horror, The Dark Tower, The Stand, America Under Siege, and New Worlds.

What do these terms mean? Well, buckle up and let's take a guided tour of the "Kingdom."

Maine Street Horror

The most comfortable setting for a King story is his home state of Maine. King's deep love of the people, land, lakes, sea, islands and culture of Maine is a keynote to his body of work.

Maine Street Horror reality stories are largely set in Maine and exist in the same "reality" as our own world. Some of these stories also occur in our timeline, but then set off on a series of events (for example the superflu of *The Stand*) that clearly have not occurred in our history. In fictional terms these must be set in an alternative universe (see The Stand and New Worlds realities later in this chapter).

The King stories fully set in Maine are among his best known. They include *'Salem's Lot, Cujo*, "Rita Hayworth and Shawshank Redemption" (made into the movie, *The Shawshank Redemption*), *It, The Dead Zone, Carrie, Dolores Claiborne, Bag of Bones, Under the Dome* and "The Body" (made into the very popular coming of age movie, *Stand by Me*).

Even stories largely set outside Maine often have at least a small Maine connection; among these is *The Stand*, which has as one of its beginning points the seaside town of Ogunquit.

King often uses the geography of both the real and his imagined Maine as virtual characters. Certainly, the towns of Jerusalem's Lot, Castle Rock and Derry have a life (and deaths) of their own. Many American horror writers, including Shirley Jackson, H. P. Lovecraft (another New Englander who clearly captured the region's topography and culture and was the creator of another imaginary town, Arkham), Edgar Allan Poe and Nathaniel Hawthorne have delivered their readers place as virtual character, and King follows in this fine tradition.

In addition to using real Maine towns and cities—such as Pownal, Bridgton, Portland, Bangor, Brewer, Durham (and its equally real Runaround Pond, in which young boys are infested with leeches in "The Body" and *Stand by Me*), Augusta, Mechanic Falls, Fryeburg, Old Orchard Beach or Lewiston/Auburn — King began creating a fictional Maine very early in his writing career.

For most readers the best-known King town is likely to be either Castle Rock or Derry. The sheer breadth and depth of a small town Maine, cut wholly from the cloth by King, is testament to his descriptive powers. To the reader most of these towns feel so real it is a shock (if, at times, a comforting one) to discover they are not. Visitors to Maine who are familiar with King's fiction are likely to find themselves driving the roads and byways of the state expecting at any turn to blunder into one of his creations.

Many of King's Maine stories involve his alma mater (and that of his novelist wife, Tabitha), the University of Maine, Orono. Dozens of characters attended it or other University of Maine campuses. "Hearts in Atlantis" is clearly set there, during the very times the Kings attended in the late 1960s. A less happy place for King's characters is Shawshank Prison, host to Red and the redeemed Andy Dufresne ("Rita Hayworth and Shawshank Redemption"); and the infamous Ace Merrill ("The Body" and *Needful Things*). Characters with mental illnesses are more likely to end up at Juniper Hill asylum, near Augusta. Inmates have included Raymond Joubert (*Gerald's Game*), Henry Bowers (*It*) and Nettie Cobb (*Needful Things*).

The fictional town perhaps best known to King readers is Castle Rock, Maine, which first appeared in the 1979 novel *The Dead Zone*. Its tragedies include the Castle Rock Strangler murders (*The Dead Zone*), a St. Bernard gone mad with rabies (*Cujo*), and explosions that destroy downtown (*Needful Things*). Human ugliness plays its havoc in *Bag of Bones*; even Tabitha King's 1993 novel *One on One* adds to the town's legacy. See the Castle Rock entry in the accompanying companion for a list of works that include the fictional town.

Fictional Derry is near Bangor, Maine, the hometown of the Kings, and is much like that small city. Derry first appeared in the short story "The Bird and the Album" (1981) and reached the mass market in *It* (1986), one of King's most popular novels. It has an even more troubled past than Castle Rock. In 1741 the entire population of Derry disappeared without a trace, according to King mythology. A collapsing water tower killed 67 people in 1985. Its worst tragedy may be the rampage against its children by a monster — which often masquerades as the clown Pennywise — every 25 years or so. The terror's most recent appearances were in 1957–58 and 1984–85, as chronicled in *It*, but in the intervening years Derry has also had a political killing (*Insomnia*) and individual human tragedy. See the entry for Derry in the companion for a list of stories that include this setting.

Jerusalem's Lot, having earlier been the site of devil-worship and also the disappearance of its entire populace in 1789, was taken over by a colony of vampires and effectively abandoned again by the living in 1975. Despite the town's destruction by fire in 1976, vampires were known to be in the area as late as 1977. A list of works may be found in the Jerusalem's Lot (Town) entry.

King chose to re-introduce a significant character from *'Salem's Lot*, Father Donald Callahan, to the Dark Tower cycle, allowing for his personal redemption. Taking an even greater risk, King introduced both the actual novel and himself as its author to the series, describing a meeting between himself and his characters Roland Deschain and Eddie Dean at his own real 1977 home in Bridgton. In the final Dark Tower novel, an even more important interaction occurs between King and his characters.

Clearly King is very familiar and comfortable with his own home state. After all, he has avoided the celebrity traps of New York and Los Angeles and continued to live in the last northeastern city before America gives way to the Canadian Atlantic provinces (although he has had a second home in Florida for some years). This familiarity of and love for Maine resonates deeply in these tales.

The Stand

Stories in The Stand Reality relate to the fundamental change of world history following a devastating superflu epidemic. These appear in various versions of *The Stand*, as well as the short story "Night Surf."

The timeline established in King's fiction for the superflu has been altered not once but twice. When the original version of *The Stand* was published in 1978, the flu epidemic was said to have struck in June 1980. Certain later paperback editions moved this to a new timeline of June 1985.

The first version was heavily edited by the publisher for financial reasons and King was dissatisfied with the result. When King's brand power over his publisher resulted in his being able to have the story re-published as he had originally intended, in a 1990 *Complete and Uncut* edition, the timeline moved once again, to June 1990. King also wrote a movie script, which was never produced, and the screenplay for the 1994 television mini-series *The Stand* (no year was provided in that version but it was certainly set no earlier than 1990).

As many fictional events in the Maine Street Horror, America Under Siege and even Dark Tower Realities occur in our world after the varying superflu dates, it follows that The Stand Reality is in fact an alternate reality and timeline.

The Stand itself, one of King's greatest novels (and perhaps the one most loved by his readers), is initially set in small town America (as they are overwhelmed by death) and New York. Readers are then taken on something of a tour of the empty heartland as the survivors who support good (or "the White," as King would have it) congregate around Mother Abagail Freemantle in Boulder, Colorado, and the forces of evil join Randall Flagg in Las Vegas (not that King was making any social commentary in the choice of cities).

Apart from the variations of *The Stand* itself "Night Surf" is part of this reality, linked as it is by the same superflu, given the street name Captain Trips. "Night Surf" was first published in *Ubris*, a University of Maine literary magazine, in the spring of 1969. King substantially revised the tale for its appearance in a men's magazine, *Cavalier*, in August 1974 and made further minor revisions for its appearance in his collection *Night Shift* (1985). The use of the term "Captain Trips" to describe the superflu clearly indicates that the story is a progenitor of *The Stand*. "Captain Trips" is a nod to the nickname of Jerry Garcia of the rock group the Grateful Dead.

The other direct ancestor of *The Stand* is King's poem "The Dark Man," which King has revealed depicts the epic novel's anti-hero, Randall Flagg. In an interview with Waldenbooks in July 2003, King had this to say: "Actually, Flagg came to me when I wrote a poem called "The Dark Man" when I was a junior or senior in college. It came to me out of nowhere, this guy in cowboy boots who moved around on the roads, mostly hitchhiking at night, always wore jeans and a denim jacket. I wrote this poem, and it was basically a page long. I was in the college restaurant ... I wrote the poem on the back of a placemat."

In the Dark Tower novel *Wizard and Glass*, Roland and his ka-tet, along with Flagg, briefly visit another reality that had also been devastated by Captain Trips. That place is strangely like our world but is clearly not ours and had not been even before the superflu struck. It therefore appears the superflu leaked across realities.

The Dark Tower

King officially recognizes the Dark Tower Reality. The list of his novels and collections initially included in *Wolves of the Calla* was the first to highlight those works connected to the Dark Tower mythology. King also refers to the seven novels and related stories that make up the Dark Tower cycle (a term he also uses) as his magnum opus. Readers who followed the main character, Roland, from 1978 through 2004 and beyond know what King means. More detailed information about the reality's genesis is available in the section on *The Dark Tower*.

America Under Siege

King stories are set not only in Maine or in other worlds but all over the United States and, sometimes, in other countries. Despite the odd foreign intrusion, the vast majority of the non–Maine stories are sent in the U.S. and involve people in dire situations, hence the name for another reality, "America Under Siege."

The America Under Siege works are linked by their common location in our physical world and in our "normal" timeline. When a story deviates into a timeline in which the world as we know it fundamentally changes (e.g., *The Stand*, "The End of the Whole Mess") it may be classified in another reality.

Many "America Under Siege" Reality stories are very mainstream in form, a trend in King's writing that has been accelerating since the mid–1990s. Examples include "All That You Love Will Be Carried Away" or "That Feeling, You Can Only Say What It Is in French." King's rare but often powerful crime genre stories, such as "Man with a Belly," are also part of this grouping.

From sea to shining sea, King certainly spreads the problems around. New York, a large and often faceless city, is the setting for mayhem ("The Ten O'Clock People," "Lunch at the Gotham Café"), mystery ("The Breathing Method," "The Man Who Would Not Shake Hands"), murder ("The Man Who Loved Flowers," *The Plant*, "Sneakers") penance ("Blind Willie") and even some good ("Dedication"). Large cities such as Los Angeles (*The Talisman*), Las Vegas ("Dolan's Cadillac"), Seattle (*Rose Red*) and imaginary urban areas such as Harding (*The Running Man*) also play host to King tales.

However, and as always with King, it is small towns and semi-rural locations that quickly come to mind when considering his assault on America through supernatural means ("Children of the Corn") or the simple despair of life ("All That You Love Will Be Carried Away"). Isolated towns and homes such as Gatlin, Nebraska, deep in the cornfields; or Travis, Indiana (*Sleepwalkers*), serve as wonderful backdrops for the doings of supernatural creatures; or the very human horrors at the Wilkes' farm (*Misery*) and at Santa Donato, California ("Apt Pupil").

Evil has visited Junction City, Iowa ("The Library Policeman"), a future home of Leland Gaunt; and Desperation, Nevada (*Desperation* and *The Regulators*). The young Jack Sawyer barely survived the horrors of small town Oatley, New York (*The Talisman*); visitors to Rock and Roll Heaven, Oregon, do not have the luxury of departing ("You Know They Got a Hell of a Band"); and there were once serious dangers in the flashing lights emanating from a shed in Statler, Pennsylvania (*From a Buick 8*).

The apparently idyllic French Landing, Wisconsin (*Black House*), is nothing of the sort. The killer agents of The Shop (a sort of rogue CIA) have worked their homicidal ways in Lakeland, Ohio (*Firestarter*), and Falco Plains, New York (*Golden Years*). And a killer car once terrorized Libertyville, Pennsylvania (*Christine*). In this reality it is not only towns in which King binds readers to the tale. It is here that Cold Mountain Penitentiary (*The Green Mile*) and the Overlook Hotel (*The Shining*) may be explored.

By the way, in an audience question and answer session, never ask King (or preferably any other author) where he gets his ideas. Apart from wasting your breath it tends to disappoint, if not irritate, King. His answer will often be that he buys them in a small shop in Utica. Perhaps some people even believe him? In fact, Utica appears often in King's fiction and was the crossover point for Clyde Umney ("Umney's Last Case"). Bobbi Anderson (*The Tommyknockers*) grew up there and Alan Pangborn (*The Dark Half*, *Needful Things*) was once a policeman in the town.

Despite King's close connection with Maine, he has certainly spread his literary wings to almost every part of the United States, especially Colorado and more recently Florida.

New Worlds

From time to time King has taken his readers on trips to "New Worlds" reality of science fiction or fantasy. While fantasy seems to be a strong genre for King, it is also fair to say that science fiction is not. His few published SF stories lack the depth and impact of his other work and are not rated highly against other writers in that genre.

In some of these tales the world takes a permanent turn for the worse through scientific arrogance ("The End of the Whole Mess") or nuclear war (in the unpublished novel "The Aftermath").

In yet others parallel dimensions or realities impinge upon ours. The Dark Tower cycle tells readers there are places where the walls between realities are "thin" and this proves to be the case in a section of London ("Crouch End") and Poplar Street in Wentworth, Ohio (*The Regulators*). *Kingdom Hospital* is set in a reality eerily close to but clearly not our own (there the New England Robins, rather than the Boston Red Sox, lose the World Series on an error).

While not yet a teenager Jack Sawyer discovered the Territories, a reality achingly close to ours, and set out across them and the U.S., on a great quest (*The Talisman*). The Territories is an agrarian monarchy using magic as a replacement for science. Jack returned there, near death, as a middle-aged man (*Black House*). King and Peter Straub, co-authors of these two books, intend to complete the trilogy of Sawyer stories, although no date has been set. Straub has indicated the last book would likely be set in the Territories, populated as it is by twinners and other wondrous creatures.

In certain tales the alternate worlds are of some charm, yet danger is always close at hand. *Eyes of the Dragon* is set in Delain, the place from which James and John Norman of "The Little Sisters of Eluria," a Dark Tower novella, hailed. In *Eyes of the Dragon*, Flagg is rumored to come from Garlan, and in the Dark Tower cycle John Farson began his evil rampage in that same Mid-World kingdom.

Once these New Worlds are exposed to King's characters, there is often no return (take the example of Trooper Ennis Rafferty of *From a Buick 8* or Norman Daniels, who got too close a look at Rose Madder's land); and sometimes characters return with more than they bargained for ("I Am the Doorway" or "The Jaunt"). Others are saved from a messy end ("Beachworld") and yet others not (also "Beachworld").

Interlinked Realities

It is relatively easy to link all of King's realities to one another. This may or may not be intentional on King's part. However, he clearly enjoys linking stories and deliberately linked, for instance, our world to Roland's All-World.

Trying to link each reality is as simple as the old "six degrees of separation" game. For instance, The Stand reality is linked by Abagail Freemantle's home town of Hemingford Home, Nebraska, to "Children of the Corn" (an America Under Siege story) and also, through Flagg, to both the Dark Tower and New Worlds realities (*The Eyes of the Dragon*). *The Stand* also has strong connections, through towns in Maine, to the Maine Street Horror reality.

Clearly Roland's Dark Tower reality crossed directly into both Maine Street Horror and America Under Siege in the latter three Dark Tower novels, although it is possible to argue that neither the Maine and certainly not the New York presented in those tales are actually those in which we readers live.

Many geographical locations (both real and imaginary) stand astride a number of King's realities. For instance, Topeka, Kansas, holds some importance in The Stand Reality, in New Worlds via *The Running Man*, and in The Dark Tower's *Wizard and Glass*. Stovington, Vermont, is important in *The Shining* of the America Under Siege Reality, and is the site of Stu Redman's imprisonment in The Stand Reality.

Characters also cross realities. Randall Flagg is the primary shifter here, appearing in the Dark Tower, New Worlds, and The Stand realities. Father/Pere Callahan transited from Maine Street Horror (*'Salem's Lot*) to The Dark Tower's last three novels, and Ted Brautigan has managed appearances in both The Dark Tower ("Low Men in Yellow Coats," *The Dark Tower*) and America Under Siege realities (*Black House*). Jack Sawyer, from the America Under Siege reality (*The Talisman*) and once but a visitor to the New World of the Territories, is now a permanent resident there (*Black House*).

In summary, since his earliest writing days King has been creating realities in his fiction; he formally recognizes the Dark Tower Reality, listing stories that are part of it; many of King's best loved stories are set in the Maine Street Horror Reality; non–Maine stories are part of the America Under Siege Reality; King's fantasy is superior but his science fiction is not; and King deliberately links his stories through character, place and reality.

John Coffey, Carrie White and the Mainestream Redemption

Many of King's fans came to him through movie screens. The author of this book was one of the earliest, but far from the last. He saw *Carrie* one Friday evening and went out the next morning looking for that book but came home with *'Salem's Lot*, igniting a life-long addiction to all things King. This is but one example of millions who found King through the screen. Millions more were readers first but all have had a rocky ride as to quality from that first movie in 1976 to this very day. For every great movie, such as *The Shawshank Redemption* and *The Green Mile*, there is an awful disaster such as *The Mangler* or a disappointment like *Dreamcatcher*. Some movies have been remade — sometimes with better results, sometimes not.

The first King adaptation was the movie that set his career alight — *Carrie*. Since then, and as of mid–2010, around 120 movies and television adaptations of King's material have been released.

But not all are available to the public — King established the concept of a Dollar Baby short film in the 1980s. His policy is to charge a one-time rights fee of $1 for a short story to budding filmmakers who apply through his office. They are required to send him a copy of the short film and can only show it at film festivals and the like. The films cannot be released commercially without King's written permission, and of course, he retains the full movie rights to the tale itself.

The first Dollar Baby was a success. Frank Darabont's *The Woman in The Room* impressed King so much he allowed Darabont the rights to "Rita Hayworth and Shawshank Redemption." Darabont then wrote and directed *The Shawshank Redemption*, which proved a huge critical and commercial success.

Putting these Dollar Baby productions to one side, readers will be familiar with a broad range of King's movies. Each of these productions is noted in the entry for the story from which it was adapted. Despite this, many viewers may be unfamiliar with the more obscure adaptations that are available on DVD or even on videotape — for instance, *Dolan's Cadillac* or *Riding the Bullet*.

King also has a mixed experience with television — he has had some highly rated episodes (the first episode of *Kingdom Hospital* garnered over fourteen million viewers), but also some ratings flops (*Kingdom Hospital*, on balance, and *Golden Years*, for example). Perhaps the most successful in terms of quality is *Storm of the Century*, while budget constraints are obvious in the generally faithful and entertaining adaptations directed by Mick Garris—*Desperation, Stephen King's The Stand* and *Stephen King's The Shining*. *Nightmares and Dreamscapes: From The Stories of Stephen King*, which adapts eight King stories, contains some of the better screen adaptations ever made (notably "Battleground"); others, such as the remakes of *Carrie* and *'Salem's Lot*, are quite acceptable. Whether King will write directly for television again is doubtful — he seems to have been genuinely hurt by ABC's appalling treatment of *Kingdom Hospital* and, after all, he has plenty of other writing to do, without being drawn back into the political milieu that is television production.

Viewers are fortunate that some directors just "get" King (and that King has supported them, as well as becoming their friend). Frank Darabont has made four King movies— the aforementioned Dollar Baby, *The Woman in the Room* — and two of the most acclaimed King adaptations thus far, *The Shawshank Redemption* and *The Green Mile*. He also wrote all three (which shows), as well as the less successful but still high quality *The Mist*.

Mick Garris is another of these directors. He directed *Stephen King's The Stand* and *Stephen King's The Shining, Riding the Bullet* and *Desperation*. He wrote *Ghosts* (a Michael Jackson vehicle) from King's story, and *Riding the Bullet*; he also directed *Sleepwalkers* and *Quicksilver Highway* (which adapts "Chattery Teeth" and a Clive Barker tale).

Another director is one of the greatest, Stanley Kubrick (*The Shining*). Other prominent directors include Scott Hicks (*Hearts in Atlantis*), Rob Reiner (*Stand By Me* and *Misery*), John Carpenter (*Christine*), David Cronenberg (*The Dead Zone*), Tobe Hooper (the original *Salem's Lot*), Brian de Palma (*Carrie*), zombie expert George A. Romero (*Creepshow* and *The Dark Half*), and Brian Henson (*Battleground* episode of *Nightmares and Dreamscapes: From the Stories of Stephen King*).

Great writers such as William Goldman (*Butch Cassidy and the Sundance Kid*) have adapted King for the screen — in Goldman's case *Dreamcatcher, Hearts in Atlantis* and *Misery*.

King also often writes new material, for instance *Storm of the* Century, *Rose Red* and *Golden Years*, has adapted his own work (*Desperation, The Stand, The Shining, Pet Sematary*) and even adapted works for the screen based on another writer's material (*Kingdom Hospital*). An episode of *The X-Files* was even made from King's teleplay (see "Chinga"). Many of his screenplays, including an adaptation of Ray Bradbury's classic tale *Something Wicked This Way Comes*, have not been produced, and each of these is covered in the second section of this book.

Other great screenplays have been written by Frank Darabont (*The Green Mile, The Shawshank Redemption, The Mist*), Jeffrey Boam (*The Dead Zone*) and Tony Gilroy (*Dolores Claiborne*).

Many great actors have graced King adaptations, including Jack Nicholson (*The Shining*), Kathy Bates (*Misery, Dolores Claiborne* and *The Stand*), Morgan Freeman (*The Shawshank Redemption* and *Dreamcatcher*), Tim Robbins (*The Shawshank Redemption*), Ian McKellen (*Apt Pupil*), Tom Hanks (*The Green Mile*), Johnny Depp (*Secret Window*), James Caan (*Misery*), Lauren Bacall (*Misery*), Richard Dreyfuss (*Stand By Me*), Martin Sheen (*The*

Dead Zone and *Firestarter*), Christopher Walken (*The Dead Zone*), George C. Scott (*Firestarter*), Anthony Hopkins (*Hearts in Atlantis*), Michael Clarke Duncan (*The Green Mile*), and Tim Curry (*It*).

Other well known actors to appear include Drew Barrymore (child star in *Firestarter* and *Cat's Eye*), Sissy Spacek (*Carrie*), John Travolta (*Carrie*), Rob Lowe (*The Stand* and the TV remake of *Salem's Lot*), Christopher Plummer (*Dolores Claiborne*), James Cromwell (*The Green Mile*), Gary Sinise (*The Stand* and *The Green Mile*), Ray Walston (*The Stand*), Molly Ringwald (*The Stand*), Max von Sydow (*Needful Things*), Ed Harris (*Needful Things, The Stand, Creepshow*), Jimmy Smits (*The Tommyknockers*), Marg Helgenberger (*The Tommyknockers*), Steven Weber ("You Know They Got a Hell of a Band" [*Nightmares & Dreamscapes* mini-series TV episode], *Desperation*, "Revelations of 'Becka Paulson" [*The Outer Limits* TV episode], and *The Shining*), Jeffrey DeMunn (*The Green Mile, Storm of the Century, The Shawshank Redemption* and *The Mist*), David Morse (*The Green Mile, The Langoliers* and *Hearts in Atlantis*), Rebecca de Mornay (*The Shining*), Miguel Ferrer (*The Stand* and *The Night Flier*), Jennifer Jason Leigh (*Dolores Claiborne*), Timothy Hutton (*The Dark Half*), Ron Perlman (*Desperation* and *Sleepwalkers*), Alice Krige (*Sleepwalkers*), Pierce Brosnan (*The Lawnmower Man*), Frances Sternhagen (*Golden Years* and *Misery*), Tim Matheson (*Sometimes They Come Back*), Richard Thomas (*It*), John Ritter (*It*), Fred Gwynne (*Pet Sematary*), Kiefer Sutherland (*Stand By Me*), River Phoenix (*Stand By Me*), Corey Feldman (*Stand By Me*), John Cusack (*Stand By Me*), Emilio Estevez (*Maximum Overdrive*), Gary Busey (*Silver Bullet*), James Woods (*Cat's Eye*), Heather Locklear (*Firestarter*), Louise Fletcher (*Firestarter*), Linda Hamilton (*Children of the Corn*), Robert Prosky (*Christine*), Tom Skerritt (*Desperation* and *The Dead Zone*), Herbert Lom (*The Dead Zone*), Colleen Dewhurst (*The Dead Zone*), Hal Holbrook (*Creepshow*), Leslie Nielsen (*Creepshow*), Ted Danson (*Creepshow*), Shelley Duvall (*The Shining*), Piper Laurie (*Carrie*), David Soul (*Salem's Lot*) and James Mason (*Salem's Lot*).

Even Michael Jackson headlines one effort (*Ghosts*) and Arnold Schwarzenegger another (*The Running Man*). And that's not to mention King's own cameo appearances.

One of the most interesting aspects of King's output is its variety, and this is particularly enlightening for those who write King off as "that horror writer" (one wonders if they read much at all). They are often shocked to find some of their favorite movies, such as *The Green Mile, Stand By Me* or *The Shawshank Redemption* are actually from King tales.

The following is a list of the publicly available movie and TV productions made from King's stories, his characters, or "sequels" (some so loosely connected as it is possible to be) as of the end of August 2010. They are sorted by genre to allow readers to more easily choose their viewing pleasure.

Horror

The best movies in this genre (in this author's opinion) are *The Shining* (1980 movie); *The Dead Zone*; *Carrie*; *Storm of the Century*; and *Pet Sematary*. Other films and television shows in the horror genre worthy of mention are: *Cat's Eye*; *Christine*; *Creepshow*; *Cujo*; *The Dark Half*; *Desperation*; *1408*; *Ghosts*; *Haven* (TV series); *It*; *Kingdom Hospital* (TV series); *The Mist*; *Needful Things*; *The New Twilight Zone* — "Gramma" (TV episode); *Nightmares and Dreamscapes: From the Stories of Stephen King* (TV series); *Riding the Bullet*; *Salem's Lot* (1979); *Salem's Lot* (2004); *Silver Bullet*; *Sleepwalkers*; *Stephen King's The Dead Zone* (TV series); *Stephen King's The Shining* (1997, TV); *Stephen King's The Stand*; and *The X-Files* — "Chinga" (TV episode).

Of arguably lesser quality are the following: *The Boogeyman*; *Carrie* (TV, 2002); *Children of the Corn* (1984); *Children of the Corn* (TV, 2009); *Children of the Corn: Revelation*; *Children of the Corn V: Fields of Terror*; *Children of the Corn: The Gathering*; *Children of the Corn 666: Isaac's Return*; *Children of the Corn III: Urban Harvest*; *Children of the Corn II: The Final Sacrifice*; *Creepshow 2*; *The Diary of Ellen Rimbauer* (TV); *Disciples of the Crow*; *Graveyard Shift*; *The Mangler*; *Monsters* — "The Moving Finger" (TV episode); *Quicksilver Highway*; *The Rage: Carrie 2*; *A Return to Salem's Lot*; *Rose Red*; *Sometimes They Come Back*; *Sometimes They Come Back ... Again*; *Sometimes They Come Back ... For More*; *Tales from the Darkside: The Movie*; *Thinner*.

Science Fiction

In this author's opinion, one film stands above them all in this genre: *Firestarter*. Of medium quality are the following: *Firestarter: Rekindled* (TV); *Golden Years* (TV series); *The Outer Limits*—"Revelations of Becka Paulson" (TV episode); and *The Running Man*.

What might be considered B grade, or worse, science fiction includes: *Dreamcatcher*; *The Langoliers*; *The Lawnmower Man*; *Maximum Overdrive*; *Tales from the Darkside* — *The Word Processor of the Gods*; *The Tommyknockers*; and *Trucks*.

Mainstream or Mystery

The best films in this genre are: *The Green Mile*; *Dolores Claiborne*; *Hearts in Atlantis*; *Misery*; *The Shawshank Redemption*; and *Stand By Me*.

Of fairly medium quality would be: *Apt Pupil*; *The Dead Zone* (TV series); *Dolan's Cadillac*; *Secret Window*; *Tales from the Darkside*—"Sorry, Right Number" (TV episode); and *The Woman in the Room*.

King has also had mixed success with screenplays he has written that have been produced (he's also written many that have not). *Stephen King's The Stand* and *Stephen King's The Shining* are true to the original material, if a little flat. *Golden Years* was a flop (probably deservedly), as was *Kingdom Hospital* (quite the opposite). *Storm of the Century* is an outstanding success.

King has appeared in many movies and TV programs, most related to his own work and mostly in cameo roles. These are: *Creepshow*, *Maximum Overdrive* (the only movie he has directed), *Pet Sematary*, *Golden Years*, *Sleepwalkers*, *The Stand*, *The Langoliers*, *Thinner*, *The Shining* (mini-series), *Storm of the Century*, *Rose Red*, *Kingdom Hospital* and *Gotham Café* (adaptation of *Lunch at the Gotham Café*). Non-King adaptations include *Knightriders*, *Creepshow 2*, an episode of *Frasier* and another of *The Simpsons*, *Fever Pitch* and *Diary of the Dead*.

King loves the movies—he's been attending them since childhood (see *Danse Macabre* and *On Writing*) and, even today, sees dozens of movies in the theater every year. He has written about the art form since some of his earliest published efforts (for instance, his "Stephen King's Garbage Truck" columns in *The Maine Campus*) and continued in his *The Pop of King* columns in *Entertainment Weekly* magazine.

Readers who wish to investigate King's reportage in this area should read *Stephen King: The Non-Fiction* by Rocky Wood and Justin Brooks (Cemetery Dance Publications, 2009), where three chapters are dedicated to the matter and his opinions about other pop culture, particularly television, literature and music.

There readers can learn that in King's very first "Garbage Truck" column he praised

Bette Davis' performance in *Hush ... Hush, Sweet Charlotte*; that he considered *Psycho* one of the best movies of the 1960s; he gave his views on *Easy Rider* at the time it was released; and he stated that *The Wild Bunch, Bonnie and Clyde* and *The Graduate* were the seminal movies of the sixties. Or that in his "The Pop of King" columns he argues that "movies matter" (*Mystic River* is given as a proof-point in the 14 November 2003 column); gives his views on *The Passion of the Christ*; reveals his favorite movie lines; provides his regular review of the year in movies (*Shrek 2* was one of his favorites in 2004); and offers an analysis of how the Oscars work.

Stephen King and Literary Tradition

King's success has brought him comparison to some of the great and popular writers of English fiction (William Shakespeare, Charles Dickens, Robert Louis Stevenson), American fiction (Mark Twain) and of course horror (Edgar Allan Poe, H. P. Lovecraft). Whether it is a comparison of their body of work, or indeed of individual classic tales, King could be said to rate strongly in this company. Today, a majority of high schools in the U.S. teach English using King's works, and he is studied in universities (doctoral dissertations and master's theses are regularly written about King's work).

Why is this? When King first published he was little known, could potentially have been a flash in the pan, and of course was pegged as a "horror writer" (which was out of fashion despite the long and honored history of the genre).

But, as the years passed King progressed in literary opinion and began to receive acknowledgement for the high quality of his writing as well as the sheer power of his stories. Even the august magazine *The New Yorker* regularly publishes his tales. Until the end of the last century awards came mainly from within the horror, science fiction and fantasy literary communities. Recognition from one's own peers is likely to have brought King a certain degree of satisfaction, considering his early roots as a hard-core fan and consumer of these genres.

Many of those who read King in their youth in time became teachers and university lecturers and professors, editors, publishers and critics. By the first decade of the twenty-first century this generation was able to influence decisions about the teaching of King, criticism of his work, and the giving of awards.

The Bram Stoker Awards have been given since 1987 by the Horror Writers Association, the peak writers' group in that genre. King won the Bram Stoker Award for Best Novel for *Misery* (in a tie with McCammon's epic *Swan Song*), *The Green Mile, Bag of Bones, Lisey's Story* and *Duma Key*; Best Fiction Collection for *Four Past Midnight* and *Just After Sunset*; Best Long Fiction for "Lunch at the Gotham Café"; and Best Non-fiction for *On Writing*. Through 2009 he had been nominated a further 18 times. In 2003 he received the association's Lifetime Achievement Award.

The World Fantasy Awards are nominated by members of the World Fantasy Convention and selected by a panel of judges to acknowledge excellence in fantasy writing and art. King won the Convention Award and the Short Fiction Award, for "The Man in the Black Suit." In 2007 he received the Grand Master Award from the Mystery Writers of America. The Grand Master Award recognizes important contributions to the mystery genre over time, as well as a significant output of consistently high quality.

The British Fantasy Society has awarded King the August Derleth Award for Best

Novel in 1983 (*Cujo*), 1987 (*It*), 1999 (*Bag of Bones*) and 2005 (*The Dark Tower*); Best Short Story for "The Breathing Method" in 1983; and a Special Award in 1981.

Stepping outside genre to more mainstream honors, King (and Stuart O'Nan) won Quill Awards in 2005 for *Faithful* and King was nominated for *Cell* in 2006. The O. Henry Awards are an annual collection of the year's best stories published in American and Canadian magazines and written by American or Canadian authors. King won first prize in 1996 for "The Man in the Black Suit." In doing so he joined the likes of William Faulkner, Irwin Shaw, Truman Capote, John Cheever, John Updike, Joyce Carol Oates, Bernard Malamud, Saul Bellow and Alice Walker as winners of the year's best stand-alone story.

Even greater recognition was accorded in September 2003, when the National Book Foundation announced it would award him its 2003 Medal for Distinguished Contribution to American Letters at the National Book Foundation awards ceremony and benefit dinner. The medal was presented to King, who then delivered the keynote address to some 1,000 authors, editors, publishers and friends of the book industry. Previous recipients include Saul Bellow, Studs Terkel, John Updike, Ray Bradbury, Arthur Miller and Philip Roth.

A statement from the foundation said, "Stephen King's writing is securely rooted in the great American tradition that glorifies spirit-of-place and the abiding power of narrative. He crafts stylish, mind-bending page-turners that contain profound moral truths—some beautiful, some harrowing—about our inner lives. This award commemorates Mr. King's well-earned place of distinction in the wide world of readers and booklovers of all ages." According to a press release from the foundation dated 15 September 2003, King stated, "This is probably the most exciting thing to happen to me in my career as a writer since the sale of my first book in 1973." King and thriller writer John Grisham once purchased their own tickets to the annual National Book Awards presentation by the foundation, King telling *The New York Times* for September 15, 2003 ("A Literary Award for Stephen King"), "that was the only way we were going to get in the door."

There is no doubt King has contributed to a revival in reading generally, and for many teenagers and young people taking up reading as a pleasure for the first time in their lives. In spite of his popular and critical success King is uncomfortable with being compared to other writers, but it is also true that, as the years have passed, more and more critics, academics and others have found themselves drawn to pass comment upon King's position in the pantheon of writers. His output will stand the test of time as both popular fiction and as the subject of academic study. Courses teach King works across the high schools and colleges of the U.S. Teachers and professors have come to understand that they can offer King stories that not only help teach the art of creative writing but actually engage their students.

In fact, King has become the Dickens of our times—popular with readers, although initially unpopular with certain critics. As time passed many of Dickens' works became the standard fare of entertainment. Characters such as Scrooge, Nicholas Nickleby and Oliver Twist, and stories such as *A Tale of Two Cities* and *Great Expectations* are now embedded in our culture.

Fellow horror writer (and sometime collaborator) Peter Straub has something of real relevance to add at this point: "I think the Dickens allusion is always a double-edged sword. Tremendous popularity inevitably evokes contempt. [King's] real merits, which are those of a hugely talented novelist born with an instinct for narrative, great intelligence, empathic insight into his fellow human beings and a visionary imagination, often go unremarked. If he had been a crime writer, he would have been canonized long ago."

King himself has commented upon his status as a "popular" writer: "How do I deal with the prejudice? I don't. There is a simple fact of life in English-speaking literature, and it's this: a huge rock cropped up in the second half of the 18th century, and the river of literature split into two streams around it: popular fiction and literature. That rock was the gothic novel.... The only literary figure strong enough to bridge the created gap was Charles Dickens, and the literati of his day basically sneered at him as your classmates sneered at the work I do" (from "She's Got Mail: Symposium on the Nature of Genre and Pleasure in the 21st Century" by Emma Straub, in *The Spook*, February 2002).

There is also much of Mark Twain about Stephen King. Twain was a master of creating characters who were young and of creating new twists on old themes. He helped bring a new American style of writing to English literature. His body of work is now standard study throughout the American education system. King has all these attributes, being the most visible and popular of writers reflecting the mainstream American culture of the last forty years. Nathaniel Hawthorne, whose portrayals of New England are still among the richest ever written, was also prominent in establishing a truly American literary voice. There is no doubt King has continued Hawthorne's tradition.

Perhaps Dr. Michael Collings, noted King critic and former professor of English at Pepperdine University in California, writing in Spignesi's *The Essential Stephen King*, put it the most succinctly: "William Shakespeare was the Stephen King of his generation." After all, Shakespeare wrote plenty of horror—just read *Macbeth* with its witches and ghosts, or *Hamlet*—and created some of the most famous characters of all time. In an era when the popular theater served in place of what in the twentieth century became cinemas, Shakespeare's productions were some of the most popular of his day.

The Dark Tower— *King's Magnum Opus?*

King's *The Dark Tower* cycle, can be described as an apocalyptic sci-fi fantasy western. Its very genre-crossing nature has simply added to its appeal, and it may well be that the Dark Tower stands a century from now as King's greatest literary achievement. Many fans and critics argue *The Dark Tower* cycle is King's great work. Why?

It is King's longest work, both in terms of storytelling content (seven novels, a novella, a number of short stories and dozens of links to his other tales) but also in the length of time he took to write the work—34 years between 1970 and 2004 (or even longer if one considers further tales such as *UR*, published in 2009). It also represents one of his most compelling tales, with some of his strongest characters and, undoubtedly, some of his best writing.

But it is the fact that the series encompasses so much of King's life and his canon that best supports the argument. A fictional version of King himself appears in the cycle (this meta-fiction particularly irritated certain critics, but King has argued it came naturally as the tale unfolded). Much of his work is linked (consciously or unconsciously) to the cycle, making it the center of his fictional universe.

Let's understand more about the cycle, its origins, King's motives, and how his magnum opus came to be. The author relates something of the origins of the cycle in his introduction to the revised edition of the first Dark Tower novel, *The Gunslinger*, titled "On

Being Nineteen (and a Few Other Things)". From as early as his reading of J.R.R. Tolkien's classic *The Lord of the Rings* in 1966 and 1967, King had determined to write something as sweeping,

> but I wanted to write my own kind of story.
>
> Then [in 1970], in an almost completely empty movie theater ... I saw a film directed by Sergio Leone. It was called *The Good, The Bad and the Ugly*, and before the film was half over, I realized what I wanted to write was a novel that contained Tolkien's sense of quest and magic but set against Leone's almost absurdly majestic Western backdrop.... And, in my enthusiasm ... I wanted to write not just a *long* book, but *the longest popular novel in history*. I did not succeed in doing that, but I feel I had a decent rip; *The Dark Tower*, volumes one through seven, really comprise a single tale.

From its inception King did indeed have high hopes. In the 1982 afterword to *The Dark Tower: The Gunslinger*, he wrote that his brief synopsis for the action to follow the first novel "suggests a length approaching 3000 pages, perhaps more." (In fact, the original first edition page counts of the seven novels exceed 3,500 pages).

Dark Tower reality stories are primarily set in an alternate reality/world, sometimes known as "All World." In that world the anti-hero/hero, Roland Deschain, the last of the gunslingers and a knight-warrior of sorts, is on a thousand year-long quest to find and save the Dark Tower.

In *Stephen King's The Dark Tower: The Complete Concordance*, King's research assistant and later collaborator on the *Dark Tower* comics, Robin Furth, defines the Dark Tower itself as

> a looming gray-black edifice which is simultaneously the center of all universes and the linchpin of the time/space continuum. All worlds and all realities are contained within its many levels.... The line of Eld, of which Roland is the last, is sworn to protect the Tower. Yet a terrible illness affects this structure, one that is often compared to cancer.... The Tower is held together by a network of magical magnetic forces—rays, known as Beams ... the Beams, Portals and mechanical Guardians are breaking down. If the weakening Beams collapse and the Tower falls, all creation will blink out of existence.

The Dark Tower itself is in End-World (a part of "All World"), the same geographical location that appears in King and Peter Straub's second joint novel, *Black House*. Ted Brautigan (of "Low Men in Yellow Coats," filmed as *Hearts in Atlantis*) and other Breakers (a type of psychic slave), toiling under the yoke of the Crimson King (the nemesis of The White, or all that is Good), were reluctantly hard at work, trying to break the Beams, until released by Roland and his "ka-tet" (a group bound together by fate) shortly before Roland finally arrived at the tower.

The first appearance of a Dark Tower story was the short story, "The Gunslinger" in *The Magazine of Fantasy and Science Fiction* of October 1978. However, King had been working on his magnum opus since 1970 and took Robert Browning's 1855 epic poem "Childe Roland to the Dark Tower Came" as his initial inspiration. The various short stories that would become the first novel, also called *The Gunslinger*, originally appeared in *The Magazine of Fantasy and Science Fiction* in 1978, 1980 and 1981 and were then combined into the novel, which was first published in a limited edition in 1982. A mass-market edition did not appear until 1988. It was only then that some King fans came to know of the epic. Supporters quickly became addicted, demanding more of the author at every opportunity.

According to King's afterword to *The Dark Tower: The Gunslinger*, when he wrote the first words of the cycle on green copy paper his wife-to-be had given him, "I was living in a scuzzy riverside cabin ... and I was living all by myself — the first third of the [first novel] was written in a ghastly, unbroken silence.... Those two factors, the challenge of that blank green paper, and the utter silence ... were more responsible than anything else for the opening lay of The Dark Tower." This is exactly what the reader perceives in the opening section, a vast, silent space, yellow-green in a hideous form of near dead geography.

In the same piece, he says the attraction of the cycle never left him after that night in June 1970; indeed, "I came back to the gunslinger's world when *'Salem's Lot* was going badly ... and wrote of the boy Jake's sad ending not long after I had seen another boy, Danny Torrance, escape another bad place in *The Shining*. In fact the only time when my thoughts did not turn at least occasionally to the gunslinger's dry and yet somehow gorgeous world (at least it has always seemed gorgeous to me) was when I was inhabiting another that seemed every bit as real — the post-apocalypse world of *The Stand*." And, as early as the afterword to *The Drawing of the Three* he wrote, "This work seems to be my own Tower, you know; these people really haunt me, Roland most of all."

By 1997, in the afterword to *Wizard and Glass*, King was fully admitting the pull the cycle has on him: "Roland's story is my Jupiter — a planet that dwarfs all the others (at least from my own perspective), a place of strange atmosphere, crazy landscape, and savage gravitational pull.... I am coming to understand that Roland's world (or worlds) actually contains all the others of my making"; and that there are places in Mid-World for Randall Flagg, "even Father Callahan, the damned priest from *'Salem's Lot* ... who wound up dwelling on the border of a terrible Mid-World land called Thunderclap." King wrote that Mid-World is where all these characters finish up: "Why not? Mid-World was here first, before all of them, dreaming under the blue gaze" of Roland Deschain's eyes.

King added to the Dark Tower cycle with the novels *The Drawing of the Three* in 1987; *The Wastelands* in 1991; and *Wizard and Glass* in 1996 after what some fans found to be an excruciating wait, due to the cliffhanger ending of the previous book. Another lengthy break, as King worked to find the way to finish the epic, occurred over the next seven years. It was only after his near-death experience (later incorporated into the cycle) that he was able to finish the series with *Wolves of the Calla* (2003); *Song of Susannah* (2004); and finally *The Dark Tower* (released on 21 September 2004, the author's 57th birthday).

As time passed and to keep hungry fans happy, King had published *The Bear* (1990), an "excerpt" from *The Wastelands*, although that story was heavily revised before being included in the novel. He also released a Dark Tower novelette, "The Little Sisters of Eluria" (1998), later collected in *Everything's Eventual*, and began to refer explicitly to Dark Tower mythology in his mainstream stories. The major references were in *Insomnia* (1994); "Low Men in Yellow Coats" and "Heavenly Shades of Night Are Falling" (both collected in *Hearts in Atlantis*, 1999); and *Black House* (2001). King provided further sustenance to Dark Tower addicts by giving them free on-line excerpts: "Calla Bryn Sturgis" (from *Wolves of the Calla*, in 2001) and "Callahan and the Vampires" (from *The Dark Tower*, in 2004); and allowed the publication of the short story "The Tale of Gray Dick" (2003), excerpted from *Wolves of the Calla*, although the story was slightly revised from what would be the novel's appearance, so as not to give away a plot line.

In June 2003, King published a revised and expanded edition of the cycle's first novel, *The Gunslinger*. He explains the reasoning for the rewrite in his foreword to that edition: "Although each book of the Tower series was revised as a separate entity, I never really looked at the work as a whole until I'd finished Volume Seven, *The Dark Tower*. When I looked at the first volume ... three obvious truths presented themselves. The first was that *The Gunslinger* was written by a very young man, and had all the problems of a very young man's book. The second was that it contained a great many errors and false starts, particularly in the light of the volumes that followed. The third was that *The Gunslinger* did not even *sound* like the later books—it was, frankly, rather difficult to read. All too often I heard myself apologizing for it, and telling people that if they persevered, they would find the story really found its voice in *The Drawing of the Three*."

Dark Tower and King experts alike also link *Eyes of the Dragon* (published in 1984 in limited edition and 1987 in mass market edition) to the Dark Tower cycle, through the magician Flagg and certain "lands" mentioned.

The Dark Tower Cycle is made up of seven novels and one novella and is supported by a number of other stories that directly link to this reality. A full understanding of the Dark Tower can be achieved by reading each.

Dark Tower *Stories*	*Related Tales*
I: The Gunslinger	*Insomnia*
II: The Drawing of the Three	"Low Men in Yellow Coats"
III: The Waste Lands	"Heavenly Shades of Night Are Falling"
IV: Wizard and Glass	*Black House*
V: Wolves of the Calla	*Eyes of the Dragon*
VI: Song of Susannah	"The Mist"
VII: The Dark Tower	*UR*
The Little Sisters of Eluria	

On 30 November 2009, King posted a note on his official Web site suggesting he might write another Dark Tower novel, tentatively titled "The Wind Through the Keyhole." He said it would be "a new Mid-World book (not directly about Roland Deschain, but yes, he and his friend Cuthbert are in it, hunting a skin-man, which are what werewolves are called in that lost kingdom)." It would therefore fit between the events described in the flashback scenes from *Wizard and Glass* and *The Gunslinger*.

Finally, there are a series of official graphic novel adaptations of parts of the Dark Tower cycle (including parts untold in King's novels). Written by King's former research assistant, Robin Furth, each is signed off by King to ensure it is consistent with his vision. (Further details are provided in the entries that follow.)

So, if magnum opus really means an author's "great work," then *The Dark Tower* surely is Stephen King's.

Stephen King:
A Literary Companion

Abagail Freemantle

Abagail Freemantle, an African American woman, was born in the late 19th century in **Hemingford Home, Nebraska**, and lives her entire life there until the superflu wipes out most of the world's population in ***The Stand***. Soon after the disease strikes, people start to dream of "Mother Abagail," and those with good intentions are drawn to her, first at her home and later to Boulder, Colorado (the Boulder Free Zone). She tasks **Stu Redman**, **Larry Underwood**, Ralph Brentner and **Glen Bateman** with confronting **Randall Flagg**. Edgar Freemantle (***Duma Key***) is distantly related to her (according to their creator).

On the Screen: Emmy Award winner Ruby Dee is brilliant as Mother Abagail in *Stephen King's The Stand*.

Ace Merrill

John "Ace" Merrill is one of King's minor recurring villains. A local thug in Castle Rock, he appears as a threat to **Gordie Lachance** and his friends in "**The Body**"; as a tough guy in "**Nona**"; as a significant character in ***Needful Things***; and is mentioned as being held in **Shawshank Prison** in "**The Sun Dog**." He is the nephew of the equally nasty **Reginald "Pop" Merrill**.

On the Screen: Kiefer Sutherland is great in the role in the movie *Stand by Me* (based on the novella "The Body") and that may explain why the character does not appear in the film version of *Needful Things*.

After the Play

"After the Play" was an epilogue to ***The Shining***, which was merged into the novel. King says the full version has been lost. He did add an epilogue to the tale in ***The Shining*** (**Mini-series Screenplay**), which updates Danny Torrance's life to the time of his graduation day.

The Aftermath

The Aftermath is the first novel King completed, in 1963, the year he turned 16. King has made it clear it will never be published, as he regards it as juvenilia. The manuscript is held in the Special Collections department of the **Raymond H. Fogler Library** at the University of Maine in Orono, the author's alma mater. Written permission from King is required to access this work and is generally only given to researchers.

In this science fiction tale a young man survives a nuclear war that devastates parts of America. After the trials of attempting to survive as a loner, Larry Talman joins the Sun Corps, a group trying to use military and bureaucratic means to re-establish order. He and a friend uncover the secret of the corps and begin to plan its downfall.

Unsurprisingly, the writing is of an immature teenager, and is clearly influenced by King's view of fascism, H.G. Wells' *War of the Worlds*, and Isaac Asimov's *Foundation* series. The tale is the progenitor of King's many apocalyptic tales, such as *The Stand*.

Alan Pangborn

Alan Pangborn became sheriff of **Castle Rock** in 1980, taking over from **George Bannerman**. He'd previously worked as a police officer in Utica, New York. He first appears as an important character in *The Dark Half* and there is married to Annie. He is a major character in *Needful Things*, where he and his friend Polly Chalmers determine to stand up to Leland Gaunt and his spells. He is briefly mentioned in "**The Sun Dog**" and *Gerald's Game*.

On the Screen: Ed Harris plays Alan in *Needful Things*; and Michael Rooker played the same role in *The Dark Half*.

Alfie Zimmer

Alfred (Alfie) Zimmer is the protagonist of "**All That You Love Will Be Carried Away**." A traveling salesman, he is married to Maura and father to Carlene. He collects graffiti and records it in a notebook. In despair at what his life has become, he contemplates taking his life one January night at a motel in Lincoln, Nebraska.

On the Screen: The character has appeared in four separate **Dollar Baby** adaptations, and is played by Craig Sidell in *The Secret Transit Codes of America's Highways*; movie critic Joe Bob Briggs in *All That You Love Will Be Carried Away*; and Kent Vaughan in *All That You Love*.

All That You Love Will Be Carried Away

Originally appearing in *The New Yorker* for 29 January 2001, "All That You Love Will be Carried Away" was collected in *Everything's Eventual*, with minor variations.

Alfie Zimmer, a traveling salesman, stops at a motel for the night. He is planning suicide but is forced to consider what to do with his notebook full of collected graffiti. The last entry might be mistaken for a suicide note and the entire contents might seem just a little crazy. A disturbing tale with hints of redemption, it is leavened by the humor contained in the graffiti Zimmer collects, largely from public toilets across America. This is very much King in mainstream fiction mode.

Movie: Four **Dollar Baby** movies have been made from this story, the best of which carries the same title as the tale. Directed by James Renner, it stars B-movie critic Joe Bob Briggs as Alfie Zimmer. The others are *The Secret Transit Codes of America's Highways* (2003), *All That You Love* (2004) and another effort with the same name as the story, also produced in 2004.

All-World

Although this is not certain, All-World appears to be the name of **Roland Deschain**'s world in **The Dark Tower cycle**. All-World is closely aligned to Planet Earth (although apparently not the version of Earth in which we live) but it is the only world in the entire universe in which **The Dark Tower** takes its physical form. It encompasses **Mid-World**, **In-World**, **Out-World** and **End-World**. All-World was once united under one high King, Roland's ancestor, Arthur Eld. The term is actually only used in *The Dark Tower IV: Wizard and Glass*, *The Dark Tower VI: Song of Susannah* and *The Dark Tower VII: The Dark Tower*.

American Vampire

American Vampire is a comic book series launched by Vertigo (an imprint of DC Comics) in May 2010. This is King's first original comic script. Each of the five issues in the first arc contains one story by King and one by series creator Scott Snyder. After that first arc King had no further involvement. It is likely the first five issues will be collected as a graphic novel and it is most unlikely the material will ever appear in a King collection.

King's tales revolve around Skinner Sweet, a vicious outlaw who is made vampire in 1880, and follows his adventures into the 1920s. Sweet is a peculiarly American vampire, created in the Old West, powered by the sun and with fangs more like a rattlesnake than a traditional European vampire. In one interesting link, King starts the story in Sidewinder, Colorado (a town he created), which is the closest town to both **The Overlook Hotel** (*The Shining*) and the farm belonging to **Annie Wilkes** (*Misery*).

Genesis: Series creator Snyder originally sold his idea to DC Comics, then approached King for a blurb. The author enjoyed the tale so much he suggested he'd be willing to contribute to future issues. Naturally enough, this excited Snyder and the editors at Vertigo, who agreed. King said he was excited to deal with a new form of vampire: "It's really the vampire as American capitalist gone totally wild."

Comic: The comics were published from May 2010 by Vertigo, an imprint of DC Comics. They are easily accessible from specialist comic stores, on-line or via the secondary market.

Anderson, Bobbi *see* Bobbi Anderson

Andre Linoge

The mysterious Andre Linoge is the protagonist of *Storm of the Century*. He mysteriously appears on **Little Tall Island**, near Machias, Maine, as a snowstorm approaches; it is so severe the island is cut off from the rest of the world. He casually murders Martha

Clarendon and shows no concern at being arrested by the island's part-time constable, Mike Anderson. He simply advises that if they give him what he wants he will leave. It is entirely unclear if Linoge is even human.

On the Screen: Colm Feore is at his brilliant best playing Linoge in *Storm of the Century*.

Andros, Nick *see* Nick Andros

Andy Dufresne

Andy Dufresne is unjustly jailed in "**Rita Hayworth and Shawshank Redemption**" for the murder of his wife and her lover. He is sent to Maine's **Shawshank Prison**, where he meets "Red." Red had murdered his wife by cutting the brake lines on her car, which she crashed traveling down Castle Hill in **Castle Rock, Maine**. Andy refuses to bow to the brutality of prison life and slowly builds a new life, while constantly dreaming of the outside world.

On the Screen: Tim Robbins plays Andy perfectly in *The Shawshank Redemption*.

Annie Wheaton

Teenage autistic girl Annie Wheaton is also telekinetic, telepathic and psychokinetic. Joyce Reardon believes Annie has the power to wake up the Rose Red house in *Rose Red* and takes her on an expedition there. At the age of five she'd made stones rain on her neighbors' house after their dog bit her.

On the Screen: Kimberly J. Brown plays Annie Wheaton in *Rose Red*.

Annie Wilkes

Annie Wilkes is a registered nurse who apparently suffers from manic depression; she is living on an isolated farm not far from the **Overlook Hotel** in Colorado when she comes across a badly injured **Paul Sheldon**. Stunned to find she has saved the man who created her favorite literary character, Misery Chastain, she holds him captive and demands he write another "Misery" novel, just for her. Indeed, she describes herself as Sheldon's "number one Fan." Her unsavory past is revealed, along with her fascinating interplay with Sheldon, in *Misery*.

On the Screen: Kathy Bates deservedly won an Academy Award for her portrayal of Annie in *Misery*.

Apt Pupil

One of four original novellas in **Different Seasons**, "Apt Pupil" appeared as "Apt Pupil: Summer of Corruption." The horror in this tale centers on how far from humanity an individual can stray, if allowed. **Todd Bowden** discovers his elderly neighbor **Arthur Denker** is actually the Nazi war criminal Kurt Dussander (The Blood Fiend of Patin). Todd blackmails Denker into telling him the gory details of his war crimes at German concentration camps and their warped relationship begins to escalate.

In an interesting link, Dussander purchased stocks through **Andy Dufresne**, the banker falsely imprisoned in "**Rita Hayworth and Shawshank Redemption.**"

Genesis: Written in the two weeks immediately after King completed *The Shining*.

Movie: The 1998 movie includes a brilliant portrayal of Denker/Dussander by Sir Ian McKellen. Much overlooked, this movie is well worth viewing.

Arnie Cunningham

Arnold Richard (Arnie) Cunningham is a major character in *Christine*. Seeing an old, beaten-up 1958 Plymouth Fury for sale, he immediately falls in love with the car and buys it on the spot. Unable to keep the car at home, Cunningham takes it to a garage to bring it back to original condition. Soon the car, named Christine, seems to take on a life of its own. Dennis Guilder and Leigh Cabot try to break the car's hold over their friend Arnie.

Genesis: The name of the character appears to be a nod to Richie Cunningham, of *Happy Days* TV fame.

On the Screen: Keith Gordon appears as Arnie in the 1983 film.

Arthur Denker

Arthur Denker is a major character in the novella "**Apt Pupil.**" He is **Todd Bowden**'s elderly neighbor but he has a secret — the sort of secret few elderly men in California have. The consequences after Bowden uncovers Denker's past drive the tale.

On the Screen: Sir Ian McKellen is simply brilliant in the role in the 1998 film. Nicol Williamson played the role in a movie version that was never released.

Autopsy Room Four

"Autopsy Room Four" was a short story first published in **Six Stories** and collected in **Everything's Eventual**. Howard Cottrell awakes, can hear voices and feel people moving him about, but cannot move. A smell seems strangely familiar, almost like rubber. The last thing he remembers is playing golf at the Derry Municipal Country Club and losing his ball in the rough. And now he realizes he's in a body bag and an autopsy is about to be performed — on him! Readers can put themselves in Howard's place as the terror builds. King chose **Derry, Maine**, as the setting for this tale. Derry, of course, is subject to cyclical visits by **Pennywise**, as chronicled in *It*.

Television: Adapted as an episode for TNT's *Nightmares and Dreamscapes: From the Stories of Stephen King*. Richard Thomas (John Boy from TV's *The Waltons*, who also appeared as **Bill Denbrough** in *It*) stars as Howard Cottrell; Greta Scacchi is Katie Arlen. While not the best episode of the series, it is watchable.

Genesis: King credits an *Alfred Hitchcock Presents* TV episode as inspiration for this story and notes his "more — shall we say modern? — method of communicating liveliness" than the original's single tear; along with his joy in being able to use a snake breed — the "boomslang," from one of Agatha Christie's Miss Marple tales.

Ayana

"Ayana," a short story first published in *Paris Review* magazine for Fall 2007, is collected in **Just After Sunset**. This mystic tale is reminiscent of **The Green Mile**. A man survives an apparently hopeless struggle with pancreatic cancer after a blind young girl visits him. If indeed he has received a gift, the miracle may not yet be spent.

Genesis: Reflecting on the subject of the afterlife and God, King says, "When we ask questions about God, one near the top of the list is why some people live and some die; why some get well and some do not. I didn't want to write about answers. I wanted to write about questions. And suggest that miracles may be a burden as well as a blessing."

The Bachman Books

This is a collection of King's first four novels written under the pseudonym **Richard Bachman** (and the best way for any reader to access the one that will never be republished as a stand-alone book—*Rage*). The others are *The Long Walk*, *The Running Man* and *Roadwork*. From 1985 editions included the non-fiction piece "Why I Was Bachman," which was replaced from 1996 with the much more interesting "The Importance of Being Bachman." The collection is now out of print but can easily be found at online second-hand bookshops.

Bag of Bones

Often overlooked by King's readers but undoubtedly one of his greatest works, this is novel is a classic and erotic ghost story of great ingenuity, and is at the same time one of his most moving. *Bag of Bones* deals with grief, love and the damage the secrets of the past can inflict. Mike Noonan, best-selling author from **Derry, Maine**, and his wife Jo live an idyllic life until she suddenly dies from a brain aneurysm. Mike discovers she'd had kept her pregnancy secret and had met an unidentified stranger near their summer home on Dark Score Lake in Western Maine. He suffers writer's block, along with vivid nightmares of their lake house, Sara Laughs. Hoping to deal with both problems, he moves to the lake and is drawn into two awful conflicts—one threatening a beautiful young widow and her daughter; and another, the roots of which are set deep in the past, involving Negro blues singer Sara Tidwell.

The novel won the Bram Stoker Award for Superior Achievement in a Novel from the Horror Writers Association and the August Derleth Award (Best Novel) from the British Fantasy Society. King says at the beginning of the "On Living" section of *On Writing* that his own family's summer house in western Maine is "very much like the one Mike Noonan comes back to in 'Bag of Bones.'"

The appearance of **Castle Rock** and Derry in this tale links it to a large portion of King's Maine fiction. He also mentions previously appearing characters such as **Thad Beaumont (*The Dark Half*)** and eight other notable characters from earlier works. The continued use of such links between his works endears King to his "constant readers."

Genesis: The tale is partly tribute to *Rebecca*, a novel by Daphne Du Maurier, and contains numerous quotes and references to it. In the tale the novelist Thomas Hardy is said to have claimed, "The most brilliantly drawn character in a novel is but a bag of bones," but Noonan himself thought one of his teachers had made that up. As there is no evidence Hardy did actually say anything of the sort, we must assume it was actually King or one of his teachers who came up with the saying.

The Ballad of the Flexible Bullet

This strange and not entirely satisfying short story first appeared in *The Magazine of Fantasy and Science Fiction* for June 1984 and is collected in **Skeleton Crew**. "The Ballad of the Flexible Bullet" revolves around a strange creature, a Fornit, that writer Reg Thorpe thinks lives in his typewriter. As a result Thorpe develops strange beliefs, and his actions begin to threaten everyone around him.

Bannerman, George *see* George Bannerman

Barlow, Kurt *see* Kurt Barlow

Bateman, Glen *see* Glen Bateman

Battleground

Originally published in *Cavalier* magazine in September 1972, "Battleground" is collected in **Night Shift**. John Renshaw is a hit man for "the Organization," charging a minimum of $10,000 per job. His latest victim is Hans Morris, the owner of a toy company. On returning to his apartment he finds a package containing a G.I. Joe Vietnam Footlocker, made by the Morris Toy Company, which had been sent by Morris' widow. Renshaw finds himself under attack by the miniature army. One of King's lesser known tales, it is nonetheless a fun read and deserves wider attention.

Television: The best episode from the TV series, *Nightmares & Dreamscapes: From the Stories of Stephen King* (2006). A brilliant teleplay by Richard Christian Matheson and a tour de force performance by William Hurt as Renshaw make compelling viewing. Available on DVD.

Beachworld

Certainly one of King's lesser stories, this science fiction tale (with strong horror undertones) was originally published in the Fall 1984 edition of *Weird Tales* and later collected in **Skeleton Crew**.

In "Beachworld," a spaceship crashes on a world entirely covered with sand. Rand, one of two survivors, loses his mind and believes the dunes form a living entity. Colleague Bill Shapiro calls for a rescue ship. What will it find?

Trivia: King once argued the opening line ("Fedship ASN/29 fell out of the sky and crashed") is one of the best pulp-magazine story lines ever.

The Bear

"The Bear" forms part of **The Dark Tower III: The Wastelands** but was originally published in *The Magazine of Fantasy and Science Fiction* for December 1990. This was billed as a "Special Stephen King Issue" and included the first appearance of "**The Moving Finger**."

This version of "The Bear" is significantly different from that in the novel. Those wishing to read it, particularly Dark Tower completists and fans, will be able to purchase a copy from online booksellers or specialist magazine traders, as *The Magazine of Fantasy and Science Fiction* is collectable in its own right.

Beaumont, Thad *see* Thad Beaumont

Before the Play

"Before the Play" is the deleted prologue of **The Shining**. It was first published in *Whispers* magazine as a short story in August 1982 — readers will prefer this uncut version. Two sections with adult content were deleted for republication in the *TV Guide* issue for 26 April to 2 May 1997, which coincided with the debut of *The Shining* mini-series that week.

It is effectively a collection of five stories, loosely connected by **The Overlook Hotel**. Four of the scenes are set at the hotel and the remaining one in **Jack Torrance**'s childhood. Not only do the scenes provide fascinating background about the Overlook, but also of Jack's motivations and his later behavior as an adult.

The five loose stories, which King calls "scenes," start with the building of the hotel in 1909 and the tragic results. They continue with a visit by a honeymooning couple twenty years later (this scene includes one of the scariest cameos in all of King's canon), and then gives previous unknown detail from the hotel's famous masquerade ball. Probably the most important section deals with an incident from Jack (Jackie) Torrance's childhood, and the piece closes with another horrific incident from the hotel's bloody history, one readers of *The Shining* will recognize. Readers will enjoy the rich history that this piece adds to *The Shining* myth; perhaps King will one day include this tale in one of his collections, or create an expanded version of the novel.

Copies of the *TV Guide* version, which is illustrated, are relatively easy to find online; the *Whispers* version can be found if you search thoroughly enough.

"**After the Play**" was an epilogue to *The Shining* but was merged into the novel.

The Beggar and the Diamond

One of King's more obscure offerings, collected in **Nightmares and Dreamscapes**. In "The Beggar and the Diamond" archangel Uriel is sad at the lot of an old beggar, so God tries to improve the man's life.

Genesis: In a note in the collection, King explains, "This little story — a Hindu parable in its original form — was first told to me by Mr. Surendra Patel, of New York City. I have adapted it freely and apologize to those who know its true form, where Lord Shiva and his wife, Parvati, are the major characters."

Ben Hanscom

Ben Hanscom grows up as a fat boy in **Derry, Maine,** and as an adult works as an architect and lives near **Hemingford Home, Nebraska.** In 1957–58 he and his friends, **Bill Denbrough, Mike Hanlon, Beverly Marsh, Richard Tozier, Stanley Uris** and **Eddie**

Kaspbrak form "the Losers Club" in the novel *It*, in an attempt to fight **Pennywise**. He also appears in **"The Bird and the Album"** and is mentioned in *Insomnia*.

On the Screen: John Ritter (*Man About the House*) plays Hanscom in *It*.

Ben Mears

Benjaman (Ben) Mears is the protagonist in *'Salem's Lot*. A writer, he spends five years of his childhood living in **Jerusalem's Lot**, Maine. Two years after his wife Miranda is killed in a motorcycle accident, he returns to the town, only to find the isolated rural location holds a developing threat. In the face of danger Ben forms friendships in The Lot with Susan Norton, **Mark Petrie**, Matt Burke and Jimmy Cody. More of Ben's history is revealed in *The Dark Tower V: Wolves of the Calla*, which also features **Father Donald Callahan**, who had been the Catholic priest in the town.

On the Screen: David Soul (*Starsky and Hutch*) plays Ben in the 1979 version; and Rob Lowe (who also played Nick Andros in *The Stand*) plays the role in the 2004 production.

Ben Richards

In the novel *The Running Man* it is 2025 and everyone watches Free-Vee game shows. **Ben Richards** decides to try out in the hope of winning money to buy medicine for his sick baby. He is accepted for "The Running Man," the big money game show where contestants are hunted to their deaths, and now must fight for his life and that of his family.

On the Screen: Arnold Schwarzenegger is Ben Richards in the movie *The Running Man*, which has little connection with the original story.

Beverly "Bev" Marsh

Beverly Marsh is living in **Derry, Maine,** in 1957–58 when she and her friends, **Bill Denbrough, Ben Hanscom, Richard Tozier, Mike Hanlon, Stanley Uris** and **Eddie Kaspbrak** form "the Losers Club" in the novel *It*, in an attempt to fight **Pennywise**. Her father often beats her. As an adult she marries Tom Rogan, who is also violent towards her. She returns to Derry in 1985 when Mike Hanlon calls the Losers Club back. She also appears in **"The Bird and the Album"** and is mentioned in *Dreamcatcher*.

On the Screen: Annette O'Toole played Bev in *It*.

Big Driver

"Big Driver" is a novella from King's 2010 collection, *Full Dark, No Stars*. According to his Web site, "Mystery writer, Tess, has been supplementing her writing income for years by doing speaking engagements with no problems. But following a last-minute invitation to a book club 60 miles away, she takes a shortcut home with dire consequences."

Big Wheels: A Tale of the Laundry Game (Milkman #2)

There are two versions of this short story. The first was published in *New Terrors 2* in 1980 (reprinted in *New Terrors*, 1982). King substantially revised it for collection in *Skeleton Crew*. "Big Wheels: A Tale of the Laundry Game (Milkman #2)" is closely linked to "Morning Deliveries (Milkman #1)," as both tales were adapted from an aborted King novel, *The Milkman*. One significant character, Milligan, undergoes a given name change from one version of the story to another—from Spider to Spike. The changes between the two versions are not critical to the overall story but are so wide-ranging readers are encouraged to seek out the earlier version as an example of how King can create two alternatives for one tale.

In the story, friends Leo Brooks and Rocky Rockwell drive around drunk one evening in 1969 trying to find someone to inspect Rocky's 1957 Chrysler. They happen on Bob's Gas and Service, owned by Bob Driscoll, an old school friend of Rocky's, and soon the three of them are drinking. As Rocky and Leo leave, Rocky thinks he sees his ex-wife's new partner's milk truck approaching. Blind drunk and speeding, he swerves.

Genesis: In *On Writing*, King describes one of his real fellow workers at the New Franklin Laundry in Bangor (prior, of course, to his writing success) and names him as Ernest "Rocky" Rockwell.

Bill Denbrough

William (Bill) Denbrough's younger brother George is killed by **Pennywise** in 1957 in the novel *It*. Bill stutters a lot as a child but loses the disability in his adulthood—only when he comes back to **Derry, Maine** does it return. As a consequence he is also known as "Stuttering Bill." He and his friends, **Michael Hanlon, Benjamin Hanscom, Beverly Marsh, Richard Tozier, Stanley Uris** and **Eddie Kaspbrak** form "the Losers Club" in an attempt to fight Pennywise. Bill's childhood bicycle, "Silver," will serve him well in adulthood, after he becomes a successful writer and marries actress Audra Phillips. Bill is also mentioned in "**The Bird and the Album**," *Dreamcatcher* and *Bag of Bones*.

On the Screen: Richard Thomas (*The Waltons*) plays Bill in *It*.

Bill Shearman

Bill Shearman is the protagonist in the *Hearts in Atlantis* version of "**Blind Willie**."

Bill Shearman looks like any normal businessman as he travels to work at Western States Land Analysis in New York City. But he secretly changes his appearance and clothing each workday by sneaking into his second office, Midtown Heating and Cooling, and becoming William Shearman. From there he goes into a public toilet, takes out a cane and dark glasses, reverses his coat and magically transforms into William J. "Blind Willie" Garfield, a beggar. Why would a man undertake such a transformation every work day?

Billy Halleck

Grossly overweight lawyer Billy Halleck knocks down and kills an old gypsy woman in *Thinner*. He has himself cleared by using contacts in the legal community. As he leaves court an elderly gypsy man touches him and mutters one word—"thinner." From that day on, Halleck starts to lose weight at a startling rate. At first, he's happy but as time passed he realizes the weight loss is not going to stop. Convinced he's under a gypsy curse, he must track the gypsies down.

On the Screen: Robert John Burke plays the role in the movie.

The Bird and the Album

"The Bird and the Album" was published in *A Fantasy Reader: The Seventh World Fantasy Convention Program Book* in 1981. Thanks to the editor's introduction some sources claim it to be an excerpt from Chapter 13 of the novel *It*. Actually, the story was published five years before the novel, and King substantially rewrote it for the novel, where it appears as the beginning of Chapter 14.

In the tale friends meet after twenty-five years in **Derry, Maine**. **Eddie Kaspbrak, Ben Hanscom, Mike Hanlon, Bill Denbrough**, Beverly and Richie discuss some of the terrible things they are starting to remember from their childhood. One of their former friends, "a guy named **Stan Uris** ... couldn't make it." (The surnames of **Beverly Marsh** and **Richard Tozier** are not given in this story).

At the time the original was published, readers were intrigued but had to wait another five years for the context in which to place this slightly less than 3000 word piece. This was the first published mention of **Derry, Maine**.

The difficult to find convention book appears for sale at specialist King booksellers on rare occasions. While it is really not necessary for every fan to read this version, hardcore King fans and the many who rate *It* as one of King's greatest works won't want to miss the additional descriptions that appear in this version.

Black House

Black House, written with Peter Straub, is one of the most important novels in King's canon. The sequel to *The Talisman*, it can be read as a stand-alone story. The main links between the two novels are the main character, **Jack Sawyer**, and an alternate world, **The Territories**.

On the likelihood of a third book in the "Territories" series, Straub had this to say: "Given the tendency of fantasy novels to parcel themselves out in units of three, it would be entirely reasonable to propose a third part to the Talisman series. After all, the first book is set more or less equally in this world and the Territories; the present book takes place mainly in this world; and the third could be set mostly in the Territories. There's a nice balance in that structure."

In the tale a child-killer is stalking the small town of French Landing, Wisconsin. Known as "The Fisherman," he has abducted, murdered and even eaten parts of small children. The chief of police asks Jack Sawyer, a retired policeman, for help. Sawyer, now in his 30s, remembers little of the adventure he'd faced as a 13-year-old child crossing the country to secure the Talisman.

Helped by a group of locals known as the Thunder Five, his old friend Speedy Parker, and multi-personality DJ **Henry Leyden**, Sawyer begins searching for the killer and the mysterious Black House, which may be the key to the whole mystery.

Not only is this is a tremendously exciting story with great sub-plots but, for the first time, a direct link between the Dark Tower Universe and The Territories is outlined. For instance, **Mid-World** and **End-World** are mentioned. Parkus speaks of many worlds all linked and of "ka": "This business concerns the Dark Tower," he says. There are dozens of other links to that cycle both in this book and in the Dark Tower novels King wrote after *The Talisman*, proving his intent to link the Talisman and Dark Tower universes.

There are also many links to other King fiction, including *Rose Red*, the *Hearts in*

Atlantis stories, *Insomnia*, *Desperation*, "The Sun Dog," *The Tommyknockers* and *Lisey's Story*.

The multitude of characters in this tale adds much to its depth, for instance DJ Henry Leyden (a man of many characters) is one of the most memorable minor characters in King's canon (or Straub's for that matter). Overall, this is a complex tale, beautifully written by two masters of their craft and a must read for all King fans.

Genesis: Straub had this to say about inspirations, "We have certain tastes, *Tom Sawyer* meant a lot to both Steve and I when we were kids. *Bleak House* meant to a lot to us in our adulthood. Dickens in general had a big effect on Steve and myself. The title *Black House* is a deliberate reference to *Bleak House*. We sure as hell didn't try to hide it."

Black Ribbons

A collaboration with musician Shooter Jennings, *Black Ribbons* was released as a concept audio album of the same title in March 2010. King reads the story, playing the character Will O' the Wisp, a radio talk-show host being phased out due to government censorship. King's character talks about a doomsday future for America between the music of Jennings' band, Hierophant.

Genesis: Jennings, son of Waylon Jennings, conceptualized the album and sent a script to King. King rewrote and changed the original, recorded the material and sent a typed transcript to Jennings.

Album: *Black Ribbons* (2010) by Shooter Jennings and Hierophant. Drea De Matteo (*The Sopranos*), Jennings' fiance at the time the album was recorded, plays the high priestess.

Game: In 2010 a game based on the album was live at www.shooterjennings.com.

Blaisdell, Claiborne, Jr. *see* Claiborne Blaisdell, Jr.

Blaze

King first wrote the novel *Blaze* in 1973, tried to rewrite it at some point possibly in the 1990s, and finally reworked it for publication under his **Richard Bachman** pseudonym in 2007. Royalties go to the Haven Foundation, which King set up to make "grants to freelance writers and artists experiencing career-threatening illness, accident, natural disaster or other emergency or personal catastrophe."

The final published novel features **Claiborne Blaisdell, Jr.** (Blaze), a dim-witted but lovable small time criminal. He and his partner, Rockley, have been planning to kidnap a baby who is heir to a shipping fortune. Even after Rockley is knifed to death in a bar, Blaze continues to have "conversations" with him and determines to proceed with the kidnapping.

Blaze's back-story is the most interesting part of the tale — he'd suffered horrific head injuries when his father assaulted him as a child, and readers learn of his tragic upbringing in an orphanage and the manner in which he drifts into petty crime.

King writes this tale with great sympathy, although some of the faults from his earliest draft do appear in the final product. A minor novel, it is nevertheless a short and interesting study of a very sympathetic main character. There are flashes of King's own upbringing in the area in which the tale is set, along with the powerful feel of hardscrabble life in post-war rural Maine.

Genesis: King wrote this novel just before **Carrie** and offered it to Doubleday along with **'Salem's Lot**, but they wisely chose the latter. It then stayed in King's trunk for three decades. He tells more of the story in his "Full Disclosure" introduction to the novel.

Blind Willie

Originally published in *Antaeus* magazine (1994), the story was completely rewritten by King for its appearance in **Hearts in Atlantis** so it would fit the story line of that collection.

In the collected version of "Blind Willie," a man undergoes a daily transformation. Each day businessman **Bill Shearman** enters his New York City office, changes his appearance and emerges as "Blind Willie" Garfield, a beggar who collects cash from passersby. The story revolves around why a man would act in such a manner. A poignant tale, it is only slightly more powerful as part of the Vietnam influenced storyline of the collection. In the earlier version of the tale it is Bill Teale who becomes "Blind Willie" Teale each day.

Blockade Billy

William "Blockade Billy" Blakely was an outstanding baseball player but today he's forgotten. In fact, he was the first — and only — player to have his existence completely removed from the record books, according to the novella "Blockade Billy." Blakely had a deep, dark secret — one more scandalous than any modern sports controversy.

"I love old-school baseball," Stephen King said of the book, "and I also love the way people who've spent a lifetime in the game talk about the game. I tried to combine those things in a story of suspense. People have asked me for years when I was going to write a baseball story. Ask no more; this is it."

The novella combines King's love for and knowledge of America's pastime with his ability to tell a very dark tale.

Genesis: Cemetery Dance publisher Rich Chizmar (who had published various editions of King books, such as **From a Buick 8** and books about King) and King corresponded about baseball for 20-odd years before 2010. King thought the book would be a perfect fit for the publisher because of Chizmar's love of the game.

Blood and Smoke

Blood and Smoke (Simon and Schuster Audio, 1999) is an audio book. Stephen King reads all three short stories. At the time, "**Lunch at the Gotham Café**" had been published, but "**1408**" and "**In the Deathroom**" appear here for the first time. All three were later collected in **Everything's Eventual**. Hearing King read his own stories adds a level of interest to each tale.

The Blue Air Compressor

One of King's stranger stories and probably not one of his best, "The Blue Air Compressor" was originally published in *Onan*, a student literary magazine at the University of Maine, in January 1971, shortly after King graduated. He allowed it to be republished in *Heavy Metal*, an "adult illustrated fantasy magazine," in July 1981.

King introduces himself as the writer early in this story. It is a rarity for King to mention himself in his fiction and in this case it is very deliberate and self-conscious. It's interesting that he chose not to remove or rework these interjections when the story was republished. They have an air of pretension that is most unlike King, and while in the original publication (which also carried his poem "**In the Key-Chords of Dawn**") this may have worked due its "student" nature, it fails completely in *Heavy Metal*.

In the story Gerald Nately, a writer, rents a seaside cottage in Maine. After arriving at Mrs. Leighton's nearby house, he finds her to be a very large woman. Obsessed with her weight, he writes a story about her, "The Hog." Nately shows signs of mental instability and debates with himself whether to let his subject read the story. He's decides to do so but finds her reading it without permission. Events spiral from there. The final scene is the most interesting and original in the otherwise forgettable tale.

Possibly due to its quality, King has never allowed this story to appear in one of his collections. It is virtually impossible to find an original *Onan* copy, except at very high price through a specialist King bookseller. *Heavy Metal* is generally available from online sellers.

Genesis: Inspired by an EC Comics story, with further influence of Edgar Allan Poe.

Bobbi Anderson

Roberta "Bobbi" Anderson is an author of western novels who discovers processed metal buried in the woods near her home in **Haven, Maine**. She begins to dig it out and, as she does, is compelled to construct strange devices. **Jim Gardener**, an alcoholic poet and Anderson's lover, helps her dig but is immune to the strange side effects. One of Bobbi's books, *Rimfire Christmas*, is mentioned in the uncut version of *The Stand*.

On the Screen: Marg Helgenberger plays Bobbi in the telemovie.

Bobby Garfield

Eleven-year-old Bobby forms a friendship with **Ted Brautigan** when Ted moves into the apartment house in which he and his mother live in "**Low Men in Yellow Coats**." They will have adventures together before Ted moves on. **Carol Gerber** is Bobby's putative girlfriend, **John Sullivan** is his best friend, and each will lead interesting lives.

Bobby also appears or is mentioned in "**Blind Willie**," "**Hearts in Atlantis**," "**Heavenly Shades of Night Are Falling**," "**The New Lieutenant's Rap**," "**Why We're in Vietnam**," *The Dark Tower VI: Song of Susannah* and *The Dark Tower VII: The Dark Tower*.

On the Screen: Anton Yelchin plays young Bobby in the movie *Hearts in Atlantis* and David Morse plays the adult version.

The Body

This is one of the most beloved of all King tales, particularly in the filmed version. Many fans do not know it included two previously published King tales—"**Stud City**" (published in *Ubris*, a literary magazine at his college, University of Maine, for Fall 1969) and "**The Revenge of Lard Ass Hogan**" (*Maine Review* magazine, 1975). Both were heavily revised in this version.

King first began to write "The Body" in 1968 and completed the manuscript in 1974, but it was not published until the release of ***Different Seasons*** in 1982, in which it appeared as a novella.

In the tale four young boys undertake a memorable odyssey. **Gordie Lachance** is a successful author looking back to 1960, when he and three friends had left **Castle Rock** searching for the body of Ray Brower, a boy their own age who had been hit by a train.

On the way Lachance told the others stories he called "Stud City" and "The Revenge of Lard Ass Hogan." The boys face an adventurous, dangerous trip, and their bonds will be tested.

This coming-of-age tale is linked to other Castle Rock stories by characters such as Cujo, the possibly crazy **Ace Merrill**, and **George Bannerman**. King deliberately links the story to many other Maine tales, including "**It Grows on You**," "**Mrs. Todd's Shortcut**," ***Pet Sematary***, ***The Dark Half***, "**Graveyard Shift**," ***Blaze***, ***'Salem's Lot*** and "**Hearts in Atlantis**."

Genesis: In ***On Writing***, King recalls the first time he publicly told the story that most ascribe as inspiration for "The Body." Making it clear he does not recall the events himself (he is recalling his mother's story), readers learn that another child, aged just four, had been run over by a slow-moving freight train while playing with or near King ("years later, my mother told me they had picked up the pieces in a wicker basket"). The tale has clear autobiographic overtones, with Gordie Lachance very clearly an idealized young Stephen King. The scene where the boys are attacked by leeches at Runaround Pond is based an incident when King was growing up at the real **Runaround Pond** in Durham, Maine.

Movie: Stand by Me. One of the best loved adaptations of any King work. Directed by Rob Reiner with actors Wil Wheaton (*Star Trek: The Next Generation*), the late River Phoenix, Corey Feldman (*The Lost Boys*), *24*'s Kiefer Sutherland (as Ace Merrill), Richard Dreyfuss (*Jaws*) and John Cusack.

The Bone Church

This poem appeared in *Playboy* magazine in November 2009.

A man describes an expedition aimed at finding an elephant graveyard. The jungle they must traverse is so difficult, and the expedition faces such tragedy, that the geography itself becomes a character.

Copies of the magazine containing this highly evocative piece are easily found at online sellers.

The Boogeyman

One of King's earliest commercially published stories, it first appeared in a men's magazine, *Cavalier* (March 1973), and is collected in ***Night Shift*** (1978).

A progenitor of much King fiction, "The Boogeyman" is predictable but also reaches heights of pent up suspense that prove how adept a young King was at using this technique to enthrall an audience. In the tale, Lester Billings feels responsible for the deaths of his three children. They had been afraid of the boogeyman they believed lived in their closet, and to assuage his guilt, he determines to visit a psychiatrist.

The story has been featured three times as **Dollar Baby** short films and once as a stage play performed in Scotland but has yet to appear in any mainstream adaptation.

Genesis: King says this story is about both the fear of the dark and the fear for someone close.

Movie: Dollar Babies of the same name were produced in 1982, 2006 and 2010.

Bowden, Todd *see* Todd Bowden

Brautigan, Ted *see* Ted Brautigan

The Breathing Method

This original novella from **Different Seasons** is paired with "**The Man Who Would Not Shake Hands**," as both are presented as stories told in an unnamed New York gentlemen's club on East 35th Street, where older men gather to tell tall tales and true. Six characters appear in both stories as working at or attending the club.

In "The Breathing Method," a doctor, Emlyn McCarron, tells the story of a single young pregnant woman, Sandra Stansfield, who came to him for help in 1935. She paid cash up front before the delivery of her baby and McCarron introduced her to the Breathing Method, the forerunner of the modern Lamaze breathing method, which had once been used by certain American Indian tribes. But tragedy and a bizarre outcome await the birth.

It was winner of the Best Short Story award from the British Fantasy Society in 1983. The tale has not been adapted for the stage or screen.

Genesis: King wrote the story for Peter Straub (co-author of **The Talisman** and **Black House**) and his wife, Susan, immediately after completing **Firestarter**. It may have been inspired by Straub's Chowder Society Men's Club in his classic novel *Ghost Story*; King says, "That men's club really is a metaphor for the entire storytelling process."

Brooklyn August

King has a well-known love-affair with baseball (see in particular **Faithful**), and has written about the sport in the non-fiction form since as early as 1969. The Boston Red Sox is his team, but he also has a deep appreciation of America's pastime. A real pitcher crossed into King's fiction in **The Girl Who Loved Tom Gordon**.

This poem is a wistful and elegiac homage to the Brooklyn Dodgers' last season in New York (1956). It's a must read for baseball and poetry fans alike.

It appears in **Nightmares and Dreamscapes** (1993), which also includes the non-fiction essay "**Head Down**," which is the only time King has ever included previously published non-fiction in one of his fiction collections.

Trivia: Most fans would not know it was first published in 1971 an obscure magazine, *Io*, and not republished until Tyson Blue's *The Unseen King* was released in 1989.

Burlingame, Jessie *see* Jessie Burlingame

But Only Darkness Loves Me

In 2002 I was researching King's papers at his alma mater, the University of Maine, when I discovered a number of stories previously unknown in the King community. This one is a two-page story fragment labeled as by Stephen and Joseph King. King's oldest son, Joseph Hillstrom King (see **King, Joseph**), would become an award-winning horror writer in his own right using the pseudonym Joe Hill.

In the few words from this story that remain, we find a boy talking to a beautiful girl in a bar in Ledge Cove, Maine. She is too beautiful to look at directly, except in quick glances. She invites him back to her hotel but he only agrees to go to the lobby, not her room. The few words are mysterious and have a "**Nona**"-like quality.

Readers can check out the two pages at the Special Collections Unit of the University's **Raymond H. Fogler Library**. Ask for Box 1012.

Cain Rose Up

King's first version of this short story appeared in the Spring 1968 edition of *Ubris*, a literary magazine at the University of Maine, Orono. Considering King was a student there at the time of publication, it is not surprising he choose to completely rewrite it for **Skeleton Crew** 17 years later. In fact, the original text is almost unrecognizable in places. The extra maturity in King's writing clearly shows in the later version. The *Ubris* version is difficult to find but may be photocopied at the university's **Raymond H. Fogler Library**.

In the tale student Curt Garrish takes his .352 Magnum rifle out of the university gun storage room. He acts normally until he reaches his dormitory room, where he begins shooting.

This tale reflects King's fascination with the lone gunman, which would be more fully developed in **Rage**. Of course, any student writing such a tale today and offering it for publication in the school or university magazine is likely to be investigated or ordered into counseling.

Genesis: A response King got to this story was his first, and King had this to say: "In it, a student who has just lost his girlfriend (a good deal of student writing tends to be about student loving, and the loss of same) goes bonkers and starts shooting people from the window of his dorm room. It wasn't a very good story — and since the victims were on their way to the caff when the shooting started, their deaths might have been deemed mercy killings — but this kid I've never seen before had not only read it but liked it. He liked my story! I think that was when my career actually began." The story itself is partly inspired by the killing rampage of Charles Whitman at the University of Texas in Austin in 1966. King once said of the power of his writing to keep him sane, "I know that guy Whitman. My writing has kept me out of that tower."

Calla Bryn Sturgis

"Calla Bryn Sturgis" was first released on King's official Web site in August 2001. King offered the story free of charge as a thank you to long-suffering fans of **The Dark Tower cycle**, who had by then been waiting four years since **The Dark Tower: Wizard and Glass**.

Readers were told it was a prologue to a new, fifth novel in the series, but it was hinted this version would not be the final form in the upcoming book. In fact, so as not to give away certain events in the novel, there had been some careful editing and changes.

The tale was delivered in a substantially different form as the prologue "Roont" when **The Dark Tower V: Wolves of the Calla** was published more than two years later, in November 2003.

Both versions feature the return of King's benighted character, **Father Donald Callahan** of **'Salem's Lot**, known in the Calla as Pere Callahan. Many years earlier King had said that, despite the Catholic priest having last been seen on a bus out of **Jerusalem's Lot**, he had not finished with the character, and he would reappear in some future story.

King's serious fan base was delighted and intrigued by both the story and Callahan's appearance. Perhaps as a result of this positive reaction the author also allowed another section of the novel to appear before release, "**The Tale of Gray Dick**," also in an altered version.

The story no longer appears on King's Web site and, as it was never published in a paper form, those wishing to access a copy will need to contact a King collector or fan who has retained it in electronic format.

Callahan, Donald *see* Father Donald Callahan (aka Pere Callahan)

Candleton, Earl *see* Earl Candleton

The Cannibals

"The Cannibals" is a manuscript King attempted and abandoned twice before resurrecting the concept as the novel **Under the Dome**. The first attempt, actually titled "Under the Dome," was in 1978. His second, with "The Cannibals" title, was while filming **Creepshow** in Pittsburgh (1981). King says the "almost five hundred pages" he wrote that time "turned up — battered, and with some pages missing, but mostly complete — in the summer of 2009."

To help promote the novel *Under the Dome,* King released two sections of the original manuscript of "The Cannibals" in 2009, noting that some "Internet writers have speculated on a perceived similarity between *Under the Dome* and *The Simpsons Movie*." Releasing part of "The Cannibals" was intended to "demonstrate I was thinking *dome* and *isolation* long before Homer, Marge, and their amusing brood came on the scene."

In the 120-odd pages released by King, a group of apartment building residents slowly realize they are trapped in the building, while the outside world seems to appear and disappear. At the time of writing both sections were available from www.stephenking.com.

Carol Gerber

Eleven-year-old Carol Gerber is **Bobby Garfield's** putative girlfriend in "**Low Men in Yellow Coats**." Her life does not take a standard course, as readers learn in the stories "**Blind Willie**," "**Hearts in Atlantis**," "**Heavenly Shades of Night Are Falling**," "**The New Lieutenant's Rap**," and "**Why We're in Vietnam**," and she is mentioned in **The Dark Tower VII: The Dark Tower**.

On the Screen: Mika Boorem plays Carol in the movie *Hearts in Atlantis*.

Carrie

The movie adaptation of King's first novel, *Carrie*, brought King to the attention of this author and many others for the first time. He began writing it in 1973 but famously threw the first pages in the trash, from which they were recovered by his wife, Tabitha King (see **King, Tabitha**), who encouraged him to continue. *Carrie* was published by Doubleday in April 1974 with little fanfare; the paperback rights were sold to Signet for $400,000 (by terms of his contract King got half) but the book failed to make either hardback or paperback best-seller lists until the smash-hit movie was released. After the movie, readers bought enough copies to drive the paperback to number 3 on *The New York Times* best-seller list in January 1977 (however, it was not King's first best-seller — *'Salem's Lot* had reached number 1 just a few months earlier).

As King's first novel it is important, but remarkably few King fans have actually read the book. It is written as an epistolary novel, a series of documents making up the tale; many readers find this form (also seen in *Dracula*) difficult. It is a remarkably short but deeply compelling novel and begins King's long tradition of dealing successfully with characters some distance from his white, educated, male existence.

Carrie White is dominated by her religious fanatic mother, **Margaret White**, and tormented by fellow students at Ewen Consolidated High School in Chamberlain, Maine. Carrie has a secret — telekinetic powers re-awakened when she is shocked by her first period, an event she had not expected, as her mother regarded all forms of human sexuality as an abomination and had therefore neglected to provide any form of sex education.

Carrie's classmate, Sue Snell, feels guilty after Carrie is humiliated by other girls when she has that first period in the school showers. She asks her boyfriend, Tommy Ross, to take Carrie to the school dance and Carrie accepts. However, other students who had been punished over the shower incident see the chance for revenge. The scene is set for the "Black Prom."

Genesis: King says he got an idea for a short story about a girl with telekinetic powers in the late fall or early winter of 1972 ("the idea had actually been kicking around my head since high school, when I read a *Life* magazine article about a case of poltergeist activity in a suburban home"). When he first attempted the tale he found that "ghosts of my own began to intrude; the ghosts of two girls, both dead, who eventually combined to become Carrie White." In the introduction to a new paperback edition of *Carrie* in 1999, he relates the unfortunate histories of these two girls — one a student at Durham Elementary with King who was treated badly by other students because her family was so poor as to afford her only one outfit for school per year; and a girl who lived in Durham with her mother. When King visited the house he was struck by a huge and "grisly" crucifix in their living room; she was regarded as different not only for the religious beliefs but a feeling of "Strange! Not like us! Keep away!" she gave off. He says the first girl committed suicide and the second died alone of an epileptic seizure; neither survived high school, and these ghosts "kept insisting that I combine them" in this tale.

Though frightened as he was of the world of young girls he "would have to inhabit ... and the level of cruelty I would have to describe," he and Tabby needed quick cash for living expenses, so he attempted the tale. When he threw the "half-completed first pages of the story into the wastebasket ... Tabby asked me what I had been working on. I told her a short story, but it had gone bust.... Perhaps she saw something in my face.... All I know is she went into my little writing room, took the pages out of the wastebasket ...

read them, and suggested I go on. I did, mostly to please her." He closes by saying he wished that the two dead girls "were alive to read it. Or their daughters."

Movie: Brian De Palma's 1976 film *Carrie* is often credited with putting a rocket under King's nascent career. The film is a tremendous stand-alone example of the 1970s horror genre and stars Sissy Spacek as Carrie, Piper Laurie as Margaret White and John Travolta as Billy Nolan, Carrie's date for the prom. *The Rage: Carrie 2* (1999) is loosely based on Sue Snell's character and should be avoided.

Television: In 2002 NBC ran a three hour mini-series, *Carrie*, that also failed to reach the quality of the original movie. It starred Patricia Clarkson (***The Green Mile***) and Emilie de Ravin (*Lost*).

Stage: *Carrie* has appeared on stage both as a play and a musical. Famously, the musical version was a complete disaster when presented on Broadway in 1988.

Carrie White

Carrieta (Carrie) White is one of King's best-known characters, partly due to the movie version of the novel, ***Carrie***. A fat girl (which will surprise movie-goers), she is dominated by her religious fanatic mother, **Margaret White**. She has darkish blond hair, is fifteen, and knows little of her own sexuality when her first period suddenly strikes in the showers after gym class. From a young age she also had telekinetic abilities. These, combined with an act of treachery, result in events the town of Chamberlain, Maine, will never forget.

Genesis: When King first attempted to write *Carrie* he found that "ghosts of my own began to intrude; the ghosts of two girls, both dead, who eventually combined to become Carrie White." He has written about the unfortunate histories of these two girls in his book ***On Writing***). One was from a dismally poor family, was taunted at school, and later committed suicide. The second was from a very religious family and died alone of an epileptic seizure.

On the Screen: Sissy Spacek is memorable as Carrie in the original 1976 movie, while Angela Bettis plays the character in the 2002 TV remake.

On Stage: Carrie White has been played by Linzi Hateley (U.S. and U.K. musical, 1988); Morgan Cambs (2009 musical); Sherry Vine (2006 stage show); and Erik Ransom (2010 stage show). The last two presentations were "drag shows."

Castle Rock, Maine

Sometimes known simply as "The Rock," this is the town most closely associated with King, so much so that King once disavowed himself of writing of it, declaring ***Needful Things*** "the last Castle Rock story." Fortunately, he later recanted and brought "The Rock" back to a limited appearance schedule. King has sketched the history of Castle Rock since its initial appearance in ***The Dead Zone*** in 1979. It has been the site of many tragic events, including the Castle Rock Strangler murders (*The Dead Zone*); a rampage by the rabid dog **Cujo**; the destruction of much of the downtown by explosives (*Needful Things*); and lesser but more human ugliness (***Bag of Bones***). Tabitha King (see **King, Tabitha**) added to the fictional history of Castle Rock in her 1993 novel *One on One*.

Castle Rock is said to be the seat of Castle County, Maine's smallest county. The following are the important Castle Rock stories. Readers may wish to follow this order of publication to achieve the full benefit of enjoying Castle Rock and its history: *The Dead*

Zone, **Cujo**, "The Body," "Gramma," "Mrs. Todd's Shortcut," "Nona," "Uncle Otto's Truck," ***The Dark Half***, "The Sun Dog," *Needful Things*; "**It Grows on You**," *Bag of Bones*; "**The Man in the Black Suit**" and ***Under the Dome***.

Genesis: The April 1985 issue of the King fan newspaper, also *Castle Rock*, published by King's sister in law Stephanie Leonard, confirmed that king got the name from William Golding's book *Lord of the Flies*, which King read as a teenager.

Trivia: A small New England mill town in western Maine, Castle Rock is west of Pownal in the Lakes Region, and is about 30 miles from Norway and 20 from Bridgton. Bangor is 160 miles to the northeast. For reasons that remain unclear, King set **Sleepwalkers** in the town of Castle Rock, Indiana. And in his unproduced screenplay of *The Dead Zone* it morphed into Cleaves Mills, Maine.

The Cat from Hell

Despite being first published in 1977, King did not allow this short story to be collected until **Just After Sunset**, 31 years later.

In this tale a hit man is hired to kill a cat. Drogan, who owns a large pharmaceutical business that had killed 15,000 cats in tests, hires John Halston to kill his house cat. Drogan suspects Sam the Cat of playing a part in the deaths of his sister Amanda, her friend Carolyn Broadmoor and his hired man, Dick Gage. Halston readily accepts the task.

Genesis: Nye Wilden, the fiction editor at the men's magazine *Cavalier*, sent King a photograph of a house-cat, "a startling close up of a snarling face, half black, half white." It would be the illustration for a story, for which he wanted King to write only the first 500 words; readers would complete the tale as part of a competition. King wrote an entire story and says the ending "echoed the ending of Poe's *The Black Cat*. At any rate, that was the only time I ever wrote a story to order—and from a photograph, at that. Whew! That was one scary housecat." King's original 500 word starter was published in the March 1977 edition of *Cavalier*, and his complete version was in the June 1977 edition.

Movie: "The Cat from Hell" segment in *Tales from the Darkside: The Movie* (1990) adapts this tale. The screenplay is by zombie fame director George A. Romero, but the segment itself is instantly forgettable.

Cat's Eye

King's original screenplay was released as the movie *Cat's Eye* (or *Stephen King's Cat's Eye*) in 1985. The script has three basic parts—a wrap-around story, "**The General**," and adaptations of King's tales "**The Ledge**" and "**Quitters, Inc.**," but in this version both are significantly different from the original stories. "The General" section is also notably different in this screenplay from the version published later.

In the tale a woman blames her cat for her daughter's death, not knowing an evil five-inch tall creature had stolen the girl's breath. The cat escapes the woman's insane rage and wanders the city, observing the clash of wills between two men, both of whom are forced to negotiate the narrow ledge of a tall apartment building, and is captured by a very unusual quit-smoking company before escaping again to a suburban home. There the cat is given the name General and faces another confrontation with the evil creature, the result of which will determine whether another young girl will live or die.

The screenplay is difficult to find but copies do circulate in the King community and are sometimes available from online King specialists.

Genesis: Dino De Laurentiis asked King to create another vehicle for Drew Barrymore in mid–1983, during the shooting of *Firestarter*, in which the young actress starred. King's initial treatment over fifteen pages was titled *The Cat*.

Movie: Not one of the best King adaptations, it does showcase a young Barrymore. Perhaps the best fun a viewer can have is watching out for multiple King nods—look for references to *Carrie*, *Cujo*, *Christine*, *Pet Sematary* and *The Dead Zone*.

Cavell, Douglas "Duddits" *see* Douglas "Duddits" Cavell

Cell

This 2006 novel is one of King's swings into science fiction and post-apocalyptic fiction (his most famous and best offering here is *The Stand*).

Comic book artist Clayton Riddell from Maine is on Boylston Street, Boston, beginning to celebrate his first big break in the publishing business when the world as he knows it begins to disintegrate around him. Suddenly what is later known as "The Pulse" strikes—driving everyone who uses a cell phone into a form of zombie. Trapped and a long way from home, Clay and the few fellow survivors who are lucky enough to not to have used a cell phone must try to survive in this sudden new world of horror and death. Clay tries to make it back to Maine, hoping his son has not become another victim.

Perhaps not King's best work, *Cell* is still a lot of fun and there are plenty of gory, and tense, scenes for the reader to savor. To promote the book, Internet bookstore Amazon released "the chilling first chapter of a work in progress" in the form of "The Pulse" on 7 July 2005. "The Pulse" was massively revised for the novel.

So many readers wrote to King's Web site about what they perceived as an unresolved ending to the novel that he felt obliged to post an explanation. As this is a "spoiler," readers can look up the message dated March 24, 2006, at www.stephenking.com/stephens_messages.html.

Genesis: King says he came out of a hotel in New York, saw a woman talking on a cell phone, and thought, "What if she got a message over the cell phone that she couldn't resist, and she had to kill people until somebody killed her?" Then he considered what would happen if everyone on a cell phone got the same message. Normal people would see the chaos and in turn call their loved ones on cell phones, "so the epidemic would spread like poison ivy."

Chambers, Jake *see* Jake Chambers

Charles Decker

In the novel *Rage*, Placerville High School student Charles Decker hears voices whispering terrible instructions. He hits a teacher with a pipe wrench at school and is expelled. Two months later Charlie returns to school armed and forces his fellow students into a series of potentially lethal mind-games.

Charlie

"Charlie" is a partial short story King wrote while still living at Bridgton, Maine, in the 1970s. Only six pages exist and the story ends in the middle of a paragraph. It is one of King's few attempts at pure science fiction; he may have sent it for publication but accepted its rejection on the basis it lacked any real science and was not much more than a horror tale set in space.

In the story a copper miner on Asteroid 419C (that is, 419C for "Charlie") finds incredibly valuable pink cubes. But before he can leave the asteroid an alien creature attacks and traps him in his hut. The miner called the creature Charlie, presumably after the asteroid itself, and fights it for four months. But Charlie finally breaks the airlock door and we last see the miner becoming ever more desperate.

It is very unlikely King will ever complete this story and few will ever read it, as it is held in a "Restricted" box at the Special Collections Unit of the University of Maine's **Raymond H. Fogler Library**. King's written permission is required to access the manuscript.

Charlie McGee

Charlie McGee is the young daughter of Andy McGee and his wife Vicki, both of whom had been subject to government drug experiments in **Firestarter**. Charlie is born with the ability to start fires with her mind and this brings her to the attention of **The Shop**, who kidnap her and her father. She forms a friendship with **John Rainbird**, one of her captors, but Charlie is determined to save her father and escape.

On the Screen: Drew Barrymore played Charlie in the 1984 film; Marguerite Moreau features in the role in the 2002 TV remake.

Chattery Teeth

There are two versions of this story. The first was published in *Cemetery Dance* magazine in Fall 1992 — that version can be found in *The Best of Cemetery Dance* (Cemetery Dance Publications, 1998) and *The Best of Cemetery Dance*, Vol. 1 (Roc, 2000). The story was significantly revised for **Nightmares and Dreamscapes**.

In the tale, Bill Hogan, a traveling salesman driving to Los Angeles, stops at a small store in the desert. He picks up a pair of broken novelty chattery teeth — and a hitchhiker. When the hitchhiker attempts to rob Bill, matters take a very strange turn.

Movie: "Chattery Teeth" is one of three stories in the compilation TV movie *Quicksilver Highway*. Mick Garris wrote the screenplay and directed.

Children of the Corn

In written form, "Children of the Corn" (or "Stephen King's Children of the Corn") is one of King's most powerful supernatural tales, but an increasingly atrocious series of films has dimmed the cachet of the tale for many fans.

The short story was first published in *Penthouse* magazine for March 1977 and collected the next year in **Night Shift** (that version has minor textual variations).

Burt and Vicky Robeson are driving the back roads of Nebraska when they run over the body of a boy lying on the road. Driving into the apparently abandoned town of **Gatlin**,

Nebraska, they are suddenly surrounded by vicious children, intent on capturing them — or worse. What could have happened in this town and can Burt and Vicky survive?

King's originality shines through in this tale, which should not be missed by those who enjoy his early horror offerings.

Genesis: Inspired by William Golding's classic, *The Lord of the Flies*.

Movies: The first adaptation was the 1983 short film *Disciples of the Crow*. It is best described as a very ordinary movie. However, it did win the Gold Hugo Award at the Chicago Film Festival. Readers can view it as one of two movies on the videocassette *Two Features from Stephen King's Night Shift Collection* (1991); or on *A Trilogy from Stephen King's Nightshift Collection*.

The much better known film version is 1984's *Children of the Corn* (also *Stephen King's Children of the Corn*), widely regarded as one of the worst King adaptations ever (King once listed it as one of the ten worst movies of all time). It is notable as the first feature movie made from a King short story. The screenplay for the movie was credited to George Goldsmith.

Children of the Corn (Unproduced Screenplay)

King wrote a screenplay for his short story "**Children of the Corn**" that was never produced. George Goldsmith, who did write the screenplay, allegedly based his version on King's. A series of films followed based on the same premise, making this one of King's most famous tales.

Chinga

King originally wrote a screenplay for an episode of *The X-Files*, under the title "**Molly**." Chris Carter, the creator of the series, added and significantly changed material, and both writers were credited with the new teleplay, "Chinga," making Carter one of King's few collaborators.

In the story an FBI agent visits an unnamed small Maine coastal town on a break. Earlier, Polly Turner's fisherman father found a doll in a lobster pot and gave it to his daughter. He was killed three days later in a freak boating accident involving a grappling hook.

People begin to act strangely around the doll, clawing their eyes, suffering strange accidents, and killing themselves in odd and gruesome ways. Polly is thought to be autistic and it's unclear whether the doll or Polly is causing the mayhem. Agent Scully intervenes with the aid of the local police chief, but it's a race against time to save the townsfolk, Polly and her mother.

While the screenplay has not been published, copies freely circulate in the King and *X-Files* communities.

Television: "Chinga" first aired on 8 February 1998 as an episode of *The X-Files*. It appears on the DVD for Series Five.

Chip Coombs

King keeps journals in which he writes thoughts and stories. Four incomplete stories were in King's handwriting in just such a journal at the **Raymond H. Fogler Library** of the University of Maine at Orono. For security reasons the journal has been moved to Box 1010 at the Special Collections Unit, meaning would-be readers need King's written permission. Other partial stories in the journal indicate it was written in the 1989–91 time frame. Using King's titles in the journal, the stories have been dubbed "**Muffe**," "**The Evaluation**," "**Movie Show**" and "Chip Coombs."

King's fascination with psychiatry as featured in "**The Boogeyman**" and central to "**Keyholes**" and "**Comb Dump**" recurs here. In this 36 page fragment Chip Coombs attends his first appointment with psychiatrist, Dr. Monica Good, at her office in downtown Cleveland. He has unspecified concerns and has requested more and more frequent electro-cardiograms from his family physician, Dr. Amos Light, who had finally referred him to Good. Coombs has also begun to lose weight.

Coombs tells the doctor he has a "dangerous friend," whom they should call "Red McFarland." He and Red attended school together in Ohio, played basketball on a championship team, and then decided to learn barbering together in Zanesville. During their six months at the barbering school they shared an apartment and a car (by this stage the reader may be wondering if Chip and Red are in fact the same person).

McFarland was very successful with women but started drinking heavily and then hitting the girls he brought home to the apartment. On graduation McFarland moved to the town of Blood, Ohio, and opened his own barber shop in a nearby mall. Coombs headed for Boston, got a job in a barber shop and stayed for seven years. Coombs returned to Ohio eleven years before his appointment with Dr. Good.

Doctor and patient schedule a second appointment for the next day. Coombs then mentions A Cut Above, a barber's shop in the Paradise Mall in Blood, which had been owned by Roger McFerry but had now gone out of business. McFerry had been running the business into the ground for four years but had suddenly returned with a nest egg. Presumably, the reader is to suspect that Red McFarland has morphed into Roger McFerry. Unfortunately, the story fragment ends at this point and it seems unlikely King will ever return to this tale.

Christine

Christine is of King's better known novels, partly through the movie version, but mainly because of King's originality in creating a haunted, or possibly evil, car. The 1983 novel reached number 1 on the paperback bestseller lists, further confirming King's rising star.

Arnie Cunningham (the surname a tip to the TV series *Happy Days*) sees an old, beaten up car for sale; he falls immediately in love and buys it on the spot. The red and white 1958 Plymouth Fury went by the name Christine. The previous owner, the rather disgusting **Roland LeBay** (one of King's more memorable bad guys), doesn't tell Cunningham that his young daughter had choked to death in the car, or that his wife had committed suicide in it.

Unable to keep the car at home, Cunningham takes it to Darnell's Garage, where he works on it almost constantly. Christine seems to take on a life of "her" own, with bits of the vehicle fixing themselves without help. Cunningham's school friends Dennis Guilder and Leigh Cabot tried to break the hold the car has over him, but she doesn't easily brook such interference.

This is no teenage angst love triangle — Cunningham does covet the beautiful Cabot, but there's a fourth entity in their relationship—a car with a mind (or soul) of its own. A tale of obsession and its results, the novel is full of deeply drawn minor characters and a setting that seems all too real.

Genesis: King says of the novel, "It's scary. It's fun, too. It's maybe not my best book—it's kind of like a high school confidential. It's great from that angle."

Trivia: In the original hardback, Christine is described as a four-door. When it was discovered that the 1958 Plymouth was only issued in a two-door model, this was revised for later printings.

Movie: *Christine* (1983). Directed by one of the premier horror and science fiction helmsmen of all time—John Carpenter (*Halloween*), this is enjoyable mainstream viewing.

Claiborne Blaisdell, Jr.

"Blaze" is the nickname of the dim-witted but lovable small-time crook, Claiborne Blaisdell, Jr., in the novel *Blaze*. He and his partner plan a kidnapping for ransom, which does not go to plan. Blaze was a normal child until his father subjected him to a beating that resulted in horrific head injuries and permanent brain damage. He is a thoroughly sympathetic character.

Claiborne, Dolores (Character) *see* Dolores Claiborne (Character)

Code Name: Mousetrap

One of King's earliest published writings, "Code Name: Mousetrap" was printed in the Lisbon High School newspaper, *The Drum*, of 27 October 1965. When teacher Prudence Grant, who had advised the paper's staff, retired in 2002 she ran across some original copies of the newspaper and one containing "**The 43rd Dream**," and sold them on eBay, thus bringing the previously unknown stories to light.

A burglar breaks into a supermarket, which is protected by a newly installed burglar alarm. Suddenly the shop itself comes awake and begins to try to trap the shocked man—can he escape the "rump roast with two glittering antenna" and its fellow attackers?

While the tale is written in the relatively immature manner of a teenager, it shows King's early fascination with the dangers of rampant technology and foreshadows "**Trucks**," *Maximum Overdrive* and "**The Mangler**," where technology suddenly becomes animate and dangerous. This is one of King's most original horror themes and, apparently, an old favorite. At this stage the story has not been published outside the school newspaper and is almost impossible to obtain.

Coffey, John *see* John Coffey

The Colorado Kid

To date, this 2005 novel has only been issued as a paperback original and is still in print. Many King fans may have missed the release, as it was not issued by his normal publishers, nor given the normal prominence by booksellers. This is a very interesting stand-alone mystery and its setting on an island in King's home state allows full rein for his empathy and understanding of his fellow Mainers. Serious King fans should read the tale, which even has possible links to **The Dark Tower cycle**.

A man's dead body is discovered on a beach. There's no identification and only the dogged work of two local newspapermen and a student turns up any clues. A year later the body is identified, but that's where the true mystery begins.

Genesis: King was originally contacted to write a blurb for the Hard Case Crime line of books but decided to write an entire short novel for this series in the style of "dime novel" crime paperback originals.

Television: The tale was adapted as the SyFy TV series *Haven*, screening from July 2010, but King said: "It looks like *The X-Files*. I don't think it looks like *The Colorado Kid*."

Comb Dump

"Comb Dump" is a 41-page incomplete and undated manuscript, which King apparently wrote in the 1980s. There is no indication that King ever continued writing it past the point at which it ends. A point of interest is the link to other tales through mention of the **Juniper Hill Asylum for the Criminally Insane** and of **Derry, Maine**.

In this story fragment a young cocaine addict decides to attend a rehabilitation clinic near Augusta, Maine. Tommy Brigham has an old black comb in his pocket when he checks in. It has three broken teeth in the middle and a little broken jagged bit at one end. The comb mysteriously starts to replicate a week later, with exact copies continuing to appear until there are six.

Readers can check out the story at the Special Collections Unit of the University of Maine's **Raymond H. Fogler Library**. Ask for Box 1012.

Coslaw, Marty *see* Marty Coslaw

Crandall, Jud *see* Jud Crandall

The Crate

"The Crate" is one of the most interesting of King's stories that have yet to appear in one of his own fiction collections. It's a quirky horror tale in the tradition of EC Comics and appeared in a men's magazine, *Gallery*, in July 1979. Within months King had included a revision of the story in his screenplay for ***Creepshow***, and the story also appeared, again revised, in the graphic collection of the same name released in 1982. In 2010 it was finally collected in mass-market form in *Shivers 6* (Cemetery Dance Publications) and this will be the most accessible form for readers.

In the tale a university janitor finds a strange crate, labeled from an 1834 Arctic expedition. After contacting a professor they open the box and a monster inside kills the janitor before retreating. In shock, Dexter Stanley confides in his friend, Henry Northrup, who devises a plan to finally deal with someone close to them both.

A raw, satisfying and rollicking tale of tragedy and release, this prose story has also been reprinted in a number of obscure anthologies.

Genesis: According to King expert George Beahm, "The original inspiration came from a real-life incident at the University of Maine at Orono, where an old crate dating back to the previous century had been discovered in the basement of one of the buildings on campus. What, King thought, could have been in that crate?"

Movie: *Creepshow* (1982), in "The Crate" segment, starring Hal Holbrook and Adrienne Barbeau.

Graphic Novel: "The Crate" segment of *Creepshow* (New American Library, 1982).

Creed, Gage *see* Gage Creed

Creed, Louis *see* Louis Creed

Creepshow (Graphic Novel)

Creepshow is a graphic novel tie-in to the movie of the same name. King also wrote the screenplay (see next entry). Published by New American Library in 1982, it contains classic EC Comics style artwork by King favorite Bernie Wrightson. The book can be found at online second-hand booksellers.

It collects two previously published King tales, "**Weeds**" (appearing here as "**The Lonesome Death of Jordy Verrill**") and "**The Crate**," along with three original pieces adapted from the screenplay: "**Father's Day**," "**Something to Tide You Over**" and "**They're Creeping Up on You**." Amazingly, not a single one of these tales appears in a mainstream King fiction collection. "Weeds" and "The Crate" are important tales in King's canon that perhaps will receive wider circulation at some point.

Creepshow (Screenplay)

King wrote the screenplay for the anthology movie *Creepshow*. It adapts two previously published King tales. "Weeds" appears in the screenplay as "**The Lonesome Death of Jordy Verrill**," along with "**The Crate**." Three original pieces are adapted from the screenplay: "**Father's Day**," "**Something to Tide You Over**" and "**They're Creeping Up on You**." The screenplay includes a "wrap-around" segment. In Centerville, Billy's father throws away the boy's First Issue Collector's Edition of the comic magazine *Creepshow*. Later, a trash collector picks the book out of the garbage and pockets it for his kids. Included among the stories shown in the actual comic book are all the segments viewers are to see in the movie. The character that introduces each segment is itself called Creepshow. This creature looks like an "old witch, or maybe a rotting corpse."

Genesis: King's participation in this project marked his first professional involvement in the film and television industry. Director George Romero and producer Richard Rubinstein came up with the idea, in the summer of 1979, of "scaring an audience so badly and so continuously that they will have to almost literally crawl out of the theater." This sure didn't happen but, inspired by the famous EC Comics, King did deliver a screenplay in the promised two months.

Movie: The tongue-in-cheek movie, a mix of drama, satire, irony and horror, was performed by an ensemble cast including Ted Danson, Hal Holbrook, Leslie Nielsen and

Ed Harris. King himself is superb as **Jordy Verrill** in "The Lonesome Death of Jordy Verrill" segment. **Joseph King** (aka **Joe Hill**) also appeared as Billy, the original owner of the *Creepshow* comic book. Directed by the creator of the zombie movie genre, George Romero, it was released in 1982.

The Crimson King

The Crimson King is **Roland Deschain**'s nemesis in **The Dark Tower cycle**, in which we discover he has been trying to kill Stephen King since the future author was very young. While he should be the most-feared of all King's villains, in fact he is quite one-dimensional and many fans were disappointed when Roland finally confronted him at **The Dark Tower** in *The Dark Tower VII: The Dark Tower*. He appeared there as an old man with an enormous waxy, hooked nose, red lips, a small scar on his right eyebrow, a luxuriant white beard and long snow-white hair. He appears much more malevolent in Marvel's comic book adaptations.

He is first mentioned in *Insomnia*. The next significant update on his situation is in *Black House*, where readers learn he is locked in a cell at the top of the Dark Tower. Of course, he plays a crucial role in the last two novels of the Dark Tower cycle. Before moving to the tower, he lived in his castle, Le Casse Roi Russe in **End-World**; those who served him included John Farson (destroyer of **Gilead**) and **Randall Flagg**. He is one of **Mordred Deschain**'s fathers (Roland is the other); and he has many nicknames, including "Los," "The Lord of the Spiders," "The Lord of the Red" and the "Lord of Discordia."

Comic: Portrayed in Marvel's *The Dark Tower* comic series.

Cross, Nadine *see* Nadine Cross

Crouch End

This Lovecraftian story was originally published in *New Tales of the Cthulhu Mythos* (Arkham House, 1980) and was heavily revised for later inclusion in *Nightmares and Dreamscapes*. Lovecraftian tales (or those of the "Cthulhu Mythos") relate to the universe created by author H.P. Lovecraft and often involve monsters or dark gods that lurk in a dimension that sometimes overlaps our reality. As those tales go, King's contribution is well regarded.

American lawyer Lonnie Freeman and his wife, Doris, intend to visit a work acquaintance while in London. On the way to the suburb of Crouch End they realize they've lost the address. Their cabby stops at a phone box, but while they are calling he drives off, leaving them stranded. After securing the address the Freemans start to walk but when they hear the sound of someone in trouble behind a hedge Lonnie goes to investigate. Doris hears strange noises and Lonnie screaming before he bursts through the hedge yelling for her to run. Suddenly the suburb becomes strange and unfamiliar even to overseas visitors. Where are they, and what are they running from?

There are similarities between this Cthulhu Mythos reality and at that of *The Talisman* and *The Dark Tower* series, each involving different worlds. One character proposes a theory that Crouch End is in a place where the boundary between dimensions is "thinner" than in most places.

Television: "Crouch End" episode on *TNT's Nightmares and Dreamscapes: From the Stories of Stephen King*. Competently delivered and fairly true to King's vision.

Genesis: In mid–October 1977, Stephen and **Tabitha King** were invited to dinner with Peter Straub in the London suburb of Crouch End. But they got lost and this served as King's inspiration for this tale. In the fictional version there is mention of a husband who went out for a pack of fags (English slang for cigarettes) and just never came back. This is how King's father left his family, when Stephen was but two years old.

Cujo (Character)

Cujo is a five-year-old St. Bernard and a key character in the novel of the same name. He is gentle — a good dog, but contracts rabies after being bitten by a bat, then slowly loses his mind (King does a tremendous job of putting readers inside the head of this conflicted creature and it is impossible not have empathy for his plight). He becomes a threat to all in the area around the isolated Camber family farm. Donna Trenton and her son, **Tad Trenton**, find themselves trapped at the farmhouse in a broken down car, with the massive, deranged dog nearby.

The following section of the novel says it best: "Cujo slept. He lay on the verge of grass by the porch, his mangled snout on his forepaws. His dreams were confused, lunatic things. It was dusk, and the sky was dark with wheeling, red-eyed bats. He leaped at them again and again, and each time he leaped he brought one down, teeth clamped on a leathery, twitching wing. But the bats kept biting his tender face with their sharp little rat-teeth. That was where the pain came from. That was where all the hurt came from. But he would kill them all."

Cujo is also mentioned in **"Mrs. Todd's Shortcut,"** "The Sun Dog," *Pet Sematary*, *Needful Things*, "The Body," *The Dark Tower* and *The Dark Half*.

On the Screen: Five different dogs played Cujo in the film of same name; he makes a brief cameo appearance in the film *Cat's Eye*.

Cujo (Novel)

This **Castle Rock, Maine**, novel is closely linked with other Maine tales such as *The Dead Zone*, through both its setting and characters such as Sheriff **George Bannerman**. It is one of King's better known tales, partly due to the movie adaptation and partly due to the fact that the eponymous character has entered the common cultural myth. It won the August Derleth Award (Best Novel) for 1982 from the British Fantasy Society and the hearts of readers worldwide.

Donna Trenton, her husband Vic away on a business trip and both of them angry over her recent affair, takes her ailing Pinto out to the isolated Camber property to be serviced. But the Camber family's dog, **Cujo**, a good and gentle St. Bernard, has been bitten by a rabid bat while chasing a rabbit. The disease has taken hold and Cujo, having lost his mind, keeps Donna and her young son, Tad, trapped in the car on a lethally hot summer's day in Castle Rock.

The story features a remarkably sympathetic Cujo's thought processes, and the scenes from the Monster in the Closet section (where **Tad Trenton** tries to convince his parents a monster is living in his closet) reminds the readers of their own childhood fears. Joe

Camber is another of the thoroughly believable, and totally unlikable, rural Maine characters King delivers so well, particularly early in his career.

Movie: *Cujo* (1983). Based on King's own screenplay for which he did not receive final credit, there are genuinely terrifying scenes in one of the better big-screen King adaptations. See also **Cujo** (**Unproduced Screenplay**).

Genesis: One day King went to an isolated farm where he'd heard he could get his motorcycle serviced. When he got there a St. Bernard approached him and attempted to bite his hand, before his owner hit it with a socket wrench. He got to thinking about what might have happened if the mechanic had not been there. He mixed that thought with memories of the first new car the Kings ever owned, a Pinto, with which they had problems starting from time to time. Finally, he wondered what would happen if the dog was not just mean, but rabid.

In *On Writing*, King (detailing his drug and alcohol addiction) writes: "At the end of my adventures I was drinking a case of sixteen-ounce tallboys a night, and there's one novel, *Cujo*, that I barely remember writing at all. I don't say that with pride or shame, only with a vague sense of sorrow and loss. I like that book. I wish I could remember enjoying the good parts as I put them down on the page."

Movie: *Cujo* (1983) starred Dee Wallace and is a very competent and compelling adaptation.

Cujo (Unproduced Screenplay)

There is an interesting history to the final screenplay for the 1983 movie adaptation of King's early novel *Cujo*. After King wrote the first draft, responsibility passed to two other writers. The Writer's Guild of America denied King a writer's credit after one of those lodged a protest. King said later, "I was in England at the time and I just didn't have time to mess with it." In the end, the movie version is only slightly different from King's first draft screenplay.

For King fans, the main interest in this screenplay are changes he makes from the novel, especially the ending, which was changed to suit audience sensibilities. One result is that Sheriff **George Bannerman** apparently lives in alternate King universe realities.

Readers can check out this screenplay at the Special Collections Unit of the University of Maine's **Raymond H. Fogler Library**. Ask for Box 2316.

Cullen, Tom *see* Tom Cullen

Cunningham, Arnie *see* Arnie Cunningham

The Cursed Expedition

This piece of juvenilia appears in *People, Places and Things*, along with six other King tales. Two astronauts travel to Venus and find breathable air, perfect temperature and delicious fruit. Keller calls it the Garden of Eden but Bullford has his doubts, which are confirmed when he finds Keller dead.

King returned to the "living planet" theme with "**Beachworld**."

Cycle of the Werewolf

Originally intended to be a calendar, that project finally became a limited edition book, published by Land of Enchantment in 1983, evocatively illustrated by Bernie (or Berni) Wrightson. It was republished as a mass market paperback in 1985 and this is the form fans can easily access.

King also wrote a screenplay of this story, **Silver Bullet**. *Cycle of the Werewolf* and the screenplay were collected in a special paperback edition, also titled *Silver Bullet*.

In the story a werewolf stalks small town Tarkers Mills, Maine. Ten-year-old wheelchair-bound **Marty Coslaw** is an intended victim but manages to defend himself before identifying the local resident he believes responsible. Who will survive the ultimate confrontation — the brave boy, or the supernatural creature?

Another of King's love letters to small-town Maine, in the guise of very short stories told in serial form, this tale is highly entertaining and suitable for younger readers.

Genesis: Originally conceived as a calendar concept, the idea grew as King wrote what were initially to be short monthly vignettes.

Movie: *Silver Bullet* (also known as *Stephen King's Silver Bullet*). With a screenplay by King and directed by Daniel Attias, this is a competent, viewable King adaptation and is unsurprisingly faithful to the original story. Corey Haim starred as Marty Coslaw and Gary Busey as Uncle Red. Released on DVD in 2003.

Daniels, Rose *see* Rose Daniels

Danny Torrance

Daniel Anthony (Danny) Torrance is a key character in **The Shining**. The son of **Jack Torrance** and his wife, Wendy, he moves with his family to **The Overlook Hotel** high in the Colorado mountains as caretakers for the winter. But Danny has a form of psychic communication known as "the shine." When the family lived in Stovington, Vermont, his father broke his arm in a drunken rage, and he is not yet six when the family moves to the Overlook. He sees many images in the hotel and is at great risk from both a mysterious force in the building and his father.

King updates Danny's story in **The Shining Mini-Series Screenplay**, and he is mentioned in the screenplay **Storm of the Century**. **Eddie Dean** thought of him in **The Dark Tower II: The Drawing of the Three**.

On the Screen: Danny Lloyd played the role in Kubrick's movie version; Courtland Mead appeared as Danny in the television mini-series.

Danse Macabre

Danse Macabre is one of King's three volumes of non-fiction (the others are **Faithful** and **On Writing**). First published in 1981 (now becoming quite dated), it was re-issued in a slightly revised edition (to correct some initial errors) in 1983. The rarely used full title of the book is *Stephen King's Danse Macabre*.

King says the book is "intended to be an informal overview of where the horror genre has been over the last thirty years, and not an autobiography of yours truly." And so it largely is, although King does relate a number of stories from his youth to illustrate certain points and even explicates some of his dreams: "I am a writer by trade, which means that the most interesting things that have happened to me have happened in my dreams."

King makes two major arguments here. The first is about horror itself:

> The closest I want to come to definition or rationalization is to suggest that the genre exists on three more or less separate levels, each one a little less fine than the one before it ... terror on top, horror below it, and lowest of all, the gag reflux of revulsion. My own philosophy as a sometime writer of horror fiction is to recognize these distinctions because they are sometimes useful, but to avoid any preference for one over the other on the grounds that one effect is somehow better than another. The problem with definitions is that they have a way of turning into critical tools—and this sort of criticism, which I would call criticism-by-rote, seems to be needlessly restricting and even dangerous. I recognize terror as the finest emotion and so I will try to terrorize the reader. But if I find that I cannot terrify, I will try to horrify, and if I find that I cannot horrify, I'll go for the gross-out. I'm not proud.

His second argument is that there are three major archetypes in modern horror fiction: "These three are something special. They stand at the foundation of a huge skyscraper of books and films—those twentieth-century gothics which have become known as 'the modern horror story.' Like an almost perfect Tarot hand representing our lusher concepts of evil, they can be neatly laid out: the Vampire, the Werewolf, and the Thing Without a Name."

For those interested in how King became a horror writer and some of his early inspirations, reading this volume is a must. The same may be said of those deeply interested in the horror genre (King's reviews of ten major horror novels of the period alone is worth the price of the book). However, the reader only interested in his fiction may wish to give it a pass.

Despite being asked many times to issue an updated version, King demurs, indicating he regards the idea as involving too much work.

Genesis: In November 1978, King received a call from Bill Thompson, the editor who "discovered" him for Doubleday (they worked together on the five novels from *Carrie* to *The Stand*). King had left Doubleday as a result of commercial policies toward their authors and Thompson had also moved—to become senior editor at Everest House. Thompson proposed a book about the "entire horror phenomenon," but this was quickly watered down to the previous thirty years. King says in the forenote to the book, "All this is by way of acknowledging Bill Thompson, who created the concept of this book. The idea was and is a good one. If you like the book that follows, thank Bill, who thought it up. If you don't, blame the author, who screwed it up." The title apparently derives from the French "La Danse Macabre" ("Dance of Death" in English), a late-medieval allegory for the universality of death.

The Dark Half

In this novel a pseudonym literally refuses to lie down and die. **Thad Beaumont** is a successful novelist, writing both under his own name and secretly using the pseudonym **George Stark**. But he makes the fateful decision to bury Stark and to reveal the pen name to the public. In a media performance Stark is "buried" but soon the "gravesite" has been dug up and tracks lead away from it. Bodies begin to pile up and the finger of suspicion points directly at Thad Beaumont. Is it possible Stark has come to life? If so, how will the ultimate confrontation between alter egos play out?

Now regarded as one of King's lesser novels, it is nevertheless important in his canon, reflecting as it does his own battle to deal with the impact of a pseudonym —**Richard Bachman**. At the same time it's a fast-paced novel, filled with dread and placed in the familiar setting of **Castle Rock, Maine**.

Apart from the Maine locale, there are extensive links between this novel and King's other works; for instance, **Alan Pangborn** is also the sheriff of Castle Rock in "**The Sun Dog**," *Needful Things* and *Gerald's Game*. Readers are given an update on both Thad Beaumont and Alan Pangborn in *Bag of Bones*.

Genesis: King says this novel develops one of his deep interests, "the terrible attraction violence sometimes has for fundamentally good people." One inspiration is that "sometimes twins are imperfectly absorbed in the womb.... What if this guy is the ghost of a twin that never existed?"

Trivia: Donald E. Westlake wrote crime novels using the pseudonym Richard Stark from the early 1960s to the mid 1970s. This name was King's inspiration for the pen name George Stark. The original title of *The Dark Half* was to have been *Machine's Way* (Alexis Machine is a key, violent character, in two of the Stark novels). One manuscript version of the tale is headlined as "by Stephen King and Richard Bachman."

Movie: *The Dark Half* (1992). A competent adaptation directed and written by George A. Romero, the leading zombie movie helmsman and one of the most notable horror directors of all time.

The Dark Man

Probably King's most important poem, "The Dark Man" features the first appearance of the as yet unnamed **Randall Flagg**, as King confirmed in a 2003 interview. It is therefore impossible to overstate its importance in the King canon, yet the poem also stands alone as a stunning work. In only five verses King delivers a horrific spectral being, fully formed to prey on our subconscious. Serious King readers must not miss this poem.

First published in the University of Maine literary publication *Ubris* (Fall 1969), it was reprinted in another small magazine, *Moth*, the following year, along with two other King poems, "**Donovan's Brain**" and "**Silence**." It has never been included in one of King's books but can be found in a collection of horror poems, *The Devil's Wine* (Cemetery Dance, 2003). The original *Ubris* may be photocopied at the **Raymond H. Fogler Library**.

The Dark Tower Cycle

King outlines the origins of what many regard as his magnum opus, the Dark Tower cycle, in his introduction to the revised edition of **The Dark Tower I: The Gunslinger**, titled "On Being Nineteen (and a Few Other Things)." Inspired after reading J.R.R. Tolkien's classic *The Lord of the Rings* in 1966 and 1967, he wanted to write something equally sweeping, but in his own way. In 1970, a film directed by Sergio Leone, *The Good, The Bad and the Ugly* inspired King to capture Tolkien's sense of quest and magic in a western setting. Another major inspiration is Robert Browning's 1855 epic poem "Childe Roland to the Dark Tower Came."

Despite King and many fine critics regarding The Dark Tower cycle as King's greatest work, the vast majority of King's fan base is still not familiar with the series of seven novels that make up the cycle, along with "**The Little Sisters of Eluria**." Many other King tales were written with specific Dark Tower intent—for instance, **Insomnia**, "**Low Men in Yellow Coats**," "**Heavenly Shades of Night Are Falling**" and **Black House**—and others were retro-fitted by King into the reality, such as **'Salem's Lot**. Readers and fans wishing to have a complete understanding of King's canon simply cannot do so without having read the complete Dark Tower cycle.

Why have so many fans missed this literary treat? Two notable explanations present themselves. First, many fans appreciate King's horror output and view the series with suspicion, as it is often classified as fantasy. In fact, it is a mix of fantasy, western, science fiction and horror, and utilizes the worlds created by others (e.g., L. Frank Baum's Oz) while creating its own. The series magnifies the great storytelling skills, and the creation of vibrant characters the reader can literally fall in love with, that King readers are familiar with from his horror novels and short stories.

Secondly, the first novel, *The Dark Tower I: The Gunslinger*, is, frankly, difficult to read. King admits as much in the foreword to the revised edition. However, even that edition fails to satisfy, and is difficult for many readers to access. These readers should perhaps start with **The Dark Tower II: The Drawing of the Three** before moving on to **The Dark Tower III: The Wastelands** and **The Dark Tower IV: Wizard and Glass**. By this stage most fans are deeply hooked and will make the effort to read *The Gunslinger*, the events of which are also much more important to a reader by that point. The rest of the series can then be completed in order: **The Dark Tower V: Wolves of the Calla**; **The Dark Tower VI: Song of Susannah**; and **The Dark Tower VII: The Dark Tower**.

The cycle is a tale of all Realities and all Universes but is also the personal record of Roland Deschain's triumphs and tragedies. A flawed hero, Roland is one of King's greatest characters, and his (long) tale one of King's half-dozen greatest achievements.

The official cycle of novels and stories is complemented by **The Dark Tower Graphic Novels**, which are not written by King but, as all storylines and events in them are approved by King, can be considered canon.

At this writing, the only screen adaptation of a Dark Tower related tale is the delightful movie *Hearts in Atlantis*, which is actually an adaptation of "Low Men in Yellow Coats." In September 2010, Universal Pictures, NBC and Stephen King's office announced *The Dark Tower* cycle would be adapted for the big and small screen. The plan is for a first feature film, followed by a TV series that would bridge the tale through to a second feature film. A third film is also planned. Ron Howard is set to direct both the first film and the TV series (Howard is the Academy Award winning director of *A Beautiful Mind* and is well known as the actor who played Richie Cunningham on *Happy Days*). Akiva Goldsman, who is slated to write the initial movie and the TV series, also wrote the screenplays for *I Am Legend* and *The Da Vinci Code*.

In a press release King said, "I've been waiting for the right team to bring the characters and stories in these books to film and TV viewers around the world. Ron and Akiva ... along with Universal and NBC have a deep interest and passion for *The Dark Tower* series and I know that will translate into an intriguing series of films and TV shows that respect the origins and the characters in *The Dark Tower* that fans have come to love."

Hard-core Dark Tower fans, many of whom are seriously addicted to the cycle and many of whom actually do not read King outside this Reality, are deeply concerned that any such adaptation be of the highest possible quality—Goldsman's screenwriting, Howard's direction, the casting and the investment in the overall productions will be critical to the movies and the TV series.

The Dark Tower Graphic Novels

In October 2005 King and Marvel Comics announced the Dark Tower mythos would be extended with the publication of an initial six comic arc (to be collected in a hardcover edition). A series of arcs were published from 2007 and can be also purchased in collected hardback editions. Readers should note the original comic arcs, while collected in the hardcover graphic novels, contain a lot of background material about the Dark Tower Universe that are not included in those collections. This background is described by King's former research assistant and writer of the comic series, Robin Furth. All storylines are approved by King and can be considered canon by readers.

Perhaps the most important contribution that these graphic novels make is to describe the Fall of **Gilead** (**Roland Deschain**'s home city) and the Battle of Jericho Hill (the result of which sets up Roland's entire quest), neither of which were covered in any detail in King's novels.

The comics and graphic novels may be purchased from specialist stores or on the Internet without difficulty.

To the time of writing the comic arcs/graphic novels were: *The Dark Tower: Gunslinger Born*; *The Dark Tower: The Long Road Home*; *The Dark Tower: Treachery*; *The Dark Tower: The Sorcerer* (one-shot comic, not collected); *The Dark Tower: Fall of Gilead*; *The Dark Tower: The Battle of Jericho Hill*; *The Dark Tower: The Gunslinger — The Journey Begins*; *The Dark Tower: The Gunslinger — Sheemie's Tale* (apparently a one-shot comic) and *The Dark Tower: The Gunslinger — The Little Sisters of Eluria*.

The Dark Tower (Place)

The Dark Tower is in **End-World** and is the object of **Roland Deschain**'s epic quest in **The Dark Tower cycle**. In *Stephen King's The Dark Tower: A Concordance*, Robin Furth defines the Dark Tower as

> a looming gray-black edifice which is simultaneously the center of all universes and the linch-pin of the time/space continuum. All worlds and all realities are contained within its many levels.... The line of Eld, of which Roland is the last, is sworn to protect the Tower. Yet a terrible illness affects this structure, one that is often compared to cancer.... The Tower is held together by a network of magical magnetic forces — rays, known as Beams ... the Beams, Portals and mechanical Guardians are breaking down. If the weakening Beams collapse and the Tower falls, all creation will blink out of existence.

The importance of the town to Roland's quest cannot be underestimated. It sits in a field of red roses, the Can'-Ka No Rey.

The Dark Tower I: The Gunslinger

"The man in black fled across the desert and the gunslinger followed." The opening sentence of this novel is the most famous in all of King's fiction, or non-fiction, for that matter. Written by a young scribbler with virtually no published output, it would come to symbolize an entire Reality and serve as foundation for perhaps King's most important work.

The first novel in **The Dark Tower cycle** was originally published over five serial parts in *The Magazine of Fantasy and Science Fiction* from 1978 to 1981, before being combined into the specialty press novel, first published in 1982. A mass-market edition of *The Dark Tower: The Gunslinger* was not published until 1988 and it was only from that point that King's wider fan base began to appreciate the importance of this Reality to his overall fictional output.

In 2003, King published a revised and expanded edition of *The Gunslinger*. He explains why in the foreword:

> Although each book of the Tower series was revised as a separate entity, I never really looked at the work as a whole until I'd finished volume seven, *The Dark Tower*. When I looked at the first volume ... three obvious truths presented themselves. The first was that *The Gunslinger* was written by a very young man, and had all the problems of a very young man's book. The second was that it contained a great many errors and false starts, particularly in the light of the volumes that followed. The third was that *The Gunslinger* did not even sound like the later books— it was, frankly, rather difficult to read. All too often I heard myself apologizing for it, and telling people that if they persevered, they would find the story really found its voice in *The Drawing of the Three*.

The novel itself brings readers to the trail as Roland Deschain, the last survivor of a mythic group of aristocratic gunslingers, chases his arch-nemesis. What lies behind their enmity, and why is it so important that Roland catch the mysterious man in black?

The Dark Tower II: The Drawing of the Three

In the second novel of **The Dark Tower cycle**, **Roland Deschain** wakes to finds himself on the edge of the Western Sea and under immediate threat from creatures that rise out of the water. Ill, but continuing northward, Roland finds mysterious doors that allow him entry into another world, one very familiar to readers. He meets **Eddie Dean** and a young black woman in a wheelchair who has two distinct personalities, the nice Odetta Holmes and the evil, foul-mouthed Detta Walker. Eddie and Odetta/Detta (better known as the series moves on as **Susannah Dean**) join Roland on his quest.

The Drawing of the Three is the true beginning of the love affair for the Dark Tower Reality for most fans, as the story builds pace and interesting characters join Roland. One of King's nastier bad guys, Jack Mort, appears in this tale.

King begins to link the Dark Tower to his other works for the first time when Eddie Dean recalls seeing the movie version of **The Shining** (**Danny Torrance** is specifically referred to).

The Dark Tower III: The Wastelands

The Dark Tower cycle continues in the third novel, in which **Roland Deschain, Eddie Dean** and **Susannah Dean** continue their journey. They meet and fight a diseased mechanical bear. As they travel Roland becomes more and more confused as his mind fails to deal with events surrounding **Jake Chambers**, a young boy he had let die once, and saved in another Reality. Timelines have been split and must be resolved if Roland is to retain his sanity. Meanwhile Jake knows he should have died and that he no longer belongs in his world and must somehow transit to Roland's.

The travelers reach the nightmarish post-apocalyptic city of Lud, but not before a billy-bumbler, Oy, joins them. Even if they can transit Lud and its marauding gangs alive, they must leave as passengers on a sentient but insane monorail.

Apart from the progression of Roland's tale, and the re-inclusion of Jake Chambers (one of the most important characters in King's fiction), the novel introduces Oy, who is beloved by most King readers, especially dog owners. Both will play critical roles in the future novels, as will a rose that is growing in a vacant block at the corner of 2nd Avenue and 46th Street in New York City.

King continues to link the Dark Tower Reality to his other works through simple devices such as *Inside View*, the scandal newspaper he invented, which also appears in *The Dead Zone*, "The Night Flier," *Bag of Bones*, *Desperation*, *From a Buick 8*, "Home Delivery," *Insomnia*, "Popsy" and *Needful Things*.

The opening scenes of the novel had previously been published as "**The Bear**" in *The Magazine of Fantasy and Science Fiction* for December 1990. That section was significantly rewritten for inclusion in the novel, so readers may wish to obtain the original version for comparison.

The Dark Tower IV: Wizard and Glass

The fourth novel in **The Dark Tower cycle** largely features a flashback to **Roland Deschain**'s youth, many long years before we first met him in *The Dark Tower I: The Gunslinger*. While Roland's group (now known as a "ka-tet," those bound together by fate or "ka") makes some progress in its quest for **The Dark Tower**, the vast majority of the novel is consumed with this powerful and defining part of Roland's backstory.

Roland tells his companions about his first ka-tet of other young members of **Gilead**'s aristocracy—Cuthbert Allgood and Alain Johns—and their adventures in the distant Barony of Hambry. Many memorable characters are introduced, including Roland's first love, Susan Delgado; the lovable and apparently witless **Sheemie Ruiz**; and tremendous villains including the witch, Rhea of the Coos, and the Big Coffin Hunters.

As the quest continues worlds start to meld. Finding themselves in Kansas, the ka-tet (now including **Jake Chambers**) comes upon a set of red slippers on the road to a crystal palace—it seems they have arrived in the Land of Oz. They come face to face with **Randall Flagg** (from *The Stand* and other King tales), but things may not be as they appear. Flagg reveals a shocking incident from Roland's past before the group members find themselves back on the path toward the still elusive Dark Tower.

Apart from the sheer power of Roland's backstory (one of King's most effective descriptions of deep, romantic love, and revealing Roland's motivations) the tale is notable for his introduction of many other fictional links, including Flagg and the Captain Trips superflu from *The Stand* and *Night Surf*. And the importance of **The Crimson King** (locked in a cell but controlling "Breakers" in an attempt to snap the Beams that hold the Dark Tower in place) is first revealed.

It would be six years (long years for fans of the series) before King would update Roland's story in *The Dark Tower V: Wolves of the Calla*. Many readers report this as their favorite of the entire Dark Tower series and it is very effective way of first entering the Dark Tower world—readers can start here and revert to *The Dark Tower I: The Gunslinger*, reading forward from there without encountering too many spoilers.

The Dark Tower V: Wolves of the Calla

The fifth novel in **The Dark Tower cycle** was long-awaited by fans. During the six year gap since *The Dark Tower IV: Wizard and Glass*, King had nearly been killed in an accident. But four years after the accident, King delivered *Wolves of the Calla*, and the last novel of the seven would be published within ten months.

Roland and his "ka-tet" of **Susannah Dean, Eddie Dean, Jake Chambers** and **Oy** arrive in the small town of Calla Bryn Sturgis, still on their way to the elusive **Dark Tower**. Mysterious creatures, known as Wolves, raid the town once each generation, taking one from each set of twin children from the town where most children are twins. The stolen children are returned some time later "roont," unable to do more than basic tasks. And now the Wolves are due to return, unsuspecting that a new breed of gunslingers are prepared to assist the townsfolk. Worse still, Susannah Dean's mind is coming under increasing control of an entity called Mia.

The local priest, **Donald "Pere" Callahan**, is from Eddie, Susannah and Jake's world. Stranger still, a novel arrives from that very world: **'*Salem's Lot*, by **Stephen King**, which strangely contains details of Pere Callahan's time in the town of **Jerusalem's Lot, Maine**. Despite their need to save the Dark Tower, it is time for the ka-tet to stand with the townspeople of the Calla.

King's re-introduction of Father Donald Callahan to his canon was received with high praise by fans and critics alike. The story itself becomes ever more complicated and therefore interesting for readers in this fast-paced tale, partly inspired by movies such as *The Magnificent Seven* (directed by John Sturges, who is honored in the naming of the Calla) and its predecessor, *Seven Samurai*. Among other developments are the importance of the number 19; the introduction of the author, Stephen King; the Low Men, who also appear in "**Low Men in Yellow Coats**"; and even references to the Harry Potter universe).

An excerpt from the novel, titled "**Calla Bryn Sturgis**," was published at www.stephenking.com in August 2001. In the novel it was substantially revised as the prologue. Another excerpt, "**The Tale of Gray Dick**," was published in *McSweeney's Mammoth Treasury of Thrilling Tales* in 2003. In the novel it was revised and appeared as the chapter "The Tale of Gray Dick."

The Dark Tower VI: Song of Susannah

The penultimate novel in **The Dark Tower cycle**, in which **Roland Deschain**'s progression toward **The Dark Tower** is diverted by his need to rescue **Susannah Dean**, appears to be set in the world and reality in which the novel's readers live.

Roland and **Eddie Dean** find themselves in a Maine in the year 1977, searching for the author of a novel, **'*Salem's Lot*. **Stephen King** is shocked to meet one of his unpublished characters but when recovered relates events in Roland's life, including those he had not yet written. Afterward, Roland hypnotizes King so he will not remember their visit.

Meanwhile, **Jake Chambers, (Donald) Pere Callahan** and **Oy** have arrived in a New York in the year 1999, following the trail of Susannah Dean and the creature Mia, who had taken control of the pregnant Susannah's body and much of her mind. Trying to delay the labor, Susannah convinces Mia to reveal her history and that of her "chap," the baby Susannah's body is carrying. The child, apparently Roland's, will be known as **Mordred Deschain** and will, at **The Crimson King**'s behest, grow up to slay his father, Mia claims.

The writer, Stephen King, maintains a journal in the years following Roland and Eddie's visit. In it he records his life, career and the publication of Dark Tower stories and novels. On 20 June 1999 an article in the Portland *Sunday Telegram* reports that on the previous afternoon, while walking Route 7 near his Lovell, Maine, home, King had been hit and killed by a van driven by Bryan Smith of Fryeburg.

The introduction of King as a character in his own "*uber* story" received a mixed reaction from critics, but near total support from fans and readers, due mostly to his ability to make this King a critical character to entire Dark Tower Cycle. King continues to draw links with his other fiction, including to "**The Mist**," *Eyes of the Dragon*, *Bag of Bones* and *Desperation*. Further references to the events of *'Salem's Lot* make satisfactory reading.

This novel is fast-paced and progresses the tale while introducing yet more complexity and risk for Roland and his widening group of companions and supporters. The end game is being revealed—with all the risks that continue to pile up, can Roland ever reach the Dark Tower and save all the Universes?

The Dark Tower VII: The Dark Tower

The final novel in **The Dark Tower cycle** begins with (**Donald**) **Pere Callahan**, **Jake Chambers** and **Oy** desperately trying to save **Susannah Dean** and expecting to die in the attempt. Callahan is offered an unexpected opportunity to redeem his soul. Susannah gives birth to **Mordred Deschain**, son of **Roland Deschain**, **The Crimson King**, Mia and Susannah. Will Mia's prophecy about Mordred's threat to Roland come to pass?

Reunited finally, the "ka-tet" now faces a last task before Roland can proceed to **The Dark Tower**—rescuing the Breakers the Crimson King is using in an attempt to destroy the Tower, including **Ted Brautigan** ("**Low Men in Yellow Coats**"), **Dink Earnshaw** (*Everything's Eventual*) and **Sheemie Ruiz**. Will the gunslingers succeed? If so, will Roland make it to the Dark Tower and a final confrontation with the Crimson King? And if so, who will prevail? After many long years (for Roland and readers) can the last of the Line of Eld succeed in his quest to save the Dark Tower and all Realities?

The redemption of Father/Pere Callahan, along with the reappearance of **Randall Flagg** and many characters from King's fiction, including King himself and Patrick Danville (*Insomnia*), and numerous references to events in other King novels including *The Dead Zone*, *Carrie*, *Black House*, *Cujo* and *It*, make very satisfactory reading for long-time King fans. The novel is full of poignant moments, some of which will bring even a hardened reader to tears, but as always, King's fiction is entirely honest. Every great saga must have an ending, and this one is perfect.

Dave Duncan

"Dirty Dave" Duncan was once Ardelia Lortz's lover in the novella "**The Library Policeman**." His life spiraled downward, and by the time of the tale he was an alcoholic (hence the nickname), but he plays an important role and is one of the more sympathetic and interesting of King's creations.

The Dead Zone

One of the best-known, well-loved and compelling of King's novels, *The Dead Zone* was King's first number 1 bestseller on *The New York Times* hardcover list in 1979. It also hit number 1 on the paperback list in 1980, the first King book to be number 1 on both lists.

Johnny Smith is a young man with a bright future — a new teaching job and the love of a new girl — Sarah Bracknell. But events from his past, along with a bizarre run on a carnival wheel of fortune seem to combine to destroy that promise. Johnny enters a long coma after a car crash and awakes to find he's lost his girlfriend but gained pre-cognitive powers. Those powers, which he did not seek and cannot avoid, will put everyman Johnny Smith on the road to collision with tragedy and evil, leaving him to confront his own mortality.

In this novel King introduces Sheriff **George Bannerman**, the politician **Greg Stillson**, the Castle Rock Strangler and the iconic town of **Castle Rock, Maine.** Castle Rock would become intimately familiar to King's "constant readers"; Bannerman would play a key role in *Cujo* and appears in many King stories, including "**The Body**"; Stillson is remembered as one of King's most interesting human villains; and the Castle Rock Strangler murders cannot be erased from the memory of any reader. Even this early in his career King was busily building links to his other works—for instance at one point Smith taught at Stovington Preparatory Academy in Vermont — **Jack Torrance** of *The Shining* once taught there, and Stovington is the site of the Plague Control Center where **Stu Redman** was held in *The Stand*.

Smith is one of the most sympathetic among all of King's characters, and King's naming of the character is perfect — he is the "everyman" that so often enriches American fiction.

Genesis: Parts of the novel are barely disguised autobiography — Johnny Smith and Sarah Bracknell attended the University of Maine at Orono (as did Stephen King and Tabitha Spruce, who would be King's wife) and may be King's idealized memory of their youth. King's motivation was a "what if?" — in this case, "What if a man was able to have this ability to see the future? The secondary thing was the visualization of this guy taking a test paper from a student and saying, 'You gotta go home right away. Your house is burning down.'"

Movie: The Dead Zone (1983). This compelling film is regarded by many as a classic. Directed by David Cronenberg, it has an outstanding cast, with a young Christopher Walken playing Johnny Smith, Brooke Adams as Sarah, Tom Skerritt as Bannerman, Herbert Lom as Sam Weizak and Martin Sheen brilliant as Greg Stillson.

TV Series: The Dead Zone or *Stephen King's The Dead Zone* ran over 81 episodes and six seasons from 2002 through 2007. Created by Michael Piller (various *Star Trek* series), the franchise had strong ratings and critical reviews although "based on Stephen King's *The Dead Zone* characters" might be the best description of the continuing storyline. Anthony Michael Hall played Johnny Smith; Nicole de Boer was Sarah Bracknell Bannerman; Chris Bruno was Sheriff Walt Bannerman, and David Ogden Stiers portrayed the Rev. Gene Purdy. All seasons are available on DVD.

The Dead Zone (Unproduced Screenplay)

Genesis: When Dino De Laurentiis purchased the production rights to *The Dead Zone*, he asked King to write a script but rejected the 1982 submission as "too complex." The movie was later produced with an entirely different screenplay.

One of the most interesting aspects of this script is King's decision to move Frank

Dodd's killings from his archetypal town, **Castle Rock, Maine**, to the town of Cleaves Mills, also in Maine (the town where the protagonist **Johnny Smith** was living in the novel when he went into a coma). By changing the town, King was also obliged to change the media name for the killer from the "Castle Rock Strangler" to "The Destroyer." Of course the question remains, why move this part of the action from Castle Rock at all? There are a number of other "alternative realities" in the script.

The screenplay can be read at the Special Collections Unit of the University of Maine's **Raymond H. Fogler Library**. Ask for Box 2317.

Dean, Eddie *see* Eddie Dean

Dean, Susannah *see* Susannah Dean

The Death of Jack Hamilton

This delightful story was first published in *The New Yorker*, a highly regarded magazine for which King has delivered a handful of pieces, and is collected in **Everything's Eventual**. In the tale career criminals, including the infamous John Dillinger, entertain a dying member of their gang. Artfully weaving fact with fiction, King delivers a tale that, while largely mainstream, is layered with humorous components and a slight touch of the fantastic. This departure from standard King fare can be enjoyed even by those who normally look down their literary noses at popular fiction.

Genesis: King was listening to an audio book about John Dillinger and heard that one of his gang members, Jack Hamilton, had been shot in the back. "Then all this other stuff happens to him ... I thought, I don't need [the author] to tell me what happens and I don't need to be tied to the truth. These people have legitimately entered the area of American mythology. I'll make up my own shit."

Decker, Charles *see* Charles Decker

Dedication

This rather nasty short story was first published in the anthology *Night Visions 5* (Dark Harvest, 1988), but King completely re-wrote it for inclusion in **Nightmares and Dreamscapes**.

Martha Rosewall, a housekeeper at the Le Palais hotel in New York, proudly brings her son's first novel in to show her workmates. After work she relates the events surrounding her son's birth to her friend Delores. Full of magic, violence and one rather disgusting event of a sexual nature, this is a very unusual King tale.

Two other unsatisfactory King stories appeared in the original anthology: "Sneakers" and "**The Reploids**." Readers seeking the original version, edited by Douglas Winter, will also find it published in the books *Dark Visions* (Gollancz, 1989) and *The Skin Trade* (Berkley, 1990).

Most likely due to the heavy sexual content of this piece, it has not been adapted for the screen. Adult readers should have no problem with the content but when guiding younger readers, discretion is advised.

Genesis: King says "Dedication" articulates his unease about famous, talented people who are "utter shits in person."

Dees, Richard *see* Richard Dees

Denbrough, Bill *see* Bill Denbrough

Denker, Arthur *see* Arthur Denker

Derry, Maine

Derry is near Bangor, Maine, on which it is in fact modeled, and fundamentally replicates that small city, which is also the Kings' "home town." It was first mentioned in "**The Bird and the Album**" (1981) and had its mass-market debut in one of King's best-loved (and longest) novels, *It* (1986).

According to King's mythology, in 1741 the entire population of Derry disappeared without trace. Sixty-seven people died when the water tower collapsed in 1985. Mysteriously, the town appears to have collective memory loss, considering the rampage against its children by a monster, often masquerading as the clown **Pennywise**, every quarter century or so (most recently in 1957–58 and 1984–85). That was chronicled in *It*, but in the interludes between the creature's rampages Derry has also been the site of a political killing (***Insomnia***) and individual human tragedy. As recently as 2001 there was further evidence of the clown-monster Pennywise's survival (***Dreamcatcher***), meaning the creature may return around 2011.

These are the main Derry stories, best read in order of publication: "The Bird and the Album" (revised and later included in *It*); *It*; "**Secret Window, Secret Garden**," *Insomnia*, "**Autopsy Room Four**," ***Bag of Bones***, "The Road Virus Heads North" and *Dreamcatcher*.

Deschain, Mordred *see* Mordred Deschain

Deschain, Roland *see* Roland Deschain

Desperation

Desperation was originally published with the **Richard Bachman** altered reality novel ***The Regulators***, and they share many character names.

Travelers pick the wrong time to traverse the Nevada desert near the small mining town of Desperation. One by one they are abducted by the town cop and taken into the eerily quiet town and locked up. Among them are the Carver family, including the deeply religious 11-year-old David; writer John Marinville and his sidekick Steve Ames; Cynthia Smith; and Peter and Mary Jackson. They soon realize Collie Entragian is more than a mad cop — he is possessed by an evil entity. More than their lives at are stake if they cannot escape.

This is classic King drama — the conflict of God and evil, filled with madness, action and another of King's compelling mythologies. The evil entity Tak has another life in *The Regulators* and parts of this new mythology are referenced in the latter part of **The Dark Tower cycle**.

Again, King links this tale to others, in particular *Rose Madder* (through Cynthia Smith). In **On Writing** King says *Desperation* addresses "the question of why, if there is a God, such terrible things happen." (He also classifies **The Stand** and **The Green Mile** as works on this theme).

Genesis: King says he drove through a deserted town in Oregon wondering what happened to all the people (he eventually set the book in a small Nevada desert town), and says the book is about God: "I was raised in a religious household, and I really wanted to give God his due in this book. So often, in novels of the supernatural, God is a sort of kryptonite substance, or like holy water to a vampire. You just bring on God, and you say 'in his name,' and the evil thing disappears. But God as a real force in human lives is a lot more complex than that. And I wanted to say that in *Desperation*. God doesn't always let the good guys win."

Television: *Desperation*, originally shown on the ABC network in 2006. With a teleplay by King and directed by King specialist Mick Garris (**The Shining**, **The Stand**, **Riding the Bullet**), this is an underrated presentation and is well worth viewing. Tom Skerritt plays John Marinville, Steven Weber is Steve Ames, Ron Perlman (*Hellboy*) appears as Collie Entragian; and character actor Charles Durning plays Tom Billingsley.

Desperation (Screenplay)

King adapted his novel **Desperation** in a teleplay, a copy of which is held in Box 2289 of the Special Collections Unit of the **Raymond H. Fogler Library** at the University of Maine, Orono. As this box is available to the public, those interested may read the 133-page script at the library.

A later version of the teleplay was produced for a 23 May 2006 premiere on the ABC-TV network. King did three feature drafts before Mick Garris put the script into television format. Garris directed the mini-series versions of **The Stand** and **The Shining** and the films **Sleepwalkers**, *Quicksilver Highway* and **Riding the Bullet**. ABC has a long relationship with King, having delivered *The Stand*, *The Shining*, **Storm of the Century**, **Rose Red** and **Kingdom Hospital** to viewing audiences.

Television: *Desperation* was originally shown on the ABC network in 2006.

Devore, Mattie *see* Mattie Devore

Dick Hallorann

Dick Hallorann is one of the best known King characters, appearing in **The Shining**. An African American, he is a cook at **The Overlook Hotel** during the tourist season. When

Jack Torrance and his family arrive to live at the hotel during the winter, Dick forms a friendship with **Danny Torrance** when he realizes the boy also has "the shine" (a psychic ability), a friendship that will serve them both well. Dick also appears briefly in *It*, as a cook at the **Derry** Army Base.

On the Screen: Scatman Crothers is an excellent Hallorann in Kubrick's *The Shining*; while Melvin Van Peebles is serviceable in the same role in *Stephen King's The Shining*.

Different Seasons

This is an important collection of four quality novellas, each with a subtitle referring to a season. They are "**Rita Hayworth and Shawshank Redemption**: Hope Springs Eternal"; "**Apt Pupil**: Summer of Corruption"; "**The Body**: Fall from Innocence; and "**The Breathing Method**: A Winter's Tale."

Dink Earnshaw

Earnshaw is the protagonist of the story ***Everything's Eventual*** and reprises as an important if minor character in ***The Dark Tower VII: The Dark Tower***, where he is a colleague of **Ted Brautigan** and **Sheemie Ruiz**. He has strange mental abilities, which feature in both tales.

Dino

This twelve-verse poem, homage to Dean Martin, is very readable and well worth a reader's trouble tracking down. It was originally published in *The Salt Hill Journal* (a literary journal published at Syracuse University in New York) for Autumn 1994. While it has never been included in a King book, he allowed it to be reprinted in *Stephen King: Uncollected, Unpublished* (Cemetery Dance, 2005).

Genesis: In 1991 King gave a reading in Syracuse University's Landmark Theater to help raise funds for the Raymond Carver Reading Series. While there he provided the poem to *The Salt Hill Journal*'s editors.

Discordia

"Discordia" is an Internet-based **Dark Tower cycle** experience, which can be accessed at King's official Web site, www.stephenking.com. The Metro DMA production features concept and 3D artwork by Brian Stark, engineering by Eric Klotzko, and original paintings by Michael Whelan. It is produced by Marsha DeFilippo, King's long-time personal assistant, and directed by Robin Furth, who wrote *Stephen King's The Dark Tower: The Complete Concordance* (Scribner, 2006) and acted as his research assistance when he wrote the last three novels in the cycle.

Based on events from *The Dark Tower* series, it concentrates on extending the mythos to cover the "behind-the-scenes conflict" between the Tet Corporation and Sombra/NCP. New characters appear in the tale, which can be considered Dark Tower canon, in that all material was approved by King, who acted as executive producer for the project.

Do The Dead Sing?

This beautiful and haunting short story is one of the few King pieces of fiction for which the title was changed. It was originally published as "Do the Dead Sing?" in *Yankee* magazine in November 1981 and only republished in that form in *The Best of Yankee, 1935–1985*. King substantially revised the tale and collected it in **Skeleton Crew** as "**The Reach**." While the core tale does not change, the original lacked the phrase "Do you love?"

Stella Flanders has lived her entire life on Goat Island, Maine. She has never ventured to the mainland, a short distance across the Reach, as in her nearly 96 years she has never found the need. But she begins to see her long dead friends and they have a proposal for her.

Copies of *Yankee* magazine are easily secured through eBay and second-hand resellers.

Genesis: King's brother-in-law, once in the Coast Guard, told him the story of a real-life Stella Flanders who never wanted to visit the mainland.

The Doctor's Case

This short story, set in the Sherlock Holmes universe created by Sir Arthur Conan Doyle, was originally published in *The New Adventures of Sherlock Holmes* anthology (Carroll and Graf, 1987) and collected in **Nightmares and Dreamscapes**.

Sherlock Holmes and Dr. Watson are invited to attend Lord Albert Hull's study, also the scene of the rather sadistic aristocrat's murder. As the famous detective Holmes is considering the clues, his reliable assistant Watson is able to solve the crime. Forty years after Holmes' death, he will reveal just how brilliant his deduction really was, along with a dark secret.

Here King delves into another writer's universe (as he did with L. Frank Baum's Oz in **The Dark Tower cycle**, and with Edgar Allan Poe in "**The Old Dude's Ticker**"), with considerable success. The ploy of concentrating on a secondary character is the core of this interesting, if largely unimportant, tale.

Dolan's Cadillac

King struggled to get this inventive short story published independently, partly because he'd originally allowed its publication in his office-published fan newspaper, *Castle Rock*, in 1985. In 1986 he indicated in private correspondence that, despite jokes that he could publish his own laundry list, no one would publish the tale. Finally, in 1989 Lord John Press published a limited edition book that included a revision, and that version appeared in **Nightmares and Dreamscapes** four years later.

Elizabeth Robinson, a first grade teacher, is in the wrong place at the wrong time, witnessing a crime committed by James Dolan, a career criminal. She agrees to testify against him but before she can is killed in a car explosion. Her husband begins watching Dolan's movements and planning his revenge. This is a fun tale and is not to be missed by any fan, let alone those who enjoy tension in their tales.

Genesis: King has stated this tale is a riff on Poe's *The Cask of Amontillado*, a classic tale of horror and revenge.

Movie: Dolan's Cadillac (2009), screenplay by Richard Dooling (*Kingdom Hospital*). Christian Slater plays Dolan.

Dolan's Cadillac (Unproduced Screenplay)

King attempted a screenplay of his revenge caper, "**Dolan's Cadillac**," but only five pages have come to light, held in his papers at the University of Maine. The only notable information from the screenplay is that Robinson, whose wife is murdered by Dolan, acquires a first name, Dave, that was not revealed in the original tale.

Readers can check out these pages at the Special Collections Unit of the University's **Raymond H. Fogler Library**. Ask for Box 1012.

Dollar Baby

King has a policy of charging a one-time rights fee of $1 for a short story to budding filmmakers who apply through his office. They must send him a copy of the short film and can only show it at film festivals and such. Their works cannot be released commercially without King's written permission, and he retains the full movie rights to his story.

The first Dollar Baby was Frank Darabont's ***The Woman in The Room***. King was so impressed he allowed Darabont the rights to "**Rita Hayworth and Shawshank Redemption**," from which Darabont wrote and directed *The Shawshank Redemption*, one of the most loved movies of all time. Darabont has since adapted ***The Green Mile*** and "**The Mist**" into stellar films.

Why does King maintain such a policy? He is a movie buff, often seeing dozens of movies in any given year; he is a supporter of the arts in general and particularly those starting off as writers or in the movie game. And finally, he is Stephen King—an altogether different breed from many of the Hollywood and money-focused big-name authors.

Dolores Claiborne (Character)

Dolores Claiborne is the feature character in the novel of the same name. Born on **Little Tall Island, Maine**, she marries Joe St. George, a drunk and a wife beater, but shows tremendous character in dealing with his aggression. Later in life she works for a retired wealthy resident, Vera Donovan. On 20 July 1963, during a total eclipse of the sun, she has a vision of a young girl, which is matched by the vision of **Jessie Burlingame** (as her young self, Jessie Mahout) in *Gerald's Game*. She almost certainly was on the island during the events of ***Storm of the Century*** but does not appear in that tale. Dolores is a model for hard-working women who make a stand in life.

On the Screen: Kathy Bates is simply brilliant in the movie *Dolores Claiborne* (1995).

Dolores Claiborne (Novel)

This relatively short novel features one of King's most notable characters—a woman suspected of murder, not once but twice, three decades apart. *Dolores Claiborne* draws a highly realistic view of both of an individual who has lived a hard but true existence and of life on **Little Tall Island, Maine**. Harrowing in parts, but also an examination of love, this literary experience surely leaves no reader unfeeling. Certain content may be unsuitable for young readers.

Dolores Claiborne is suspected of the murder of her employer, Vera Donovan. Such suspicion falls easily upon a woman whose husband had died mysteriously on the day of a total eclipse decades earlier. However, the police are only interested in the current case and Dolores begins to talk — unfolding two stories, each a confession and each a defense. Where will the guilt lie?

This novel was originally planned as part of a trilogy called *The Path of the Eclipse*. *Gerald's Game* and a third, unwritten, novel were to be the other. The tale is deliberately linked to *Gerald's Game* through Dolores "seeing" a little girl during the eclipse.

It is King's first major work set on Little Tall Island and would not be the last. The second was *Storm of the Century*, in which Dolores is mentioned. King also links this story to other Maine tales through the mention of **Derry**, and Little Tall Island itself is also mentioned in the *Nightmares and Dreamscapes* version of "**Home Delivery**" and in the TV series *Kingdom Hospital*.

Movie: *Dolores Claiborne* (1995). This film yielded a well-deserved Oscar nomination for Kathy Bates, in the title role. Jennifer Jason Leigh and Christopher Plummer also star in one of the best King screen adaptations.

Donald Merwin Elbert

Known as "The Trashcan Man" (or "Trashie"), Donald Merwin Elbert is an important character in *The Stand*. A pyromaniac, he lives a marginalized life until the superflu strikes, when his compulsion is allowed full reign. He travels to Las Vegas to join **Randall Flagg**.

On the Screen: Matt Frewer is brilliant in the role in *Stephen King's The Stand*.

Donovan's Brain

This 24-line poem appeared in a University of Maine literary magazine, *Moth*, in 1970 along with two other King poems ("**The Dark Man**" and "**Silence**"). It has never been included in one of King's books but can be found in a collection of horror poems, *The Devil's Wine* (Cemetery Dance, 2003).

Genesis: This piece is difficult to understand unless one has read Curt Siodmak's novel or seen the subsequent 1953 film, both with the same title as the poem, and on which it is based.

Douglas "Duddits" Cavell

Douglas "Duddits" Cavell is one of the best-loved characters in King's fiction, albeit he is a character in a lesser novel, *Dreamcatcher*. Duddits suffers from Down Syndrome and, as a boy, he is saved from bullies by **Gary Jones** and his friends. This act of kindness creates a life-long friendship, which will be critical when aliens make a bid to dominate the world when the boys grow to adulthood.

On the Screen: Donnie Wahlberg plays Duddits in the 2003 film.

Dreamcatcher

One of King's lesser novels (not helped by a highly questionable movie adaptation), this venture into science fiction is nonetheless important, as it critically updates the mythology of **Derry, Maine** (*It*, *Insomnia* and other tales).

A quarter century ago four boys bravely stood together and formed a bond that remains unbroken. This year, on their annual hunting trip, a stranger arrives at their camp, sick and talking of lights in the sky. Shortly, the four men find themselves in a battle for their lives, a battle they can only win by returning to their shared past. **Gary Jones** is the center of the struggle.

This is a tale of memory, the power of the human mind, love and darkness. Despite being a relatively minor novel, it does present one of King's most lovable and memorable characters, the intellectually handicapped **Douglas "Duddits" Cavell**, along with a creature among the grossest he has ever presented.

As the tale is partly set in Derry, there are strong links to most of King's Maine fiction, including references to **Castle Rock** and **Jerusalem's Lot**. Long time King readers will be delighted by direct and specific references to events described in **It**.

Abraham Kurtz's character is an apparent homage to the *Apocalypse Now* movie character, Colonel Walter Kurtz. In another interesting note, some review copies of the novel had Al Gore as president. This was later corrected to an unnamed president, presumably after Gore was defeated by George W. Bush in the November 2000 election and its controversial aftermath.

Genesis: King wrote this book between November 1999 and May 2000, while rehabilitating from the June 1999 accident in which he nearly died. The first draft was written in longhand, using a Waterman cartridge fountain pen, which King chose in an attempt to slow the pace of his writing. He says **Tabitha King** "simply refused to call this novel by its original title, which was *Cancer*. She considered it both ugly and an invitation to bad luck and trouble. Eventually, I came around to her way of thinking, and she no longer refers to it as 'that book' or 'the one about the shit-weasels.'"

Movie: A competent adaptation with a very disappointing ending. The screenplay is by William Goldman (**Misery**, *Butch Cassidy and the Sundance Kid*) and Lawrence Kasdan. Morgan Freeman plays Colonel Abraham Kurtz; Thomas Jane is Henry Devlin; Tom Sizemore plays Owen Underhill; Damian Lewis is Gary Jones; and Donnie Wahlberg appears as Duddits Cavell.

Dufresne, Andy *see* Andy Dufresne

Duma Key

In this novel, a successful builder-contractor is horribly injured in a construction site accident. As he recovers **Edgar Freemantle** struggles with not only his physical injuries but also psychological effects, including issues of memory. His marriage ends and he moves to Duma Key on Florida's Gulf Coast to begin a new life, painting as part of his therapy. He forms new friendships, which he will need as the secrets of Duma Key begin to unfold and supernatural forces threaten any future Edgar might have thought to build.

This is a complex novel, with a powerful supernatural overlay and a dangerous ancient enemy mixing with the prosaic nature of life—accident, divorce, love, the mysteries of the human mind and friendship. Sophisticated readers will enjoy its multi-layered nature and the care King takes in its writing.

There are some links to King's other fiction—for instance a direct reference to the concept of ka, as expressed in the Dark Tower series: "Life is a wheel, and if you wait long enough, it always comes around to where it started."

This novel won the Bram Stoker Award from the Horror Writers Association for Superior Achievement in a Novel. It reached number 1 on *The New York Times* hardcover bestseller list. According to King expert Bev Vincent, it was the 30th King book (beginning with *The Dead Zone*) to reach number 1, more than any author in the history of the list, which first appeared in 1942.

Genesis: The King family has had a home in Florida for many years and King finally felt he knew enough about the locale to attempt a novel based there. There is also an obvious working out of King's feelings about his own recovery from a horrific accident.

Duncan, Dave *see* Dave Duncan

Earl Candleton

A character from "The Butterfingers" episode of the TV series *Kingdom Hospital*, Candleton is one of King's least known but most compelling and sympathetic creations. During the 1987 World Series the New England Robins baseball player drops a simple fly ball. His team loses; he gains the nickname "Butterfingers" and his life spirals downward. But redemption may be at hand.

On the Screen: Callum Keith Rennie played the role.

Genesis: Candleton may represent King's working out of Red Sox Bill Buckner's infamous error in the 1986 World Series against the New York Mets. It did not actually cost the Red Sox the championship but was an incident which grew to represent "the Curse of the Bambino" and its ongoing impact upon the Boston team.

Earnshaw, Dink *see* Dink Earnshaw

Eddie Dean

Eddie Dean is first mentioned in *The Dark Tower I: The Gunslinger*, but he first appears as a character in *The Dark Tower II: The Drawing of the Three*. A heroin addict from New York City, he is 21 when he joins **Roland Deschain**'s "ka-tet" and he is a significant figure in the balance of **The Dark Tower** cycle. He becomes **Susannah Dean**'s de facto husband and is a close friend of **Jake Chambers** and his pet, **Oy**.

Eddie Kaspbrak

Eddie Kaspbrak is an asthmatic child dominated by his mother and living in **Derry, Maine**, in 1957–58. He and his friends—**Bill Denbrough, Benjamin Hanscom, Beverly Marsh, Richard Tozier, Stanley Uris** and **Mike Hanlon**—form "the Losers Club" in the novel *It*, in an attempt to fight **Pennywise**. As an adult he owns a limousine service and returns to Derry in 1985 when Mike Hanlon calls the Losers Club back. He also appears in "**The Bird and the Album**" and is mentioned in *Dreamcatcher*.

On the Screen: Dennis Christopher played Eddie in *It*.

Edgar Freemantle

In the novel *Duma Key*, a construction site accident leaves successful builder-contractor **Edgar Freemantle** horrible physical injuries and psychological effects, including issues of memory. His marriage ends and he moves to Florida's Gulf Coast to begin a new life on Duma Key. He begins painting as part of his therapy and finds new friends, who become vital as the secrets of Duma Key are revealed and supernatural forces threaten Edgar's future.

Genesis: King stated after the novel was published that Edgar is related to **Abagail Freemantle** (*The Stand*): "He is in fact her great-great-grandson. He has no idea of his Afro-American heritage." In *The Stand* universe, all of Mother Abagail's descendants die in the superflu, clearly delineating *Duma Key* as in a different timeline.

Edgecombe, Paul *see* Paul Edgecombe

Edie Rowsmith

One of King's least known but most interesting characters, Edie Rowsmith appears in the unpublished novel *Sword in the Darkness*. A chapter in which she describes her backstory was published in 2006; see "**Sword in the Darkness**" (**Story**). In it, readers learn of a tragic series of events after she becomes a school teacher in rural **Gates Falls, Maine**, just before the Second World War.

Elbert, Donald Merwin *see* Donald Merwin Elbert

The End of the Whole Mess

Originally published in the October 1986 edition of *Omni*, this science fiction story was substantially rewritten by King for collection in *Nightmares and Dreamscapes*. Besides large narrative changes, a number of facts, characters and even timelines were altered in the newer version. The tale is interesting and the technique King uses to draw out the story is competently delivered.

Howard Fornoy sits down to write a final story — that of his brother Bobby, a genius who discovers a strange substance in the water of La Plata, near Waco, Texas. Its presence has led to very little violence in the surrounding communities. The world is apparently spiraling towards armed destruction and Bobby determines to take matters into his own hands. But, as is often the way with science, unintended consequences will flow.

Copies of *Omni* can be found online.

Genesis: Possibly partly inspired by Daniel Keyes' masterpiece novel *Flowers for Algernon* (filmed as *Charly*).

Television: The *Nightmares and Dreamscapes* version was adapted for the TV series *Nightmares and Dreamscapes: From the Stories of Stephen King* and is available on DVD.

End-World

End-World is part of **All-World**, which also contains **Roland Deschain's Mid-World**. The **Dark Tower** itself is there (***The Dark Tower VII: The Dark Tower***), Calla Bryn Sturgis borders it (*The Dark Tower V: Wolves of the Calla*), and it contains such terrible places as Thunderclap, Fedic, Castle Discordia, Le Casse Roi Russe (**The Crimson King**'s castle) and the White Lands of Empathica. Apart from **The Dark Tower cycle,** it also features in *Black House* and is mentioned in "**The Little Sisters of Eluria.**"

The Evaluation

"The Evaluation" is the title given to one of four incomplete stories found in a journal of King's that is now kept in the **Raymond H. Fogler Library** of the University of Maine at Orono. For security reasons the journal has been moved to Box 1010 at the Special Collections Unit, meaning readers need King's written permission. Other partial stories in the journal indicate it was written in the 1989–91 timeframe.

Using King's titles in the journal, the stories have been dubbed "**Muffe,**" "The Evaluation," "**Movie Show**" and "**Chip Coombs.**"

In this twelve page story fragment, psychologist Dr. Peter Judkins evaluates Edgar Roos at the Crown County Mental Hospital in New York. Roos is under arrest after killing nine people that day, two with a butcher's knife and seven with a shotgun. Initially uncommunicative, sitting strait-jacketed and chained to an oak chair that is bolted to the floor, Roos tells Judkins he might talk if Judkins takes off a band-aid covering a shaving cut.

And there the fragment ends. There is no indication King ever intended to publish this piece, which has something of the feel of the short story "**The Boogeyman.**" There are a number of pieces featuring psychiatric examinations that King has failed to complete, including "**Keyholes,**" and, from the same journal, "**Comb Dump.**"

An Evening at God's

An Evening at God's is a "one-minute play" that King wrote for a benefit event. It was auctioned on 23 April 1990 at the American Repertory Theater's Institute for Advanced Theater Training. While it has never been published, the text circulates freely in the King community.

In a newspaper interview, King described the play as "God sitting at home and drinking a few beers and St. Peter comes in with papers to pass, and God's watching a sitcom on TV. And the earth is sort of hanging in the way of the TV, and he keeps trying to look around it to see the television." This piece is clearly no more than a bit of fun social commentary.

Everything's Eventual (Collection)

This is a collection of fourteen tales, all of which had been published in some form previously. It is a mix of mainstream, horror and fantasy tales. The stories are: "**Autopsy Room Four,**" "**The Man in the Black Suit,**" "**All That You Love Will Be Carried Away,**" "**The Death of Jack Hamilton,**" "**In the Deathroom,**" "**The Little Sisters of Eluria,**" "**Everything's Eventual,**" "**L.T.'s Theory of Pets,**" "**The Road Virus Heads North,**" "**Lunch at the Gotham Café,**" "**That Feeling, You Can Only Say What It Is in French,**" "**1408,**" "**Riding the Bullet**" and "**Luckey Quarter.**"

Everything's Eventual (Story)

Initially published in *The Magazine of Fantasy and Science Fiction* for October-November 1997, this short story was republished as part of a computer game in 2000 and collected in ***Everything's Eventual***. There are a number of variations between the different versions but these are unimportant. Copies of the original magazine are easily secured online.

Dink Earnshaw is a young man with an unusual but deadly talent — he can draw pictures using special symbols and target them through messages at a specific person. The recipients of these occult communications commit suicide. Dink accepts a job at TransCorp and they use his special talent to kill people he is told are evil. Little does he suspect he is but a pawn in a much larger game. Perhaps the most important part of this story is Earnshaw's reappearance as an important although minor character in **The Dark Tower cycle**.

Genesis: The image that inspired this tale was of "a young man pouring change into a sewer grating outside of the small suburban house in which he lived." The story "came out smoothly and without a single hesitation, supporting my idea that stories are artifacts: not really made things which we create ... but pre-existing objects which we dig up."

Computer Game: Blue Byte released *F13* (also known as *Stephen King's F13*) in 2000, which includes the text of the story, screensavers, illustrations and audio files.

Eyes of the Dragon

King's personal imprint, Philtrum Press, first published the novel *Eyes of the Dragon* in 1984, in a limited edition of 1250. The mass market edition, first published in 1987, contains important differences in the text, including character changes and an entire chapter which was not included in the later edition. Copies of the Philtrum Press edition are difficult to come by — check specialist online booksellers and expect to pay a substantial price. Some libraries have copies of that earlier edition and may offer them via interlibrary loan.

King Roland of Delain has a problem: his advisor, Flagg. Flagg wants Roland's son Thomas, who is likely to do everything Flagg advises, to be heir to the throne instead of his older brother, Peter. Flagg murders King Roland and frames Peter, who is condemned to spend the rest of his life in a high tower. But he is determined not to stay.

There are obvious links to **The Dark Tower cycle**, through the land of Delain, Flagg (just Flagg, no "Randall" in this version) and many other references. King's original title was *The Napkins* and one manuscript also includes the title *The Two Princes*.

This fairy tale in the style of Grimm is the perfect introduction for any young reader to the King.

Genesis: King wrote the tale "as a story for my daughter, who likes fantasy fiction but cares not at all for tales of horror. She's read little of my work, and quite simply put, I wanted to please her, and reach her. I had an idea for something like a fairy tale — but because my daughter is 14 and a fairly sophisticated reader, it was a fairy tale with teeth."

Fair Extension

"Fair Extension" is a story from King's 2010 novella collection, ***Full Dark, No Stars***. According to his Web site, "Harry Streeter, who is suffering from cancer, decides to make a deal with the devil but, as always, there is a price to pay."

Faithful: Two Diehard Boston Red Sox Fans Chronicle the 2004 Season

Scribner published *Faithful*, by Stephen King and Stewart O'Nan (a horror novelist), in December 2004. The paperback edition, including additional material by both King and O'Nan, was released in August 2005. O'Nan wrote the larger portion of the book (in word count at least). Readers can identify each author, as King's contributions are in bold font, O'Nan's in normal font (there are also numerous e-mail exchanges with King identified as "SK").

The amazing events in both baseball and sporting history chronicled therein makes the book a must read for both King readers and sports fans. Just as King had chosen the year his son Owen played for the West Bangor Little League All-Star team, which made it all the way the regional finals, to write of Little League baseball (in **"Head Down,"** collected in *Nightmares and Dreamscapes*), the year he agreed to write a chronicle of his beloved Boston Red Sox they were able to break an 86-year fabled drought and win the World Series. Coincidence?

Genesis: The unique background is described by O'Nan:

> Steve and I have been going to games together for years. We e-mail and talk about the team all the time, and last year in August when the team got hot, Steve decided we should keep a log of our reactions to their games. [That] spring, when the season was about to start, my agent asked if I wanted to write a book about the Red Sox (every year he asks me this, but this year I'd just finished a novel and finally had the time). I said I'd write it only if Steve could be my co-author. Steve was busy, but said he'd try to contribute as much as he could. And once the season got going, his natural love for the game kicked in and he couldn't stay away.

Father Donald Callahan (aka Pere Callahan)

Donald Callahan was parish priest of St. Andrews Catholic Church in **Jerusalem's Lot, Maine**, during the events described in *'Salem's Lot*. His confrontation with **Kurt Barlow** in that novel is one of the most important (and one of the most dramatic) in King's fiction, and his creator never forgot him.

He reappears in the town of Calla Bryn Sturgis in ***The Dark Tower V: The Wolves of the Calla***, running a Christian church and working for his redemption. He is known there as "Pere Callahan" (pere is, of course, French for "father") or "Old Fella." Through the progress of *Wolves of the Calla* and ***The Dark Tower VI: Song of Susannah***, readers are updated on Callahan's life between The Lot and the Calla and his story is complete early in ***The Dark Tower VII: The Dark Tower***. His importance to **The Dark Tower cycle** is evidenced by the fact **Roland Deschain** called out his name as he approached **The Dark Tower** itself.

In an alternate reality (the deleted scenes of *'Salem's Lot*), Callahan died in the Maine town after being confronted by the vampire Sarlinov.

On the Screen: James Gallery portrayed Callahan in the 1979 TV adaptation; James Cromwell (*Babe*) played him in the 2004 TV adaptation.

Father's Day

This horror short story appears only in the graphic collection ***Creepshow***. Nathan Grantham is an evil and demanding man who had ordered his daughter's fiancé killed.

But Bedelia is now in charge, after he suffers a stroke. Revenge will be sweet, but more complicated than Bedelia expects.

Movie: *Creepshow* (1982), in the "Father's Day" segment, starring Ed Harris.

Graphic Novel: The "Father's Day" segment of *Creepshow* (New American Library, 1982).

The Fifth Quarter

This crime caper was first published in *Cavalier* magazine for April 1972, with King using the pseudonym **John Swithen**. Other than **Richard Bachman**, this is the only pseudonym King has used, and this is the only story published with that name. According to Bachman's "death notice" in the *Castle Rock* newsletter for May 1985, Swithen was Bachman's half-brother.

The story was also published in a new version in *The Twilight Zone Magazine* in February 1986. The third and final version, after King revised the story again, is collected in **Nightmares and Dreamscapes** (in that version John Swithen is a character — a folksinger and writer).

An armored car goes missing in Maine. The gang of robbers buries the loot on an island and agrees it is only to be dug up ten years later. Each of the four robbers takes a quarter of the map showing its location. Can they trust each other for an entire decade?

Original copies of *Cavalier* do appear for sale online, at a price. As a men's magazine it is rarely held by libraries. Copies of *The Twilight Zone Magazine* are less rare but may be a little difficult to find.

Genesis: In the notes to *Nightmares and Dreamscapes*, King simply writes, "Bachman again. Or maybe **George Stark**." Stark is a character in **The Dark Half**. Indeed, the plot is not dissimilar to a novel Stark is said to be writing in that King book.

Television: The *Nightmares and Dreamscapes* version of this story was adapted for the TV series, *Nightmares and Dreamscapes: From the Stories of Stephen King* and is available on DVD.

Firestarter

In one of King's earlier and lesser novels, the most memorable takeaways from this science fiction thriller include the psychotic **John Rainbird**, an agent of **The Shop** (a covert government agency King seems to have abandoned since it featured in the **Golden Years** TV series and was mentioned in **The Tommyknockers**, "The Langoliers" and the uncut version of **The Stand**).

Andy McGee and Vicky Tomlinson are college students when they take part in a secret drug experiment backed by The Shop, an ultra-secret government organization. Each gains a talent as a result; Andy's is the ability to push other people into taking actions, and they later marry. Shortly after birth, their daughter **Charlie McGee** shows her unique pyrokinetic talent, setting her teddy bear on fire. The Shop sets out to kidnap Charlie, as her parents go on the run. The consequences of capture may be more than anyone expects.

Movie: *Firestarter* (1984). Drew Barrymore appears as a child star, playing Charlie McGee. Despite a raft of name stars, the critics were not kind, but this is a serviceable adaptation. Other well known actors included George C. Scott (as John Rainbird), Heather Locklear (as Vicky McGee), Martin Sheen (as Captain Hollister), and Louise Fletcher (as Norma Manders).

Television: *Firestarter Rekindled* (2002). This is a surprisingly good television reprise, with a chilling portrayal by Malcolm McDowell as John Rainbird. Veteran actor Dennis Hopper also appears. Available on DVD.

Flagg, Randall *see* Randall Flagg

Flanders, Stella *see* Stella Flanders

For Owen

This poem appears in **Skeleton Crew** and is almost certainly dedicated to the King's younger son, Owen (see **King, Owen**). A minor piece of only passing interest.

For the Birds

This tale appeared in a collection of stories that all end with a malaproped quotation or popular phrase. In the tale the rooks of London start to become extinct and a solution is sought. As the birds had been a popular tourist attraction, the English decided to breed them in Bangor, Maine (King's hometown), and re-populate London with them.

His closing line, "Bred any good rooks lately?" became the title of the collection and was the malapropism of "read any good books lately?" *Bred Any Good Rooks Lately?* was published by Doubleday in 1986. While now out of print, the book can be purchased from secondhand booksellers.

The 43rd Dream

One of King's earliest published writings, "The 43rd Dream" was printed in 29 January 1966 edition of the Lisbon High School newspaper, *The Drum*. Prudence Grant, a teacher who retired in 2002 and who had advised the paper's staff, ran across some original copies of the newspaper and one containing "**Code Name: Mousetrap**." She sold them on eBay, thus bringing the previously unknown stories to light.

In this story a high school student tells of his dream, which has tones of a 1960s drug trip. The narrator was in his Batmobile when approached by a bum who said, "You shoot your high school teachers and forbid your birds to fly." Pursued by a crowd, he escapes from one difficult situation after another. Here readers can see some early King themes such as high school shootings (**Rage**) and possibly the sparrows from **The Dark Half**.

Readers can access the story in its original form, with a reproduction of the two pages from *The Drum*, in Bev Vincent's *The Stephen King Illustrated Companion* (2009).

Four Past Midnight

A collection of four of King's lesser novellas: "**The Langoliers**," "**Secret Window, Secret Garden**," "**The Library Policeman**" and "**The Sun Dog**."

1408

Originally published in the audio book ***Blood and Smoke***, this incredibly scary tale of haunting is collected in ***Everything's Eventual*** and ***Stephen King Goes to the Movies***. Excerpts of a draft and an earlier version appear in ***On Writing***.

Mike Enslin is the best-selling author of "haunted" location books but is unconvinced of any such phenomena. He plans to stay in Room 1408 of the Hotel Dolphin in New York City but the manager, Mr. Olin, is determined to talk Enslin out of staying overnight in that room, which has an apparent history of driving its occupants insane, or to an even worse fate.

Genesis: King says, "As well as the ever-popular premature burial, every writer of shock/suspense tales should write at least one story about the Ghostly Room at the Inn. This is my version of that story. The only unusual thing about it is that I never intended to finish it. I wrote the first three or four pages as part of an appendix for my ***On Writing*** book, wanting to show readers how a story evolves from first draft to second.... But something nice happened: the story seduced me and I ended up writing all of it." He declares the story "scared me while I was working on it."

Movie: *1408* (2007). While the movie bears little resemblance to King's story, it does have its own thrills and chills. John Cusack plays Mike Enslin; Samuel L. Jackson is Gerald Olin; and Tony Shalhoub appears as Sam Farrell.

Fran Goldsmith

Frances Rebecca (Fran or Frannie) Goldsmith is one of the most loved characters in all of King's fiction. Strong and determined, she is a role model for women and a heartthrob for men. As the novel ***The Stand*** opens she is living in Ogunquit, Maine, and has just become pregnant by Jess Rider. When the superflu devastates America, she and **Harold Lauder**, who has a crush on her, are the only two left alive in the town and must decide whether to leave or stay. When they do move on, she meets and falls in love with **Stu Redman**.

On the Screen: Molly Ringwald was badly miscast as Fran in *Stephen King's The Stand*.

Freemantle, Abagail *see* Abagail Freemantle

Freemantle, Edgar *see* Edgar Freemantle

From a Buick 8

Ned Wilcox's father, Curtis, a member of Troop D, Pennsylvania State Police for over 20 years, is killed in the line of duty in an auto accident. To help assuage his pain, Ned helps out at Troop D's barracks with janitorial tasks. There he finds his father has been keeping a strange secret from his family, a secret so bizarre that Ned finds it hard to believe. The troopers keep a strange car in a shed — a car that had been found abandoned at a local gas station with no sign of the driver. It may look like a Buick Roadmaster but its paint self-heals when scratched, and dirt and muck simply fall off it. Worse still it appears to be a doorway to some distant and alien place.

One of King's lesser-known novels, this is a compelling mystery story laced with nasty shocks. It deals with death, the fascination of danger, and people's need for answers. King's "Afterword" is not to be missed.

In a link to other King fiction, Horlicks University also appears in "**The Raft,**" *Christine*, "**The Crate**" and *Creepshow*. *Inside View*, which Bradley Roach read, is a scandal newspaper King invented. It also appears in *Bag of Bones*, *The Dark Tower III: The Wastelands*, *Desperation*, "**Home Delivery,**" *Insomnia*, "**Popsy,**" "**The Night Flier**" and *Needful Things*. The story is widely regarded as an adjunct to **The Dark Tower cycle**.

Genesis: King slipped on a steep slope near a Conoco gas station in rural Pennsylvania, narrowly avoiding tumbling into a stream, and began to wonder how long the attendant would have waited before noticing that King's vehicle was missing its driver. Within a few hours the story was set in his mind. "This story became ... a meditation on the essentially indecipherable quality of life's events, and how impossible it is to find a coherent meaning in them." After completing the first draft, King was nearly killed when hit by a vehicle while walking in rural Maine: "The coincidence of having written a book filled with grisly vehicular mishaps shortly before suffering my own has not been lost on me, but I've tried not to make too much of it." The title is said to have been inspired by the Bob Dylan song "From a Buick 6," and the tale appears to be homage to the universe created by H.P. Lovecraft's tales.

Full Dark, No Stars

King's book release for Fall 2010, it includes four "previously unpublished novellas." One is set in **Hemingford Home** (where **Abagail Freemantle** lived most of her life), a town very near to **Gatlin, Nebraska** (the setting of "**Children of the Corn**"). The stories are "**1922,**" "**Big Driver,**" "**Fair Extension**" and "**A Good Marriage.**"

The Furnace

This piece consists of the first two paragraphs of a story, written by King, and is headed "By Stephen King and...." It was published in a magazine for U.S. school students, *Know Your World Extra*, for 23 September 2005 as an offering to be completed by young readers, starting with King's scant but scary opening words.

In the two paragraphs ten-year-old Tommy is sent to get firewood from a cellar that he hates. He believes there is something alive behind the furnace and, as he is getting the wood, the door swings shut and the light goes out. The complete story appears online at www.weeklyreader.com/wys/weeklywriter_furnace.asp.

Gage Creed

Gage is the son of **Louis Creed** and his wife Rachel in *Pet Sematary*. An accident in which he is involved is part of a chain of events that may destroy the family. In *Insomnia*, one of his sneakers is found in Atropos' lair, and in *The Shining (Mini-Series Screenplay)* there is a Gage Creed orchestra.

On the Screen: Miko Hughes plays Gage in *Pet Sematary*. Stephen King plays Gage Creed, the band leader, in the TV version of *The Shining*.

Gardener, Jim *see* **Jim Gardener**

Garfield, Bobby *see* **Bobby Garfield**

Garin, Seth *see* **Seth Garin**

Garraty, Ray *see* **Ray Garraty**

Gary Jones

Gary Jones is the protagonist of the novel ***Dreamcatcher***. He befriends **Douglas "Duddits" Cavell** as a child. As an adult his body and most of his mind are taken over by an alien entity, "Mr. Gray," which he attempts to fight.

On the Screen: Damian Lewis plays the adult Gary Jones, while Giacomo Baessato is the younger version in the 2003 film.

Gary Paulson

Paulson is an obscure character in King's canon, but one of his most interesting as the protagonist in ***It Grows on You***. An elderly resident of the Bend in **Castle Rock**, he and his cronies gather at Brownie's Store to reminisce. He recalls Joe Newall and his strange compulsion to extend his house and a particularly exciting sexual memory from his puberty.

Gates Falls, Maine

One of King's earliest fictional towns, Gates Falls first appears in the short story "Graveyard Shift" (1970). It is a key location in "**It Grows on You**," "**The Revenge of Lard Ass Hogan**," ***Riding the Bullet*** and "**Sword in the Darkness**" (short story). It is also mentioned in ***Blaze***, "**The Body**," ***The Dark Half***, ***The Dead Zone***, "**Gramma**," "**Hearts in Atlantis**," "**Movie Show**," "**Mrs. Todd's Shortcut**," ***Needful Things***, ***Rage*** and ***'Salem's Lot***. Both the old and new Kingdom Hospitals were built on the site of the Gates Mills (also described as the Gates Falls Mill), so it is likely the mill (if not the town) also appears in the ***Kingdom Hospital*** reality.

Genesis: Inspired by Lisbon Falls, Maine, the town where King attended high school.

Gatlin, Nebraska

Gatlin is a small town in Nebraska and the setting for "**Children of the Corn**." It is mentioned in ***It***.

Gaunt, Leland *see* Leland Gaunt

The General

King allowed publication of one version of the "**The General**" section of his *Cat's Eye* screenplay in the Richard Chizmar edited *Screamplays* (1997). Its one of only four published King screenplays, along with *Storm of the Century*, *Silver Bullet* and *Sorry, Right Number*.

The original script has three basic parts—the wrap-around story, "The General," and adaptations of King's tales "**The Ledge**" and "**Quitters, Inc.**" This version of the "General" section is also notably different in the screenplay that generally circulates in the King community. In the actual story a cat, General, saves a little girl's life. But Amanda's parents, Hugh and Sally Ann, blame the feline for the death of her pet parakeet, not knowing the cat had been fighting an evil five inch tall creature that had intended to steal the girl's breath and kill her. The mother takes the cat to be put down but he escapes and returns to the family home, just in time to confront the creature, who is making another attempt to kill the child.

Screamplays is available from second-hand booksellers; a new edition from the same publisher, Cemetery Dance, is planned.

Genesis: Dino De Laurentiis asked King to create another vehicle for Drew Barrymore in mid–1983, during the shooting of *Firestarter*, in which the young actress starred. King's initial treatment over fifteen pages was titled "The Cat," and it is likely this largely represents what later became "The General."

Movie: *Cat's Eye* is not one of the best King adaptations, but it does showcase a young Barrymore.

George Bannerman

George Bannerman is best known as the sheriff of **Castle Rock, Maine**. He first appeared in *The Dead Zone* after he contacted **Johnny Smith** and asked for his assistance with the Castle Rock murders. Bannerman had a long career in law enforcement—he joined the police force in 1957 and was a constable in Castle Rock in 1960 ("**The Body**"). He was elected sheriff in 1972 (defeating Carl Kelso), and his career concluded in 1980 with the events portrayed in *Cujo*. He married Victoria; their only child was Katrina (she narrowly missed becoming a victim of the Castle Rock Strangler). A huge, broad shouldered man, he had a big, sloping head capped with curly dark hair and wore rimless spectacles.

In an alternate reality (King's unproduced screenplay of *Cujo*), Bannerman survived **Cujo**'s attack and went on to be elected to the Maine Senate. In yet another reality, George Bannerman is the sheriff of Cleaves Mills in King's unproduced screenplay of *The Dead Zone*, and is investigating "The Destroyer" killings. According to King, he has yet to tell the story of how Bannerman "lost his virginity in the back seat of his dead father's car."

Subsequent sheriffs of Castle Rock include **Alan Pangborn** (*Needful Things* and *The Dark Half*) and Norris Ridgewick (*Gerald's Game*, *Bag of Bones*). Nehemiah Bannerman (quite likely a relative of George) was Castle County sheriff in 1901 (*Bag of Bones*). Nickerson Campbell was sheriff in 1904 ("**It Grows on You**").

On the Screen: Tom Skerritt was the sheriff in *The Dead Zone* movie, Chris Bruno played Sheriff Walt Bannerman in *The Dead Zone* TV series, and Sandy Ward played him in *Cujo*.

George D.X. McArdle

Early in his career King attempted a humorous western novel but abandoned it after 123 pages. A copy is held in his papers at the University of Maine. Only one other attempt at this genre is known, "**Slade**."

The complex and deliberately melodramatic tale set in 1873 Missouri features Peter Crager, a stagecoach robber. As the tale opens Crager lays wounded and abandoned and is rescued by George D.X. McArdle, who is building a travelling prostitution business. McArdle's favorite story was Poe's *The Cask of Amontillado* (the inspiration for King's "**Dolan's Cadillac**").

Both Crager's and McArdle's backstories are classic King, full of adventure, setback and struggle. The backstories of his "girls," which are generally poignant, are also outlined. There is a strong humorous tone underlying the manuscript but it's hard to determine where this meandering tale is heading and it seems certain King will never return to it.

Readers can check out the story at the Special Collections Unit of the University's **Raymond H. Fogler Library**. Ask for Box 2315.

George Stark

In the novel ***The Dark Half***, Dr. Hugh Pritchard removes a growth in eleven-year-old **Thad Beaumont**'s brain. It contains an eye, part of a nostril, three fingernails and two teeth (one with a cavity). Thad grows up to become a successful writer, both in his own name and using the pseudonym George Stark. After one bestseller Beaumont decides to "bury" George Stark and reveal the pen name to the public. In a media performance, Stark is "buried," but soon the "gravesite" has been dug up and tracks lead away.

The novels written under Stark's pseudonym include *Machine's Way*, *Oxford Blues*, *Sharkmeat Pie* and *Riding to Babylon*. Stark is also mentioned in ***Needful Things*** and ***Bag of Bones***.

Genesis: Donald E. Westlake wrote crime novels using the pseudonym Richard Stark from the early 1960s to mid 1970s. This name was King's inspiration for the pen name George Stark. The original title of *The Dark Half* was to have been *Machine's Way* (Alexis Machine is a key, violent character, in two of the Stark novels). One manuscript version of the tale has the byline "Stephen King and **Richard Bachman**," echoing the author and pseudonym in the story.

On the Screen: Timothy Hutton plays both Stark and Beaumont in the 1992 movie.

George Staub

George is a character in the story ***Riding the Bullet***. He died driving a 1960s model Mustang and Alan Parker saw his headstone in a graveyard in **Gates Falls, Maine**. George may, or may not, have given Alan a lift later that night and offered him a terrible choice.

On the Screen: David Arquette plays George in *Stephen King's Riding the Bullet*.

Gerald's Game

This King psychological horror novel is not for the faint-hearted, or for young readers. It has strong sexual content and themes, highly relevant to the story but possibly inappropriate for less mature readers.

Jessie Burlingame is handcuffed to a bed at her isolated summer home on Kash-wakamak Lake, Maine, after her husband dies during a bondage session. Unable to escape, she begins to confront the demons in her present and her past, including the terrible events that occurred during an eclipse when she was a child. Unfortunately, Jessie has more immediate problems than her past, as first a wild dog, then a mysterious intruder appear in the darkening bedroom.

This novel was originally planned as part of a trilogy called *The Path of the Eclipse*. *Dolores Claiborne* and a third, unwritten novel were to be the others. The story is linked to *Dolores Claiborne* through events which occur in each tale during an eclipse. There are strong links to King's other tales, including those set in **Castle Rock**, through the appearances of multi-story characters such as Sheriff **Alan Pangborn** and Norris Ridgewick. **Juniper Hill**, the mental asylum in which Raymond Joubert was incarcerated, appears in many King tales.

Genesis: King once wrote he has "very little idea ... what scares readers.... I only know what scares me." Using that yardstick, he called *Gerald's Game* "my most successful novel since **The Shining**." He said he first visualized this story while flying to New York. It gave him three months of "broken sleeps and bad dreams," and he hoped to pass those effects on to readers.

Gerber, Carol *see* Carol Gerber

Ghost Brothers of Darkland County

Ghost Brothers of Darkland County is a musical theater collaboration between Stephen King and famed singer John Mellencamp. The tale, set in Mississippi and Louisiana in the 1940s, revolves around a family facing the residual effects of a long-ago fratricidal murder. At the time of writing the plan was to release an unusual package — a book containing the full text, along with three disks (two featuring the entire production of the spoken word script and songs performed by the cast, and the third containing songs only).

According to King's official Web site, "The story involves domestic turmoil, and is played by a stellar cast led by Kris Kristofferson, in the role of Joe, the father, and Elvis Costello, as the satanic character, The Shape."

Ghosts

Ghosts is a short (38 minute) musical movie produced in 1997. It is also known as *Michael Jackson's Ghosts*, as it stars Jackson in a variety of roles. The screenplay is by Mick Garris (**Desperation**, *Stephen King's* **The Stand**, *Stephen King's* **The Shining** and **Riding the Bullet**) was based on a story by King. No copies of that story have ever come to light. The film is certainly worth watching and is something of a thriller.

Gilead

Gilead is (or was) the seat of the Gunslinger aristocracy in **All-World** and is important to the backstory of **Roland Deschain** in **The Dark Tower cycle**. Founded by the legendary Arthur Eld, Roland's distant ancestor, it was the capital of the Barony of New

Canaan and its last ruler was Steven Deschain, Roland's father. It is mentioned in **The Dark Tower I: The Gunslinger**, but the most information is provided in **The Dark Tower IV: Wizard and Glass**. For those interested in the history of Gilead, and its fall one thousand years before Roland arrived at **The Dark Tower**, full details are given in **The Dark Tower Graphic Novels**, particularly *The Dark Tower: Treachery*; *The Dark Tower: The Sorcerer*; *The Dark Tower: Fall of Gilead*; and *The Dark Tower: The Battle of Jericho Hill*.

Genesis: Quite likely King took inspiration from the very small town of Gilead in northwest Maine. That town was named after a large number of Balm of Gilead trees in the town center.

The Gingerbread Girl

This short story was first published in *Esquire* magazine for July 2007 and is collected in **Just After Sunset**. Set on Vermillion Key in Florida, it's the tale of a mother trying to recover from her daughter's crib death. But her escape from her husband and their grief extends her troubles. This is a compact, satisfying morality tale most readers will enjoy.

Genesis: King and a friend were walking past large mansions in Florida when the friend asked if he could imagine they are left empty much of the year. King could, and mixed this with "a very simple premise: a bad guy chasing a girl along an empty beach, but, I thought, she'd have to be running away from something else to begin with. A gingerbread girl, in other words."

The Girl Who Loved Tom Gordon

This novel is a good introduction to King for young teen readers, particularly girls who are likely to empathize with the heroine. Nine-year-old Trisha McFarland becomes lost while trekking part of the Appalachian Trail with her mother and brother. Disoriented, she walks away from civilization and any hope of rescue deep into the uninhabited Maine woods. She has very little food and each night listens to baseball games on her Sony Walkman in the hope of picking up a Boston Red Sox game, in which perhaps her hero, Tom Gordon, will be pitching. As she slowly becomes delirious, "Tom Gordon" becomes her traveling companion, helping her overcome her fears. Despite this, Trisha is not out of the woods and realizes she is being followed by something that she begins to think of as "The God of the Lost."

Tom Gordon was a real closing pitcher for the Boston Red Sox at the time the book was written and published. The tale is linked to King's other Maine fiction through the names of geographical places, such as TR-90 (**Bag of Bones**).

Genesis: King wrote, "I have been writing about God — the possibility of God and the consequences for humans if God does exist — for twenty years now, ever since **The Stand**. I have no interest in preaching or in organized religion, and no patience with zealots who claim to have the one true pipeline to the Big Guy ... but it seems to me that a little girl lost in the millions of square acres of forest west of Augusta would need someone or something to come in and at least try to get the save on her behalf." Unsurprisingly, he got the idea during a Boston Red Sox baseball game at Fenway Park.

Trivia: The book was released in an abridged "pop-up" edition by Little Simon in 2004.

The Glass Floor

"The Glass Floor" an important King story but has never appeared in one of his fiction collections. It was the piece of fiction for which he first received professional payment ($35). King was but 20, and the years of rejection slips he had collected perhaps seemed to shrink a little on its receipt. Barely six or seven years of selling short stories and writing novels later, King would publish *Carrie*, and the rest, as they say, is history.

In the story Charles Wharton visits the home of his brother-in-law, Anthony Reynard, wanting to discover the circumstances of his sister's death. Initially, Reynard refuses to give details but is browbeaten into telling Wharton that Janine had fallen from a ladder in a room that is now plastered shut. Wharton demands the room be opened and, disregarding peril, enters. A workmanlike tale with a nice twist, it is worth a reader's time to seek a copy.

The story first appeared in *Startling Mystery Stories* in Fall 1967; King allowed a reprint in the Fall 1990 issue of *Weird Tales* with some minor amendments. The original appears for sale on Web sites very rarely; the second is much more available.

Genesis: King says, "I was walking down a dirt road to see a friend, and for no reason at all I began to wonder what it would be like to stand in a room whose floor was a mirror. The image was so intriguing that writing the story became a necessity."

Glen Bateman

Glendon (Glen) Pequod Bateman was an associate professor of sociology before the superflu struck in *The Stand*. He traveled to the Boulder Free Zone with his dog Kojak to meet **Abagail Freemantle**. He will face the ultimate test.

On the Screen: Played by Ray Walston in the mini-series.

Golden Years

In this screenplay King wrote for television, Harlen Williams, a 70-year-old janitor, is accidentally exposed to an explosion at a top secret government facility. Jude Andrews, an agent from the secretive government organization **The Shop** (the same organization that chased Charlie McGee in *Firestarter*) begins to cover up the incident by killing those involved, so Harlen and his wife go on the run. Meanwhile, there are signs Harlen is starting to grow younger. How will he avoid the threats of aging in reverse and being chased by a highly trained agent intent on taking his life?

This story is yet another example of a major theme in King's fiction, the disaster that may be wrought when science, often manipulated by government, spirals out of control.

Television: Produced as *Golden Years* (or *Stephen King's Golden Years*), shown as a series on the ABC network in 1991 and released on DVD in 2002. Frances Sternhagen (*Cheers*, *ER*, *Misery*) stars and King has a cameo as a grumpy bus driver. As King's first attempt at series television (the next, *Kingdom Hospital*, would not screen for another 13 years) this disappointing production stands as an important historical note to King's career.

Genesis: King was offered his own anthology-type program, where he would introduce a new story each week. But he pitched this series instead, where there was one continuing story.

The teleplay may be read at the Special Collections Unit of the University of Maine's **Raymond H. Fogler Library**. Ask for Box 2317.

Goldsmith, Fran *see* Fran Goldsmith

A Good Marriage

This story is from King's 2010 novella collection, *Full Dark, No Stars*. According to his Web site, "Darcy Anderson learns more about her husband of over twenty years than she would have liked to know when she stumbles literally upon a box under a worktable in their garage." This is a Maine story, with an early mention of **Castle Rock**.

Gordie Lachance

Gordon (Gordie) Lachance is a successful writer when he recalls events from his youth in **Castle Rock, Maine**. He and his friends overhear that a dead boy is lying near railway tracks and set out to see the corpse. In the process he also relates two stories he told those friends—"**Stud City**" and "**The Revenge of Lard Ass Hogan**." **Ace Merrill** also remembers him in *Needful Things*.

Genesis: It is clear that Gordie is at least partially based on a young Stephen King.

On the Screen: Wil Wheaton plays the young Gordie and Richard Dreyfuss his older incarnation in *Stand by Me*.

Graduation Afternoon

This very short story was first published in *Postscripts* magazine (Number 10, Spring 2007) and is collected in *Just After Sunset*. A young woman is enjoying her high school graduation party at her wealthy boyfriend's home when their world is shattered forever.

Genesis: King was inspired by a dream of a "vast mushroom cloud blossoming over New York" and says "the story is more dictation than fiction."

Gramma

Originally published in *Weirdbook* magazine for Spring 1984 this short story was substantially revised for collection in *Skeleton Crew*. Copies of this issue of *Weirdbook* are difficult to find and those seeking it should consult sellers who specialize in King's work. The tale has direct links to the fictional universe created by H.P. Lovecraft but is certainly readable on its own account.

Eleven-year-old George Bruckner has been left home alone with his grandmother. Gramma is 83, senile, fat, terminally ill and blind, yet somehow dangerous. In her youth the old woman had used "magic" books to have children and was thrown out of her job as a schoolteacher and from church as a result. While waiting for his mother to return home, George discovers that Gramma has passed on. But for Gramma and little George, death is not the end of the tale.

Henrietta Dodd is mentioned; she is an important minor character in *The Dead Zone* and the story is set in Castle View, Maine, near **Castle Rock**.

Genesis: The title character may be inspired by King's paternal grandmother, Granny Spansky (she is mentioned in *Danse Macabre*) and by the period of his childhood when his mother, Ruth King (see **King, Ruth**), looked after her elderly parents (Guy and Nellie Pillsbury) in Durham, Maine.

Television: "Gramma," a series episode on *The Twilight Zone*. The teleplay is by famed speculative fiction writer Harlan Ellison. It is available on DVD on *The Twilight Zone: Season 1* (2004).

Graveyard Shift

This short story was originally published in *Cavalier* magazine in October 1970 and collected in *Night Shift*. It is set in the Gates Falls Mill, in **Gates Falls, Maine**, which both appear regularly in King fiction, particularly the early stories.

The Gates Fall Mill, built in 1897, is closed over the Fourth of July weekend to allow the basement of the ancient industrial holdover to be cleaned. Thirty-six workers, including an itinerant named Hall, discover a previously unknown basement and make the fateful decision to go down into the dark.

Genesis: King says this story is about fear of rats, and springs from similar work he actually did at the Worumbo Mills and Weaving in Lisbon Falls, Maine. He describes the work in *On Writing* and specifically nominates this as his inspiration for this tale — one worker actually told him he'd seen rats as big as dogs.

Growing up, King was a close friend of brothers named Hall, and the name of a major character here is certainly a tip to them. King received $200 for this story in August 1970, the most he'd ever received at that time.

Movie: *Graveyard Shift* (1990). Possibly the worst film ever made from a King story. It is also known as *Stephen King's Graveyard Shift*.

Gray Matter

This short story was originally published in *Cavalier* magazine for October 1973 and collected in the *Night Shift*. It is relatively unimportant, although it is one of the few set in Bangor, Maine (in the King canon that town is normally portrayed as **Derry**). There is one possible link to King's other tales— George Kelso had once worked for the Bangor Public Works Department but quit after seeing what he thought was a large spider in the sewers (a possible precursor to *It*).

Some months earlier Richie Grenadine drank from a bad batch of Golden Light beer and had begun to change. His son approached some of his old friends for help but none were prepared for the new Richie.

Graphic: A graphic novel version of the tale is planned for ***Secretary of Dreams Volume Two*** (Cemetery Dance), illustrated by Maine artist Glenn Chadbourne.

The Green Mile

Sixty-three years after the remarkable events surrounding the most unusual prisoner he ever met, **Paul Edgecombe** relates the tale of **John Coffey** and of life and death on the Green Mile, the nickname for Cold Mountain Penitentiary's death row. Using a series of morality tales and employing a wide cast of truly memorable characters, King's novel takes the reader on a roller-coaster emotional ride. Many of his trademark themes appear — the role of group, hope, redemption, and the horrors people inflict upon their fellow man.

King undertook this project as a serial novel, with the pressures to perform that come with that choice. It was published in six monthly parts from March through August 1996, and later re-published in a combined edition. The installments were — Part 1: "The Two Dead Girls"; Part 2: "The Mouse on the Mile"; Part 3: "Coffey's Hands"; Part 4: "The Bad Death of Eduard Delacroix"; Part 5: "Night Journey"; and Part 6: "Coffey on the Mile."

Among the many wonderful characters are John Coffey (who, despite his miraculous ability to heal and restore life, is on death row); Paul Edgecombe, the superintendent of death row, who faces moral dilemmas and an interesting fate; Eduard Delacroix, whose pet mouse, Mr. Jingles, is a crucial element in the tale; the sadistic guard Percy Wetmore; and **William** "Wild Bill" **Wharton**, whose acts had placed Coffey on the Mile, and who would be deserving of any rough justice that might come his way.

This is one of ten top King novels and one of the best ways to introduce a new King reader. Take care though, as to the maturity level of younger readers, as the material has strong adult themes and can provoke emotional reactions.

The book won the Best Novel Bram Stoker Award for 1996 from the Horror Writers Association. At one stage all six parts were on *The New York Times* bestseller list. Nowhere in the story is the state in which it is set made clear (a deliberate ploy by King). Those who argue it is Louisiana — as shown in the film — are foiled by references in the book to counties; Louisiana has parishes instead. We are simply in the South.

Genesis: Readers should refer to King's introduction to the Omnibus editions for fascinating details about the development of the story and the decision to write it as a serial novel. There you find that "What Tricks Your Eye" was King's first attempt at the tale. In that version (which will never be published), as the execution date for Luke Coffey nears, he develops an interest in sleight-of-hand magic tricks. As a result, he is able to make himself disappear from the prison.

Movie: *The Green Mile* starring Tom Hanks and Michael Clarke Duncan (the latter nominated for an Academy Award for his portrayal of John Coffey). The screenwriter and director of this 1999 film, Frank Darabont, had previously directed *The Shawshank Redemption* to his own script and would later serve in the same roles for ***The Mist***. To put it simply, Darabont "gets" King — he is able to deliver on screen the exact tone and imagery King puts on paper. This is one of the top King films ever made and was nominated for four Academy Awards, including Best Picture and Best Adapted Screenplay. It receives virtually unanimous praise — testament to the two writers — as such it is one of the best ways to introduce a reader or filmgoer to the joys of Stephen King's storytelling.

Greg Stillson

Gregory Ammas Stillson is the antagonist in the novel ***The Dead Zone***. He is also mentioned in ***The Tommyknockers*** and ***The Dark Tower VII: The Dark Tower***. Johnny Smith shakes Stillson's hand when he is but a candidate for Congress and has an apocalyptic vision about the results of a Stillson presidency. After he meets Smith he is elected to Congress and, after re-election, forms the America Now Party.

On the Screen: Martin Sheen is tremendous as Stillson in the 1983 film, while Sean Patrick Flanery plays the character in the TV series.

Halleck, Billy *see* Billy Halleck

Hallorann, Dick *see* Dick Hallorann

Hanlon, Mike *see* Mike Hanlon

Hanscom, Ben *see* Ben Hanscom

The Hardcase Speaks

This poem was first published in the magazine *Contraband* on 1 December 1971, with credit erroneously given to "Stephan King." The magazine also carried a poem about vampires by **Tabitha King**. Only 66 lines long, Stephen's piece is written in the slightly delirious style of the late 1960s hippie generation, of which he was, of course, a part. It's never been included in one of King's books but can be found in a collection of horror poems, *The Devil's Wine* (Cemetery Dance, 2003). The original *Contraband* may also be photocopied at the **Raymond H. Fogler Library** at the University of Maine in Orono.

This work bears re-reading and is complex in its themes and tone, taking us into the realm of murderous insanity. In retrospect it is one of his best poems, clearly part of the King canon and another signpost in the early development of the best-selling writer.

Harlow, Maine

Harlow is one of King's fictional towns, about eighteen miles from the real city of Lewiston. It neighbors **Castle Rock** but is a key location in only a few stories: "**It Grows on You**" (the *Marshroots/Weird Tales* and *Whispers* versions), the unpublished "**Movie Show**," and *Riding the Bullet*. It does, however, have a considerable role in both *Blaze* and "The Body" and is mentioned in *Bag of Bones*, *The Dark Half*, *Gerald's Game*, "Nona," *Rage*, *Under the Dome* and "Uncle Otto's Truck."

Genesis: It is likely based on the town where King spent his later childhood and teenage years—Durham, Maine.

Harold Lauder

Harold Emery Lauder is an Ogunquit, Maine, teenager when superflu devastates the world in *The Stand*. At the time he is fat and has bad acne. He falls in love with the only remaining resident of the town, **Fran Goldsmith**, but she rejects his advances. As a group of survivors form around **Abagail Freemantle** in Boulder, **Nadine Cross** moves in with him. His work ethic in the Boulder Free Zone earns him the nickname "Hawk," but all is not what it appears.

On the Screen: Corin Nemec is suitably creepy as Harold in *Stephen King's The Stand*.

Harrison State Park '68

This, the first of King's poems to be published, appeared in the University of Maine literary magazine *Ubris* (Fall 1968). It's never been included in one of King's books but can be found in a collection of horror poems, *The Devil's Wine* (Cemetery Dance, 2003).

The original *Ubris* may also be photocopied at the **Raymond H. Fogler Library** at the university.

The poem's narrator describes a mixed bag of images, including a little girl dead on a hopscotch grid and a cow's skeleton in Death Valley, and there's an early reference to **Harlow, Maine**. Manic, yet slightly disappointing, it is however clearly King — using trademarks, famous people and gruesome themes.

Harvey's Dream

This rather derivative story was first published in *The New Yorker* magazine for 30 June 2003 and collected in ***Just After Sunset***. Some quite beautiful writing makes up for a fairly predictable storyline.

Harvey Stevens suffers a bad dream in which he receives a phone call from his daughter, Trisha. He believes she is calling to tell him one of her sisters had been killed. He wakes himself up screaming before the dream concludes. But the next day begins to mirror the dream.

Movies: Two **Dollar Baby** films have been made from this story — *El Sueno de Harvey* (2005) and *Paul's Dreams* (2007).

Genesis: King says he woke from a dream in which he didn't want to answer a phone call because "I knew — positively knew, the way you sometimes do in dreams — that someone wanted to tell me one of our children was dead." He went straight from bed to word processor and wrote the story in one sitting.

Haven, Maine

Haven, Maine, features in ***The Tommyknockers***, in which the town faces more than a casual threat from something buried long, long ago. In "**Mrs. Todd's Shortcut**" readers learn it is located between Augusta and Bangor. It is also mentioned in "**The Revelations of 'Becka Paulson**" and *It*.

This is also the name of the town in the TV series *Haven*, which is based on the book ***The Colorado Kid***.

Head Down

"Head Down" first appeared in *The New Yorker* for April 16, 1990. It represents the only piece of non-fiction King has chosen to publish in one of his mass-market collections, in this case ***Nightmares and Dreamscapes***. In the introduction to that volume, King says he included it after a great deal of thought: "I probably worked harder on it than anything else I've written over the last fifteen years." The elegiac baseball poem "**Brooklyn August**" appears in the same collection.

The essay follows the Bangor West Side team in Little League play, including King's son Owen (at 12, already six foot two inches tall, "two hundred or so pounds") (see **King, Owen**). King follows the fortunes of the team as they first win their half of the Maine District 3 Little League, then the district championship itself. This qualifies them to play in the 1989 Maine State Little League Championship Tournament in Old Town (**Tabitha King**'s hometown). Readers can find out what happened next by reading this magnificent piece, in which King moves from a deep understanding of baseball and what it is to be young and playing the sport through some philosophical views of the game and its impact, and on to powerful sports reporting.

Hearts in Atlantis (Collection)

Hearts in Atlantis is a five-story collection published in 1999. The stories are loosely linked by certain characters and by the Vietnam War era, and contain strong autobiographical overtones (and undertones). The stories are: "**Low Men in Yellow Coats**," "**Blind Willie**," "**Why We're in Vietnam**," "**Hearts in Atlantis**" and "**Heavenly Shades of Night Are Falling**." What is not well known among fans is that the last three of these stories also appear in differing versions.

Genesis: King says, "Although it is difficult to believe, the sixties are not fictional; they actually happened. I have tried to remain true to the spirit of the age. Is that really possible? I don't know, but I have tried."

Movie: The under-rated and warm-hearted movie *Hearts in Atlantis* (2001) is actually an adaptation of "Low Men in Yellow Coats" (the "Hearts in Atlantis" storyline does not appear in the movie) and of "Heavenly Shades of Night Are Falling." The screenplay is by William Goldman (***Misery***, *Butch Cassidy and the Sundance Kid*). Anthony Hopkins played **Ted Brautigan** and David Morse (***The Green Mile***) the adult Bobby.

Trivia: At different points the collection was to be titled "While We Were..." and "Why We're in Vietnam."

Hearts in Atlantis (Story)

This is one of the most warm-hearted of all King's stories, and takes both the author and his readers back to the 1960s, in King's case back to his university days in the Vietnam War protest area. Part of the collection of the same title, it is loosely related to all the other stories in the collection.

Peter Riley, a college freshman at the University of Maine in 1966 (the same year Stephen King was a freshman) becomes slowly addicted to the game of Hearts played in his dormitory. One after another, students find themselves falling behind in their work and the Hearts game becomes their only true joy in life. As those who fail their academic requirements will be subject to the draft for the Vietnam War, the consequences of their addiction are dire. Riley watches his friends fail or quit and be sent to war, and his girlfriend, **Carol Gerber**, leaves the university to care for her mother. Some students ask for transfers to other dorms to get away from the temptation. How will Riley fare?

Disabled student **Stokely Jones** (Rip-Rip) is another of the truly memorable characters King has the power to create on a regular basis. King also links other stories by the inclusion of references to **Derry** and **Gates Falls, Maine**.

The film *Hearts in Atlantis* is not an adaptation of this story, but rather of "**Low Men in Yellow Coats**" and "**Heavenly Shades of Night Are Falling**."

Heavenly Shades of Night Are Falling

This is the closing tale in the ***Hearts in Atlantis*** collection, in which all five stories are loosely connected by certain characters, and the Vietnam War era. Apart from resolving the story of certain of these characters, its greatest importance is the clue it holds to **The Dark Tower cycle**, which was incomplete at the time of its publication.

In the summer of 1999, **Bobby Garfield** ("**Low Men in Yellow Coats**") returns to Harwich, Connecticut, to attend a funeral. He meets an old friend and tells her of the secrets he has recently been entrusted with.

Movie: The under-rated and warm-hearted movie *Hearts in Atlantis* (2001) is an adaptation of "Low Men in Yellow Coats" and of "**Heavenly Shades of Night Are Falling**." The story "**Hearts in Atlantis**" does not appear in the movie. The screenplay is by William Goldman (*Misery*, *Butch Cassidy and the Sundance Kid*). Anthony Hopkins played **Ted Brautigan** and David Morse (*The Green Mile*) portrayed the adult Bobby.

Hemingford Home, Nebraska

Hemingford Home is in Polk County, Nebraska, about 80 miles west of Omaha. It is there that some survivors of the Captain Trips superflu are drawn to and meet **Abagail Freemantle** (Mother Abagail) in *The Stand*. The town is also mentioned in *It* (Benjamin Hanscom lived there between confrontations with **Pennywise**) and "**The Last Rung on the Ladder**" (Larry and Kitty grew up there). It is apparently the same town (but called simply Hemingford, Nebraska) that is the setting for "**1922**."

King also wrote an unproduced screenplay of "**Children of the Corn**," in which Vicky tells her husband Burt the road they are traveling forks ahead: "One fork goes to a place called **Gatlin**, the other one goes to a place called Hemingford Home." The town, described as just a wide place in the road, was not mentioned in the original short story.

Henry Leyden

Henry is a blind radio DJ with multiple personalities. A minor but very interesting character, he appears in *Black House* as a friend of **Jack Sawyer**. His many pseudonyms include George Rathbun, the Wisconsin Rat, Joe Strummer, Symphonic Stan, and Henry Shake. He is much beloved by King fans.

Here There Be Tygers

This is one of the earliest King stories ever published, appearing in *Ubris*, a University of Maine literary magazine, in Spring 1968. It was marginally revised and collected in *Skeleton Crew* in 1985. It is effectively impossible to find an original of the magazine, but it may be photocopied at the **Raymond H. Fogler Library** of the University of Maine, Orono.

A student at the Acorn Street Grammar School desperately needs to visit the bathroom. Strangely, Charles finds a hungry tiger, and decides to wait. Not one of his King's best short stories, it does however leave an eerie echo in the reader's mind.

Genesis: Inspired by King's "pretty scary" first-grade teacher.

Movies: Two **Dollar Baby** films have been made from the tale —*Here There Be Tygers* (2003) and *Here There Be Tigers* (2010).

Heroes for Hope

This story, partly by King, appeared in a Marvel Comic, *Heroes for Hope Starring the X-Men* (Vol. 1, No. 1, 1985), published on 1 December. King only wrote pages 10 to 12 inclusive, so King scholars regard those pages only as part of his canon. It carries little interest to King readers, other than hard-core completists, but does include some very strong King-like horror prose.

Genesis: The comic was conceived to assist with Famine Relief in Africa.

King would go on to allow many of his works to be adapted by Marvel, including **The Dark Tower**, "**N.,**" **The Talisman** and **The Stand**. Copies of the comic are easily obtained over the Internet.

Hill, Joe

Joe Hill is the pseudonym of **Joseph King**, son of **Tabitha** (see entries under **King**) and **Stephen**. Joseph Hillstrom King was named after Joseph Hillstrom (aka Joe Hill), a labor activist controversially executed for murder in 1915. It may be that his parents were inspired by the 1971 movie *Joe Hill*, as Joseph King was born in June 1972.

Through mid–2010 the following is a list of notable works he has published under that name: *20th Century Ghosts* (collection, Harper Collins, 2007), which won major awards from the Horror Writers Association, the British Fantasy Society and the International Horror Guild); *Heart-Shaped Box* (novel, William Morrow, 2007), which won the Bram Stoker Award for Superior Achievement in a First Novel from the Horror Writers Association; *Locke & Key* (comic and graphic novel series, IDW Publishing, 2008–2010); and *Horns* (novel, William Morrow, 2010).

Home Delivery

A rare zombie tale from King, this short story first appeared in *The Book of the Dead* (Mark V. Zeising, 1989). Copies of the collection are available from booksellers. The author substantially rewrote it for collection in **Nightmares and Dreamscapes**.

Maddie Pace's husband Jack is lost at sea just a month after she becomes pregnant. Maddie has barely had time to come to terms with her loss when zombies appear worldwide and began attacking and eating the living. On Gennesault Island, Maine, she and her fellow residents must pull together to protect themselves from the dead buried in the one graveyard on the island.

This is an entertaining story, delivered with an excellent sense of humor, social commentary and a good dose of good old-fashioned horror. The collected version of the tale mentions **Little Tall Island** (**Dolores Claiborne**, **Storm of the Century**).

Genesis: This tale was written to order, for the anthology of zombie tales.

Movie: A high quality, animated **Dollar Baby**, *Home Delivery*, was produced in 2006.

Graphic: An illustrated edition of the tale appears in **Secretary of Dreams** (Cemetery Dance, 2006), brilliantly drawn by Maine artist Glenn Chadbourne.

The Hotel at the End of the Road

This piece of juvenilia appears in **People, Places and Things**, along with six other King tales. As derivative as one could expect from an early teenage writer, in this 365 word story, Tommy Riviera and Kelso Black are the target of a high speed police chase. They turn up a dirt road, see an old hotel ahead and decide to stay for the night. But a twist right out of a *Twilight Zone* episode awaits the men when they wake the following morning.

Unlike the other tales in *People, Places and Things,* this story can be found in *The Market Guide for Young Writers* by Kathy Henderson (Writer's Digest Books, 1996), but only in editions from the fourth onward.

The House on Maple Street

In this short story, on returning from an overseas trip, the four Bradbury children discover a spaceship growing in the walls of their house. After discovering when the ship will launch, they hatch a plan. This science fiction tale, collected in **Nightmares and Dreamscapes**, is suitable for young readers, but there are adult elements (domestic violence).

Genesis: King explains in the notes to *Nightmares and Dreamscapes* that his wife Tabitha (see **King, Tabitha**) suggested each member of the family write a story based on a picture in the book *The Mysteries of Harry Burdick* by Chris Van Allsburg. King's effort, based on the last picture in the book, is this story. The surname of the Bradbury family is quite likely a tip to speculative fiction author Ray Bradbury (*Something Wicked This Way Comes*).

I Am the Doorway

This science fiction tale first appeared in *Cavalier* magazine for March 1971 and is collected in **Night Shift**. Strong horrific elements somehow fail to make up for a lack of empathy for the main character.

Arthur is a deep space astronaut with project Zeus and becomes infected with a strange virus during a mission to Venus. He retires to peaceful Key Caroline but his fingers begin to hurt and before long, eyes grow at the end of each one, eyes he believes are taking control of his body.

I Hate Mondays

This is a complete, unpublished five-page story by Stephen and **Owen King**. Owen is King's youngest son and a published writer. The text is immature and was probably a bit of fun for Stephen and Owen. It is unlikely that it will ever be published in any form. In this rollicking crime tale goons have captured Spike's wife and he must save her, performing a series of outstanding heroics in the attempt.

Readers can check out the two pages at the Special Collections Unit of the University's **Raymond H. Fogler Library**. Ask for Box 1010.

I Know What You Need

This powerful short story was first published in *Cosmopolitan* magazine in September 1976 and collected in **Night Shift**. Although set in Maine, it is not linked with any other of King's stories.

When Elizabeth Rogan meets Edward Jackson Hamner, Jr., for what she believes is the first time, she is almost instantly taken with his ability to understand her wants and needs. They immediately become friends, but Elizabeth dampens his romantic interests by mentioning her boyfriend, Tony Lombard. Soon after, Tony is tragically killed in a road accident. After allowing a period of grief, Ed becomes more important in Elizabeth's life. However, her roommate Alice doubts his motives, and her concerns are well grounded.

Genesis: There is a nod to H.P. Lovecraft in King's use of the fabled (but non-existent) book *Necronomicon*. Stories such as "**Crouch End**" and "**N.**" are also inspired by Lovecraftian fiction (or what many call the "Cthulhu Mythos").

Movie: A **Dollar Baby** film of the same name was produced in 2005. This was one of the stories King included in his **Night Shift unproduced screenplay**.

I Was a Teenage Grave Robber

I Was a Teenage Grave Robber was the first of King's stories to be independently published. It initially appeared in partial form in a mimeographed "fanzine," *Comics Review*, serialized over three issues in 1965. The fourth and concluding issue never appeared, but the remaining text of King's story was posted to some subscribers as printed pages. The material that appeared in the third issue (Chapters 5 and 6) is reproduced in Bev Vincent's *The Stephen King Illustrated Companion* (2009).

The next year the whole story was published in another fanzine, *Stories of Suspense*, as "**In a Half-World of Terror**." However, the text was so different as to have almost certainly been printed from a different manuscript, although the story itself remains basically the same.

The story is highly derivative of 1950s B-grade science fiction-horror movies and has both structural and internal logic problems. It focuses on the adventures of the narrator, who finds himself working for a mad scientist in the Dr. Frankenstein mode, who is ultimately destroyed by his own creation.

Genesis: King tells us something of the story's background in **On Writing**: "The first story I did actually publish was in a horror fanzine issued by Mike Garrett of Birmingham, Alabama."

A single complete set of *Comics Review* material is held in the Murray Collection at Duke University's Rare Book, Manuscript, and Special Collections Library in Durham, North Carolina. It appears that Duke holds the only original of the concluding material that was to have appeared in Issue Number 4.

In a Half-World of Terror

"**I Was a Teenage Grave Robber**" was the first of King's stories to be independently published, in a 1965 fanzine. The following year the entire story was published in a different fanzine, *Stories of Suspense*, as "In a Half-World of Terror." Though the story is the same, the details differ to the extent that the text was almost certainly printed from a different manuscript. The narrator finds himself working for a mad scientist who is ultimately destroyed by his own creation. The story is reminiscent of 1950s B-grade horror-science fiction.

Copies of this version circulate as photocopies in the King community.

In the Deathroom

This short story has an interesting publishing history in that its first two appearances were not traditional mass-market books. First released in 1999 as part of an audiobook,

Blood and Smoke, it did not see print until inclusion in the Book of the Month Club–only publication *Secret Windows* the following year. The first mass-market publication was in the collection *Everything's Eventual* in 2002.

Fletcher, a reporter for *The New York Times*, is also a contact for Pedro Nunyes and Thomas Herara, who are planning a revolution in an unnamed South American country. Fletcher's sister and other nuns had been murdered in the country some years earlier. Captured by the government, Fletcher is taken to a basement and interrogated by the chief minister of information, Escobar and his associates. There seems no hope of escape from torture and, ultimately, death.

Genesis: King says he wanted to write one of those "Kafka-esque" stories of South American interrogations, but one for which there was "a happier ending, however unreal that might be."

Movie: Two **Dollar Baby** films with the same title as the story have been produced, in 2009 and 2010.

Stage: Adapted as part of *The Blood Brothers Present ... The Master of Horror* at the Gene Frankel Theatre in New York in 2008. The entire presentation also included adaptations of "**In the Deathroom**" and "**Quitters, Inc.**," along with vignettes from "**Survivor Type**" and "**Paranoid: A Chant.**"

Graphic: An illustrated version is slated to appear in *Secretary of Dreams* (**Volume Two**) (Cemetery Dance), drawn by Maine artist Glenn Chadbourne.

In-World

In-World is part of Roland Deschain's planet, **All-World**, in **The Dark Tower cycle**. The term appears only rarely in the cycle and appears to cover the "Inner Baronies" such as New Canaan, of which **Gilead** was the capital.

In the Key-Chords of Dawn

This 18-line poem was published without a title in a literary magazine *Onan* in 1971. Even though untitled, it is referred to by the King community as "In the Key-chords of Dawn." It has never been included it in one of King's books but can be found in a collection of horror poems, *The Devil's Wine* (Cemetery Dance, 2003).

Two people fishing realize that the pastime involves more than just eating the fish and it, like life, contains other responsibilities and complexities.

Insomnia

Although one of King's major novels, in which he introduces mythology and characters that prove important in other tales, including **The Dark Tower cycle** (for instance, the first mention of **The Crimson King**), it lacks the sort of characters and storyline that remain long in the memory of readers. It is for the Dark Tower links that it is likely to hold its greatest long-term interest. King won the British Fantasy Award for the book.

Set in **Derry, Maine,** the novel is strongly linked to *It* and other Maine stories. For instance, the **Juniper Hill** asylum appears in many other tales, including *Bag of Bones* and *Needful Things*. An important reference is made to Gage Creed (*Pet Sematary*).

Elderly **Ralph Roberts** suffers a bout of insomnia and pretty soon he is almost constantly awake. Ralph and his friend Lois Chasse begin to see strange "bald doctors" as well as auras around people. They notice that whenever the bald doctors cut a string at the top of an aura the person dies soon afterwards. Derry is a town in which people die naturally, and unnaturally, and dangers are all around.

Genesis: King says he "consciously" knew he was weaving all his fictions into The Dark Tower cycle from the time he was writing this novel.

Isaac

Isaac is the "seer" in the town of **Gatlin, Nebraska**, and a notable character in "**Children of the Corn**." He was only nine when Burt and Vicky Robeson drove into the town in July 1976.

On the Screen: John Franklin played the role in the original 1984 film and in *Children of the Corn 666: Isaac's Return*. Preston Bailey appears in the 2009 TV remake.

It

This number one bestselling novel is one of King's three greatest creations (along with *The Stand* and **The Dark Tower cycle**), and no King fan or reader should miss it. Set in two significant time periods (1958 and 1984–85) and in **Derry, Maine**, this tale of bravery, love, terror, murder and the secrets of childhood will forever change a reader. The television adaptation alone has spawned a generation or more of people who fear clowns. And rightly so; of all of King's villains, **Pennywise** is perhaps the one who evokes the most visceral terror in his readers.

Derry, a small city in Maine, has an awful history, but one its residents seem to forget. A group of children who call themselves the Losers Club stand together in the 1950s against an ancient, unspeakable evil that lives in the sewers, but that will not be the end of the matter. A quarter century later **Mike Hanlon** finds himself calling his old friends— **Stan Uris, Richard Tozier, Ben Hanscom, Beverly "Bev" Marsh, Eddie Kaspbrak** and best-selling horror novelist **Bill Denbrough**. Fate has called on them again — dare they answer?

There are strong links to King's Maine fiction, including references and allusions in *Insomnia*, *Bag of Bones*, *The Tommyknockers*, *The Dead Zone*, "The Road Virus Heads North," "Secret Window, Secret Garden," and most importantly, *Dreamcatcher*. The **Juniper Hill** asylum also appears in many tales. Even **Gatlin, Nebraska**, the setting for "**Children of the Corn**," is mentioned.

Genesis: King was inspired by "crossing a wooden bridge, listening to the hollow thump of my bootheels, and thinking of *The Three Billy Goats Gruff*." When he decided to model Derry on Bangor, King says he spent on entire autumn going around town asking people about its history, "and I asked people what they knew about various places that I wanted to incorporate into the book. And I would listen to the stories. I didn't care what the truth was, you see. I cared about what people believed. I cared about the stories that they handed down from generation to generation."

Television: It (1990). This mini-series has terrified a generation and includes one of the best portrayals of a King character — Tim Curry as Pennywise. Available on DVD.

Trivia: At one point the novel was to have been titled simply "Derry." King's earlier story "**The Bird and the Album**" was subsumed into the novel, having been published five years earlier. *It* was the best-selling book in America in 1986 and won the British Fantasy Award.

It Grows on You

This fascinating short story about secrets and sickness also has an interesting publishing history. King seems to have really enjoyed this tale, having published no less than three versions (and even one of those was later altered). It was first published in *Marshroots* magazine for Fall 1973, and that text was republished with minor variations in *Weird Tales* magazine for Summer 1991. The second version was a significant revision published in *Whispers* magazine for July 1982. *Marshroots* and *Whispers* are difficult to find but may be sourced from specialist King booksellers. In the earlier versions, the story is set in **Harlow, Maine**. The third and final adaptation is a major revision of the first two, collected in ***Nightmares and Dreamscapes***.

In the tale a strange house on a hill is discussed in laconic tones. **Gary Paulson** and his cronies gather at Brownie's Store in the Bend section of **Castle Rock, Maine** and the subject turns to the house Joe Newall built. Each addition to the house seems to coincide with a death and the old men are determined to explore every fact and rumor they have heard.

There are strong links to King's other fiction through characters such as Andy Clutterbuck (***Needful Things***, ***Lisey's Story***) and places such as Homeland Cemetery in Castle Rock (***The Dark Half***, ***Gerald's Game***).

Genesis: King says the story was "written when I was very much under the influence of Sherwood Anderson's *Winesburg, Ohio* and Thornton Wilder's *Our Town*. I grew up in a small town ... and for a while in my twenties I felt an almost constant urge to capture that world of dirt roads, abandoned houses, and general stores full of old men, old baked bean supper posters, and old fly paper."

I've Got to Get Away!

This piece of juvenilia appears in ***People, Places and Things***, along with six other King tales. A fairly obvious science fiction piece, the tale is of Denny Phillips, who wakes to find himself on an atomic factory assembly line but can remember nothing. Those around him look like zombies or prisoners and he tries to escape, only to be shot by guards. Two weeks later, after being repaired and returned to work, Denny Phillips (the robot) again has the urge to get away.

King apparently re-wrote this 308-word story as "**The Killer.**"

Jack Sawyer

Jack Sawyer is the key character in ***The Talisman***. Also known as "Travelin' Jack," John Benjamin Sawyer sets off on a quest across both the United States and a "twinner" world known as **The Territories** to find the Talisman, which will save his mother's life. Only eleven, he faces great danger in both worlds and forms friendships, including with **Wolf**. In ***Black House*** he is a retired police officer living in French Landing, Wisconsin, when he is called to assist with the investigation of "The Fisherman" case in which children are being abducted and murdered. Again, he is drawn into another reality, **End-World** (which is in **Roland Deschain**'s world). After again facing dangers in both worlds, Sawyer's future is in the balance at the end of this second novel. Both co-author Peter Straub and King have indicated they hope to complete Jack's story in a third novel.

Genesis: Jack is clearly named after Mark Twain's famous title character in *The Adventures of Tom Sawyer*.

Jack Torrance

John Daniel (Jack) Torrance is one of the most important figures in King's fiction, both for his flaws as a father and husband (indeed as a man), and for his famous portrayal by Jack Nicholson in the movie version of **The Shining**. Jack Torrance's past seems to dictate his future — his father was an alcoholic and broke the boy's arm when he was young ("**Before the Play**," in which Jack is known as "Jacky"). Jack's own failure to deal with his alcoholism and his anger issues leads to he, his wife, Wendy and their son **Danny Torrance** moving to the isolated **Overlook Hotel** in Colorado for the winter, where Jack is to act as caretaker and, hopefully, to write. Jack's flaws do not stop at alcohol and violence — a part of his soul is attracted to even deeper desires, which will put his entire family at risk.

Annie Wilkes mentions Jack in **Misery**, and he is referred to in **The Dark Tower VI: Song of Susannah**.

Genesis: King once wrote that Jack Torrance's face is "to a large extent, my own." King has had his own battle with alcohol (which he revealed in **On Writing**) and this worked its way into Jack's character.

On the Screen: Jack Nicholson is brilliant as Torrance in Kubrick's movie version; Stephen Weber is quite acceptable in the role in the television mini-series.

Jake Chambers

Jake Chambers is an important character in **The Dark Tower cycle** and has an intimate familiarity with death. John Chambers is but 11 or 12 years of age when he first meets **Roland Deschain** and joins what will be his "ka-tet." Jake appears in all seven Dark Tower novels and features in one of the most critical incidents of the entire cycle in the final novel. As a member of the ka-tet, he is close friends with **Eddie Dean**, **Susannah Dean**, Roland and his own pet billy-bumbler, **Oy**.

The Jaunt

This relatively unimportant science fiction short story was first published in *The Twilight Zone Magazine* in June 1981 and was revised by King before being collected in **Skeleton Crew**. The magazine version is easily purchased from online sellers.

In 2307 the Oates family is preparing to teleport from New York to Mars using the Jaunt Service. When the process was discovered in 1987 it was also found that sentient beings must use the Jaunt while unconscious. Those who tried it awake died or went insane. One apparently claimed, "It's eternity in there." Twelve-year-old Ricky Oates listens intently to the story and determines to hold his breath to avoid taking the gas that puts Jaunt travelers to sleep.

Genesis: "The Jaunt" was originally written with *Omni* magazine in mind, but King reports they "rightly rejected it because the science is so wonky."

Jerusalem's Lot (Story)

This original story for the **Night Shift** collection provides some of the tragic history of the town of the same name, later infested by vampires in **'Salem's Lot** and "One for the Road." It is also strongly influenced by H.P. Lovecraft's stories.

Trivia: At one point King intended to title this story "The Shunned Town."

An illustrated edition of the tale appears in **Secretary of Dreams** (Volume One) (Cemetery Dance, 2006), brilliantly drawn by Maine artist Glenn Chadbourne.

Jerusalem's Lot (Town)

Jerusalem's Lot, Maine (widely known as 'Salem's Lot), is a small town 20 miles north of Portland. Founded by a splinter group of Puritans in 1710, it was incorporated in 1765. The name arose after one of Charles Belknap Tanner's pigs, Jerusalem, escaped into the woods and went wild. Tanner would warn small children away from Jerusalem's wood lot.

Jerusalem's Lot's history is best discovered by reading King's stories in the following order: "Jerusalem's Lot," **'Salem's Lot**, "One for the Road" and **The Dark Tower V: Wolves of the Calla**. The town is also mentioned in **The Dark Tower VI: Song of Susannah**, **The Dark Tower VII: The Dark Tower** and "Night Shift" (**Unproduced Screenplay**). Jerusalem's Lot and vampires are virtually synonymous in the King universe.

Genesis: The town is modeled on King's boyhood hometown of Durham, Maine.

Jessie Burlingame

The main character in **Gerald's Game**, Jessie Burlingame finds herself handcuffed to a bed in a lonely home near Kashwakamak Lake in Maine when her husband dies of a heart attack during a sex game. She soon discovers she has even greater problems than how to escape the handcuffs.

Born Jessie Mahout, she had a strange vision of a woman during a 1963 eclipse. She attended **Jack Torrance**'s alma mater, the University of New Hampshire, where **Johnny Smith** also spent time in the library. Mahout is described but not named in **Dolores Claiborne**.

Jhonathan and the Witchs

King wrote this story in 1956 or 1957, at the age of nine. It was first published more than three and a half decades later in *First Words: Earliest Writing from Favorite Contemporary Authors*, edited by Paul Mandelbaum and published by Algonquin Books of Chapel Hill (1993). The book can be found at second-hand booksellers.

Jhonathan, a cobbler's young son, is set the task of making his fortune by killing three witches (this is correctly spelled in the manuscript, but not in the title), with the penalty for failure to be death. Many adventures follow in which the young author is able to show some inventive touches. It is of tremendous interest to read this, the earliest of King's writings to come to light (the first page of the manuscript, in King's handwriting, is also reproduced).

Genesis: King relates he wrote the story for his Aunt Gert, who paid him a quarter for every story he wrote.

Jim Gardener

Jim is a poet and **Bobbi Anderson**'s lover in ***The Tommyknockers***. His career had stalled over his heavy drinking and he'd even shot his wife in the cheek, after which they divorced. He'd had a steel plate inserted into his skull after a skiing accident, and this appears to make him immune from the strange effects that occur after Bobbi begins to dig up processed metal and gets Jim to join her venture.

On the Screen: Jimmy Smits plays Gardener in the television movie.

Trivia: In one scene Gardener awakes near Alhambra Hotel at Arcadia Beach, New Hampshire, on 4 July 1988. In ***The Talisman*** Lily Cavanaugh and **Jack Sawyer** stayed at the Alhambra Inn and Gardens in Arcadia Beach, New Hampshire. The Arcadia Funworld Amusement Park is nearby and this is where Jack Sawyer first meets Speedy Parker. Some claim that Gardener met Jack Sawyer on the beach that day; however, it is clear that the boy he met is not Sawyer.

John Coffey

John Coffey ("like the drink, only not spelled the same way") is the central character in ***The Green Mile***. He arrives at Cold Mountain Penitentiary's death row (known as "the Green Mile") in 1932, convicted of raping and murdering twin girls. He's huge — 6' 8" tall and weighs over 320 pounds — a barrel-chested, bald black man, and simple. Even he had only a vague idea of his life before the killings of which he has been convicted.

But John has mysterious powers to cure disease, and even raise the dead. In fact he had not killed the twins, he'd simply come across their bodies, had not been able to save them but tragically was found in a compromising position. His powers are slowly revealed to the chief jailer, **Paul Edgecombe**, as first he cures Paul of an infection, then brings a dead mouse back to life. Risking their jobs Edgecombe and fellow guards take John from the prison to see if he can save the warden's wife, who is suffering incurable cancer.

Having witnessed John's powers and understanding his likely innocence, Edgecombe and the warden now face a dilemma — the scheduled execution.

John Coffey's initials are no accident, with King acknowledging in *On Writing* they were "after the most famous innocent man of all time." Like other Christ figures, John has suffered — his body is covered in scars; yet his story offers readers and moviegoers redemption and hope, which are so prominent in many King works. Some critics have even posited that Coffey is Christ reincarnated.

On the Screen: Coffey was played to perfection by Michael Clarke Duncan, who deservedly won an Academy Award nomination for the role. The character is probably the most loved of King's captured on screen. The scene in which John watches Fred Astaire and Ginger Rogers dance on film brilliantly captures John's childish innocence.

John Rainbird

Rainbird is one of the most psychopathic of all fully human characters in King's canon. A 6' 10" tall half Cherokee Indian, he is an assassin and operative for **The Shop**.

He'd suffered facial and eye injuries in Vietnam. After helping catch **Charlie McGee** and her father in **Firestarter**, he forms a friendship with the young girl. He is also mentioned in **Golden Years**.

On the Screen: George C. Scott is menacing in the role in the 1984 movie; Malcolm McDowell performed equally in the 2002 TV remake.

John Shooter

Mort Rainey, a successful writer, has recently divorced and is depressed when John Shooter suddenly arrives in "**Secret Window, Secret Garden**," pointing an accusing finger. Shooter claims Rainey had stolen a story that he himself had written many years previously. But is Shooter who Rainey thinks he is?

On the Screen: John Turturro plays the role in the movie *Secret Window*.

John Sullivan

John Sullivan (Sully-John) is Bobby Garfield's close friend in "**Low Men in Yellow Coats**," and he is the key character in "**Why We're in Vietnam**" — in 1970 he'd been badly injured fighting in Vietnam and would always be haunted by a particular image from that war.

He is also mentioned in "**Blind Willie**," "**Hearts in Atlantis**," "**Heavenly Shades of Night Are Falling**" and "**The New Lieutenant's Rap**." He is mentioned in the Coda to **The Dark Tower VI: Song of Susannah** and in **The Dark Tower VII: The Dark Tower**.

On the Screen: Will Rothhaar plays Sullivan in the movie *Hearts in Atlantis*.

John Swithen

One of King's two pseudonyms, the other being **Richard Bachman**. He wrote one story using it — **The Fifth Quarter**, which is collected in **Nightmares and Dreamscapes** (in that version John Swithen is a character — a folksinger and writer).

According to Bachman's "death notice" in the *Castle Rock* newsletter for May 1985, Swithen was Bachman's half-brother.

Johnny Smith

The protagonist of **The Dead Zone**, Johnny Smith was only six when he fell on the ice at Runaround Pond in Durham, Maine (the town in which Stephen King grew up and in which there is an actual Runaround Pond), and blacked out. He graduated from the University of Maine at Orono in 1970 (the same year King graduated that very institution). In late October 1970 he and Sarah Bracknell are returning from a date when he's critically injured in a car accident and lapses into a coma. He wakes up four and a half years later to find his girlfriend has moved on. He then discovers he has psychic powers, which Sheriff **George Bannerman** wishes to use in the "Castle Rock Strangler" case. John's flashes of insight now cause him escalating personal problems, and lead inexorably to the greatest dilemma of his life.

A second "alternate reality" Smith appears in King's unproduced screenplay of the novel.

Both Johnny's given and surnames are deliberately "everyman." Smith is one of King's greatest and most tragic heroes.

On the Screen: Johnny was played perfectly in the movie by Christopher Walken and in convincing style in the long-running TV series by Anthony Michael Hall.

Jones, Gary *see* Gary Jones

Jones, Stokely *see* Stokely Jones

Jordy Verrill

Jordy Verrill is a hardscrabble farmer living near Cleaves Mills, New Hampshire ("**Weeds**"), or **Castle Rock, Maine** ("**The Lonesome Death of Jordy Verrill**"), when a meteor falls on his land. Determined to make a few dollars by selling the meteor to the local college, he is infected by a strange substance. Jordy is simple-minded and it is King's description of his thoughts and motivations that make this character so compelling.

On the Screen: Stephen King plays Jordy Verrill in the movie ***Creepshow***. This is by far King's best piece of acting.

Trivia: In the ***Pet Sematary*** (**Screenplay**) the Baterman place is described as looking like Jordy Verrill's.

Jud Crandall

Judson (Jud) Crandall is the elderly neighbor of the Creeds in ***Pet Sematary***. It is he who tells **Louis Creed** about another cemetery, deep in the woods. As he realizes the consequences of his actions, he tries to warn Creed by telling the story of Timmy Baterman. Jud also knew the story of a St. Bernard dog that had gone rabid and killed some people — a clear reference to **Cujo**.

On the Screen: Fred Gwynne played Crandall in *Pet Sematary* (1989).

Jumper

"Jumper" and "**Rush Call**" were originally printed in a neighborhood newspaper, *Dave's Rag*, published by King's older brother David in Durham, Maine. The first of the two was apparently "Jumper," published over three parts in the winter of 1959–60, technically making it the earliest published of King's works (Part One was published in the December 29, 1959, issue).

Both stories were re-published in the Book of the Month Club's collection of miscellaneous King writings, ***Secret Windows: Essays and Fiction on the Craft of Writing***, in 2000. The stories were re-published as originally written, with only the spelling corrected.

In "Jumper," Robert Steppes threatens to jump off a building. Jeff Davis has been called to talk him down and decides to use unusual methods. Unsurprisingly, this is a juvenile story but shows King's early desire to be a storyteller.

The Juniper Hill Asylum for the Criminally Insane

Juniper Hill is King's most famous mental asylum, nearly as well-known as **Shawshank Prison**. Located in Augusta, Maine, it has both a Blue Ward Wing and a Red Ward and was sold by the state to a corporation in 1983. The asylum appears in **Bag of Bones**, **Cell**, "Comb Dump," **The Dark Half**, **Gerald's Game** (Raymond Joubert was incarcerated there), **Insomnia**, **It**, **Needful Things** (Nettie Cobb), "**Suffer the Little Children**" (Miss Sidley) and **The Tommyknockers**.

Just After Sunset

This 2008 collection of twelve previously published tales and one specifically written for this collection (thirteen in total) mostly contains works published in the prior five years. After three decades King finally relented and included "**The Cat from Hell**," a 1977 story. The other stories are "**N.**," "**Willa**," "**The Gingerbread Girl**," "**Harvey's Dream**," "**Rest Stop**," "**Stationery Bike**," "**The Things They Left Behind**," "**Graduation Afternoon**," "**The New York Times at Special Bargain Rates**," "**Mute**," "**Ayana**" and "**A Very Tight Place**."

A limited edition was also released, featuring a DVD collection of the 25 episodes of the online animated series based on the story "N." Copies of that edition are available from online sellers but purchasers should take care to specify the DVD is included with the sale.

Trivia: At one point the announced title was *Just Past Sunset*. King had also mused about two other titles—*Pocket Rockets* and *Unnatural Acts of Human Intercourse*.

Kaspbrak, Eddie *see* Eddie Kaspbrak

Keyholes

This partial story appears only as a 2½ page fragment in a notebook donated by King for auction in 1988 to benefit the American Repertory Theater. The notebook also contained a handwritten revision of **Silver Bullet**. Copies of the "Keyholes" pages circulate in the King community.

In the tale a man visits a psychiatrist. Michael Briggs, a construction worker, was seeing Dr. Conklin about his 7-year-old son Jeremy, but little is revealed.

The Killer

"The Killer" is effectively a rewrite of "I've Got to Get Away!" one of the stories in King and Chris Chesley's self-published collection, **People, Places and Things**. It was obviously written in King's teenage years and its only publication was in *Famous Monsters of Filmland*, issue 202, for Spring 1994. Readers wishing to access the story can purchase the magazine online.

In the story the narrator suddenly awakes on a production line, with no knowledge of how he got there, or anything of his past. While the "twist" is formulaic, this tale shows a 12- or 13-year-old King hard at work creating stories.

Genesis: King relates in **On Writing** that he'd submitted the manuscript to Forrest J. Ackerman, editor of *Spaceman*, in 1960. While the story was rejected, Ackerman kept the manuscript and King agreed to its publication in another of the veteran editor's publications decades later.

The King Family and the Wicked Witch

One of King's most obscure stories, this was published in the now-defunct Manhattan, Kansas, newspaper *Flint* on 25 August 1977. Photocopies of the story circulate in the King community but it has not been published elsewhere.

In this children's tale Witch Hazel plots against the King family, leaving four magic cookies, each of which cast a spell on a family member. Unimportant though the story is, it is fun and gives a bit of insight into the King family of Bridgton, Maine, in the long ago of 1976.

Genesis: King and the newspaper's editor attended the University of Maine together and worked on *The Maine Campus*. In 1976, while visiting King in Maine, the author gave him a copy of this story, which he'd written for his children. The next year the paper ran the story, despite concerns that some families might be offended by the word "fart." Indeed, one manuscript copy of the story is titled "The King Family and the Farting Cookie."

King, Joseph (aka Joe Hill)

Joseph (Joe) King is the son of **Stephen** and **Tabitha King**. Joseph Hillstrom King was named after Joseph Hillstrom (aka Joe Hill), a labor activist controversially executed for murder in 1915. It may be that his parents were inspired by the 1971 movie, *Joe Hill*, as Joseph King was born in June 1972. He is married with three children.

The following is a list of notable works he has published under that name through mid–2010: *20th Century Ghosts* (collection, Harper Collins, 2007), which won major awards from the Horror Writers Association, the British Fantasy Society and the International Horror Guild; *Heart-Shaped Box* (novel, William Morrow, 2007), which won the Bram Stoker Award for Superior Achievement in a First Novel from the Horror Writers Association; *Locke and Key* (comic and graphic novel series, IDW Publishing, 2008–2010); and *Horns* (novel, William Morrow, 2010).

He appeared in the movie *Creepshow* as Billy in the prologue and epilogue scenes.

King, Naomi

The only daughter and eldest child of Stephen and **Tabitha King**, she is a minister of the Unitarian Universalist Church in Plantation, Florida. She was born in 1970.

King, Owen

Owen King is the youngest son of Stephen and **Tabitha King**, he is also a writer and was born in February 1977. Stephen King's "**Head Down**" is about Owen's Little League baseball team, and most assume the poem "**For Owen**" is literally for Owen.

Owen's notable work to date is a collection of three short stories and a novella, *We're All in This Together* (Bloomsbury, 2005).

King, Ruth

Nellie Ruth King was Stephen King's mother. She married Donald King but he walked out on their family in 1949 or 1950, when Stephen was but two years old. She raised Stephen and his adopted older brother, David, single-handedly, working a number of jobs to shelter, feed and clothe the family. She died of cancer in 1974, age 59, just as King was about to hit the big-time. She was able to read *Carrie* before passing but did not live to see her son's initial success. "**The Woman in the Room**" is partly about King's angst over her illness and death.

King, Stephen (Actor)

King in the Movies: King has appeared in many movies and TV programs, most related to his own work and mostly in cameo roles. These are: *Creepshow*, *Maximum Overdrive* (the only movie he has directed), *Pet Sematary*, *Golden Years*, *Sleepwalkers*, *The Stand*, *The Langoliers*, *Thinner*, *The Shining* (mini-series), *Storm of the Century*, *Rose Red*, *Kingdom Hospital* and *Gotham Café* (adaptation of "**Lunch at the Gotham Café**"). Non-King adaptations include *Knightriders*, *Creepshow 2*, an episode of *Frasier*, one of *Breaking Bad* (as the character Richard Bachman) and another of *The Simpsons*, *Fever Pitch* and *Diary of the Dead*.

King, Stephen (Character)

King appears as versions of himself or is mentioned in the following stories: "**The Night Flier**" (but only the original version); *The Dark Tower V: Wolves of the Calla*; *The Dark Tower VI: Song of Susannah*; *The Dark Tower VII: The Dark Tower*; *The Regulators*; "**The King Family and the Wicked Witch**"; "**The Leprechaun**"; "**The Library Policeman**"; *Thinner*; *Sleepwalkers*; "**The Blue Air Compressor**" and "**Slade**."

King has written about his appearance in the latter volumes of **The Dark Tower** cycle. He expresses his dislike for the "smarmy academic term" that covers such matters—metafiction—and says he is in the story "only because" he'd known (consciously since writing *Insomnia* in 1995; unconsciously since Father Callahan left town in *'Salem's Lot*) that "many of my fictions refer back to Roland's world and Roland's story," and that since "I was the one who wrote them, it seemed logical I was part of the gunslinger's ka." ("Ka" is the term for "fate" in the Dark Tower Universe).

King, Tabitha

Tabitha King, wife of Stephen King, is also a writer. She was named after the ship her father (Raymond George Spruce) served on in World War II, *Tabitha Brown* (a troopship in service from 24 October 1942). Born in 1949, she and Stephen met at the **Raymond H. Fogler Library** of the University of Maine, Orono. They married on January 2, 1971, and have three children, **Naomi**, **Joseph** and **Owen**.

A social activist, she has published nine novels: *Small World* (Signet, 1981); *Caretakers* (Simon and Schuster, 1983); *The Trap* (Simon and Schuster, 1985), also published as *Wolves at the Door*; *Pearl* (Penguin, 1988); *One on One* (Penguin, 1993); *The Book of Reuben* (Penguin, 1994); *Survivor* (Penguin, 1997); and *Candles Burning* (Penguin, 2006), in which she completed the late Michael McDowell's novel.

Like her husband, she has created a fictional town — Nodd's Ridge, Maine — which features in all but *Small World*, *Survivors* and *Candles Burning*. *One on One* specifically references King's iconic town of **Castle Rock** and Tabitha has also mentioned **Derry** in her fiction.

Kingdom Hospital

Kingdom Hospital is an ambitious TV series project King attempted in 2004. For reasons unexplained the ABC-TV network moved the program around its schedule and at one stage put it on hiatus. While King refused to blame the network, and indicated that the slow burn type of entertainment he devised was possibly out of synch with the times, more neutral observers felt the network butchered any chance the series had of being a medium-term ratings success.

King was deeply affected by the ratings failure, later admitting, "When your greatest fulfillment in life is entertaining people, failing to do so is hurtful and dispiriting. You're listening to the voice of experience; when *Kingdom Hospital* flamed out on ABC in 2004, I felt that I'd screwed up a great opportunity. I moped for months."

The series presents the terrifying story of The Kingdom, a Maine hospital with bizarre occupants that include a nearly blind security guard, a nurse who regularly faints at the sight of blood, an apparent psychic, and a badly injured artist whose recovery is a step beyond miraculous. When patients and staff hear the tortured voice of a little girl crying through the halls, some are dismissive of any suggestion of the supernatural, others are not so sure. The bizarre history of the hospital, which is built on the site of a great mill fire a century earlier that killed many children, may be literally haunting patients and staff. And who or what is Antubis?

Readers should access the 15 hours of this series on DVD, as this is a major offering from America's favorite author, and it is unlikely the screenplay will ever be published. Core King fans will be delighted with the storylines and the quirky acting, not to mention the many links to King's other fictional canon, including **The Dark Tower cycle**, many of King's Maine geographies, and an obvious dramatization of the author's own near-death experience. The "Butterfingers" episode, featuring the character **Earl Candleton**, alone represents some of King's most heartfelt and emotional fiction and is not to be missed.

Genesis: The teleplay is based on Lars von Trier's Danish miniseries, *Riget* or *The Kingdom*.

Television: *Kingdom Hospital* (2004). The screenplay is by Stephen King and Richard Dooling; and story by Stephen King, Richard Dooling and **Tabitha King** (who came up with the storyline for one episode). King appears in two cameos — one simply as the voice of an AA sponsor, the other as TV lawyer Johnny B Goode. Released on DVD as *Stephen King Presents Kingdom Hospital*.

Trivia: King and Dooling wrote an outline for a second series but no copies of this have come to light. A companion novel, *The Journals of Eleanor Druse: My Investigation of the Kingdom Hospital Incident*, was published as "by Eleanor Druse." The novel was actually written by Rick Dooling.

King's Garbage Truck

King attended the University of Maine at Orono from the Fall of 1966, graduating in June 1970. In the latter part of his time at there, he wrote a series of columns for the college newspaper, *The Maine Campus*, under the title *King's Garbage Truck* (a title given by the editor, not the author). The forty-six *King's Garbage Truck* columns ran from February 20, 1969, to May 21, 1970.

The columns are important, as they shine a light on the young Stephen King as man and writer, remind us of student life on a campus in the heady days of the late 1960s, provide a view of his social awakening, and offer an early helping of his literary, movie, television and musical tastes.

In 1990 *The Maine Campus* planned to reprint the *Garbage Truck* columns as a separate book, claiming they held copyright. King's office demurred, legal action was threatened, and the university backed off. The best readers can do to access these often very interesting columns is to visit the **Raymond H. Fogler Library** and print them from microfiche (the originals have been stolen). A review of every column appears in *Stephen King: The Non-Fiction* by Rocky Wood and Justin Brooks (Cemetery Dance, 2008).

Genesis: King became involved in penning the columns after writing a letter to the editor, after which he was apparently convinced to contribute in a more substantive manner.

Kinnell, Richard *see* Richard Kinnell

Kurt Barlow

Kurt Barlow has been around for an unnatural period by the time he moves to **Jerusalem's Lot, Maine,** in 1975 with his assistant, Richard Straker. His career as an antiques dealer covers a grim and awful reality. His confrontation with Father **Donald Callahan** in *'Salem's Lot* is one of the most important (and one of the most dramatic) in King's fiction. As a result he is mentioned in the last three novels of **The Dark Tower cycle.**

On the Screen: Reggie Nelder plays Barlow in the 1979 version; Rutger Hauer plays the role in the 2004 production.

Lachance, Gordie *see* Gordie Lachance

Landon, Scott *see* Scott Landon

The Langoliers

This fantasy novella is collected in ***Four Past Midnight***. One of King's lesser tales, its interest lies in the contest of wills between certain characters.

American Pride Flight 29 from Los Angeles to Boston flies the unfriendly skies, as ten passengers wake to find all the other passengers and crew have disappeared, leaving behind only items of a personal nature. Off duty pilot Brian Engle takes control and lands the plane safely in Bangor, Maine, only to find the airport totally devoid of people. What appears to be safe ground is anything but, as the survivors struggle to deal with their new reality.

Genesis: The inspiration for this story was an image the author had "of a woman pressing her hand over a crack in the wall of a commercial jetliner," combined with his later realization that "this woman was a ghost."

Television: *The Langoliers* (1995). This two-part, four-hour miniseries is available on DVD as *Stephen King's The Langoliers*. In a capable presentation with questionable special effects, King makes a cameo appearance as Tom Holby.

Trivia: King is a "white-knuckle" flier and avoids the experience where possible.

Larry Underwood

Larry Underwood is one of the major characters in *The Stand*. When superflu sweeps the world, killing the vast majority of the population, Larry finds himself back in his native New York City. He's just had a hit record ("Baby, Can You Dig Your Man?") after years of trying to make it as a musician. As the shock of the apocalypse sinks in, driven by strange dreams Larry travels westward with **Nadine Cross** and a lost boy known as "Joe." After arriving in Boulder to join those drawn by **Abagail Freemantle**, he lives with Lucy Swann but is sent to Las Vegas by Freemantle to confront **Randall Flagg**.

On the Screen: Adam Storke is well cast as Larry in *Stephen King's The Stand*.

The Last Rung on the Ladder

This poignant mainstream short story is collected in *Night Shift* and is not to be missed. The two main characters lived near **Hemingford Home, Nebraska**. Shortly after hearing bad news, Larry recalls an incident when he and his sister were growing up on a farm.

Movie: A **Dollar Baby** of the same name was produced in 1987.

Lauder, Harold *see* Harold Lauder

The Lawnmower Man

This fun, minor story was first published in *Cavalier* magazine for May 1975 and collected in *Night Shift*.

After a neighbor's cat is killed under Harold Parkette's lawnmower, he decides to get rid of the mower and hire a lawn service. But after questioning the unique methods they use, Harold is in line for a service he did not order.

Television: *The Lawnmower Man* (1992). This TV movie is only loosely based on some parts of King's original story. Avoid it unless you are a Pierce Brosnan fan. Available on DVD. It is sometimes known as *Stephen King's Lawnmower Man* but the producers were barred from using King's name after a lawsuit.

Movie: *Lawnmower Man 2: Beyond Cyberspace* (1995). An atrocious sequel to the first movie, it is to be avoided at all costs. Also known as *Lawnmower Man 2: Jobe's War*. No DVD.

Movie: A **Dollar Baby** of the same name was produced in 1987.

Comic: Adapted in Marvel Magazine Group's *Bizarre Adventures*, Vol. 1, No. 29, for October 1981. Copies may be found for sale online.

Video Game: Sales Curve Interactive released a game developed by Allied Visions in

1993, titled *The Lawnmower Man*. For DOS, Sega and Super Nintendo, it was based on the 1992 movie, not King's story.

Video Game: In 1994 Sales Curve Interactive released a game it had developed titled *Cyberwar*. It is not based on any King story but is a sequel to *The Lawnmower Man* game.

Lebay, Roland *see* Roland Lebay

The Ledge

This fun but unimportant story first appeared in Penthouse magazine for July 1976 and was collected in **Night Shift**. This is the only King story in which a pigeon is a major character.

When crime boss Cressner discovers his wife is having an affair with her tennis coach, he plans revenge.

Movie: Adapted as one segment of *Cat's Eye* (1985). The screenplay is by King.

Leland Gaunt

In the horror novel **Needful Things**, in October 1991 a new store of that name opens in the town of **Castle Rock, Maine**. All who shop at Needful Things seem to find the one thing they want most. In truth, the goods they buy are usually not what they appear. Leland Gaunt, a mysterious stranger and owner of the shop, seems to know everything about everyone and the things they truly desire. But it is not the retail trade that interests Gaunt, and Gaunt himself may not be human.

On the Screen: Max von Sydow is suitably mysterious as Gaunt in the movie *Needful Things*.

The Leprechaun

This tale is known only from five pages that circulate in the King community. It begins with **Owen King** saving a leprechaun from the depredations of the family's housecat. The most interesting aspect of the story is King's wonderful description of the cat, Springsteen.

Genesis: Some researchers claim this was the beginning of a novel (apparently King lost 30 pages while riding a motorcycle) but this seems unlikely, considering the characters are members of his family. The storyline is very similar to parts of the *Cat's Eye* screenplay and it is possible King was working out aspects of that.

Leyden, Henry *see* Henry Leyden

The Library Policeman

This important and highly readable horror novella with overtones of Ray Bradbury's novel *Something Wicked This Way Comes* is collected in **Four Past Midnight**.

After being asked to fill in for a speaker at a Rotary dinner, Sam Peebles approaches the local librarian, Ardelia Lortz, who suggests some useful material. When Sam is unable to return the books to the library on time, he must face Lortz and deal with a problem much bigger than overdue fines. **Dave Duncan**, an alcoholic and Ardelia's former lover, plays an important role in the tale.

King directly links this tale with *Needful Things* through a character, and there is also mention of Paul Sheldon (*Misery*).

Genesis: This story originates from a passing remark from King's son **Owen** (now also a published author) about the "library police," who would supposedly visit if one did not return overdue books. King had also heard of the library police as a child and had spoken about them with Peter Straub in the early 1980s. As he began a tale titled "The Library Police," the real story began to unfold as King realized "something I knew already: the fears of childhood have a hideous persistence. Writing is an act of self-hypnosis, and in that state a kind of total emotional recall often takes place and terrors which should have been long dead start to walk and talk again."

Linoge, Andre *see* Andre Linoge

Lisey and the Madman

This tale first appeared in the anthology *McSweeney's Enchanted Chamber of Astonishing Stories* (Vintage, 2004) and was reprinted in *New Beginnings: A Tsunami Benefit Book* (Bloomsbury PLC, 2005). Both books are still in print. While the short story was originally said to be the opening segment of *Lisey's Story*, this turned out to be incorrect and a heavily revised version finally appeared in the novel.

Lisey's Story

Although this novel is profoundly important to King (it reads very much as a lengthy love letter to his wife, **Tabitha**) it is one of his lesser works. It is beautifully written (the author seems to have taken almost too much care in crafting it) and contains some important references for his canon, but the story is not particularly compelling. King is also working out feelings about his legacy.

Lisey Debusher Landon finds herself alone after the death of her successful novelist husband. **Scott Landon** had been a complicated man, with both demons to confront and a place he could go to escape them. As a stalker begins to threaten her safety, Lisey must confront those same demons and see if she can return to Scott's safe place.

King deliberately links both *The Talisman* and *Black House* and The Dark Tower cycle through clear references, and many Maine locations and characters are mentioned, linking works such as *The Dead Zone*, *Bag of Bones* and "The Sun Dog."

Genesis: King was hospitalized for pneumonia some years after he was hit by a van in 1999, and during that period his wife redecorated his study. When he returned to find it empty, he said "I felt like a ghost ... maybe I died. This is what the study would look like after I died. So I started to write this story about a famous writer who died, and about his wife Lisey, who is trying to get on with her life." He also says at some point it stops being a book about grieving and started to become one about the way we hide things. "From there it jumped into the idea that repression is creation, because when we repress we make up stories to replace the past."

Trivia: **Lisey and the Madman** is a different version of the opening scenes from the novel. In the novel Lisey sent Scott Landon's papers to the Special Collections Unit of the **Raymond H. Fogler Library** at the University of Maine, Orono. That very unit actually holds a collection of the papers of Stephen Edwin King. Lisey is pronounced "Lee-see."

The Little Sisters of Eluria

This important and lengthy **Dark Tower cycle** story was first published in *Legends: Short Novels by the Masters of Modern Fantasy* (Tor, 1998) and collected in **Everything's Eventual** (with some minor changes). The anthology is still in print. A stand-alone edition was released by Donald M. Grant Publishers in 2008.

Any reader seeking to understand or enjoy the Dark Tower cycle must read this story, as it both covers an important incident in **Roland Deschain**'s life between leaving **Gilead** and chasing the Man in Black across the desert in **The Dark Tower I: The Gunslinger**; and links to **The Territories** novels—**The Talisman** and **Black House**.

Roland Deschain finds himself in the town of Eluria, deserted but for green mutants who attack and nearly overcome him before he is saved by the Little Sisters, apparent nurses who take him to their hospital tent, where he finds John Norman, a fellow patient. Recovering, Roland becomes aware the Little Sisters are not as they appear and he now is at their mercy.

Comic: Marvel published a comic adaptation in 2010 and 2011, *The Dark Tower: The Gunslinger — The Little Sisters of Eluria*.

Little Tall Island, Maine

The novel **Dolores Claiborne** is set on this island (a total eclipse of the sun was observed there on 20 July 1963), as are the events of the screenplay **Storm of the Century**. While Martha Clarendon's death at the hands of **Andre Linoge** in 1989 was officially the first murder in some 70 years, there were suspicions around the deaths of **Dolores Claiborne**'s husband, Joe St. George (1963), and her employer, Vera Donovan (1992).

Gennesault Island ("**Home Delivery**") is near Little Tall Island (in fact, Mattie Pace, heroine of "Home Delivery," grew up on Little Tall). Both Jonesport and Machias are on the mainland nearby.

The Lonesome Death of Jordy Verrill

This story was originally published as "**Weeds**" in *Cavalier* for May 1976 and *Nugget* magazine for April 1979. King adapted it for the movie **Creepshow**, and that adaptation was included in a graphic novel of the same name.

Movie: *Creepshow* (1982)—"The Lonesome Death of Jordy Verrill" segment starred Stephen King as the title character.

Graphic Novel: "The Lonesome Death of Jordy Verrill" segment of *Creepshow* (New American Library, 1982).

The Long Walk

The second **Richard Bachman** paperback novel (Bachman is one of King's two pseudonyms), it is collected in **The Bachman Books** and was later re-released in a stand-alone edition (Penguin USA, 1999). This is the best of the four Bachman books published prior to *Thinner*, with a tough psychological edge and a building of empathy with certain characters.

Ray Garraty enters The Long Walk, an annual event where 100 teenage boys begin at the U.S.–Canada border and keep walking south through Maine and New Hampshire until only one walker remains. The gruesome twist to this event is that competitors have to constantly keep moving or they will be shot.

Genesis: King wrote this novel in the fall of 1966 and the spring of 1967, when he was a freshman at the University of Maine at Orono. This means it is the first written of all his published novels. He submitted it to a first novel competition in the fall of 1967 but was rejected without comment. After *Rage* was published as a paperback original, New American Library picked it up as the second Bachman novel.

Louis Creed

Louis Creed is the protagonist of *Pet Sematary*. A medical doctor, he moves to Ludlow, Maine, with his family — wife Rachel, son Gage and daughter Ellie — and takes a job at the University of Maine. Slightly over six feet tall, he is soon confronted by the strange death of a student and also learns of a local pet cemetery (misspelled "sematary" by local children). He also makes friends with neighbor **Jud Crandall**, who also reveals other information, known only to a few locals. This combination of circumstances soon puts the entire Creed family at risk. It is difficult to read the novel without having great empathy for Louis.

On the Screen: Dale Midkiff played Creed in *Pet Sematary* (1989).

Genesis: Considering the genesis of the novel, it is feasible to see Stephen King in Louis Creed.

Low Men in Yellow Coats

This important **Dark Tower cycle** story is collected in *Hearts in Atlantis* and *Stephen King Goes to the Movies*. King proves again how easily he can take readers back to their childhood, in a manner very similar to "**The Body**" (filmed as *Stand by Me*). The first tale in a collection loosely connected by various characters and the Vietnam War era, it is a warm-hearted and very realistic tale but also introduces the threat of the "Low Men" and contains mystic undertones.

It is 1960 and **Ted Brautigan** moves into the apartment building where **Bobby Garfield** lives with his solo mother Liz. Ted and Bobby become close friends, much to the Liz's disgust (although she has bigger issues to deal with). Ted has secrets and hires Bobby to read from the newspapers every day, and to keep an eye out for signs of "low men in yellow coats" in the area. Meanwhile, Bobby's friend **Carol Gerber** falls afoul of local bullies. Liz, Ted, Carol and Bobby are all at risk as Ted's secrets begin to unravel.

Genesis: Apart from being a deliberate extension of the Dark Tower mythos, this story is inspired by King's own youth in Stratford, Connecticut. The author wrote in 2009, "The fact is that 'Low Men' is only part of a loosely constructed novel, which still isn't really done ('The House on Benefit Street'), the story of what happened to Bobby's childhood girlfriend, Carol, remains to be written."

Movie: The movie *Hearts in Atlantis* (2001) is actually an adaptation of "Low Men in

Yellow Coats" (the novella "**Hearts in Atlantis**" storyline does not appear in the movie), and of "**Heavenly Shades of Night Are Falling.**" The screenplay is by William Goldman (***Misery***, *Butch Cassidy and the Sundance Kid*). Anthony Hopkins plays Ted Brautigan and David Morse (***The Green Mile***) portrays the adult Bobby.

L.T.'s Theory of Pets

This entertaining if minor story first appeared in *Six Stories* and is collected in ***Everything's Eventual***.

L.T. DeWitt delights in regaling his workmates about his "theory of pets." He often tells the story about his wife, Cynthia, or "Lulu," and the time she left him. Lulu had bought a dog named Frank for L.T., and the following year he bought her a cat, Lucy. The animals intensely disliked their intended owners but loved the person who had originally purchased them. After two years of marriage L.T. came home to find that Lulu had taken the dog and all her belongings, leaving him a note. And thereby hangs a tale.

Genesis: According to King, "The origin of the story so far as I can remember was a 'Dear Abby' column where Abby opined that a pet is just about the worst sort of present one can give anyone." It is also inspired by the interaction between his own pets (Marlowe, a corgi, and Pearl, "a rather crazed Siamese cat.") He says it is his favorite story of the collection.

Audio: King can be heard reading the story on *Stephen King Live* and *L.T.'s Theory of Pets* (both released by Hodder and Stoughton Audio Books). It's an entertaining rendition, and it's great to listen to King read one of his own tales.

Luckey Quarter

This warm-hearted short story first appeared in the national newspaper *USA Weekend* for 30 June to 2 July 1995. King updated it for publication in *Six Stories* and the mass-market collection, ***Everything's Eventual***. Readers who wish to access the original newspaper version will find that many libraries hold archives of this weekend edition of *USA Today* or can access it via interlibrary loan.

Carson City, Nevada, hotel chambermaid Darlene Pullen would like to afford braces for her daughter and a Sega system for her son. While cleaning Room 322 she comes across the standard tip envelope, nicknamed the "honeypot." All she finds inside is a single quarter and a note reading, "This is a luckey quarter! It's true! Luckey you!" But what can she do for her family with a single quarter?

Genesis: King wrote this story "longhand, on hotel stationery" in a Nevada hotel while on a Harley-Davidson motorcycle trip across America, promoting ***Insomnia***. The inspiration was a two-dollar slot chip and note left by the turndown maid.

Movie: A **Dollar Baby** film of the same name was produced in 2004.

Lunch at the Gotham Café

This darkly amusing story has an interesting publishing history. It first appeared in an anthology, *Dark Love: 22 All-Original Tales of Lust and Obsession* (Roc, 1995). King then significantly revised it for inclusion in *Six Stories* (a limited edition). The first time it was available in practical mass-market form was as part of the audio book ***Blood and Smoke***, released in November 1999 (in the *Six Stories* version). The first mass-market printed release was in **Everything's Eventual**.

Steven Davis' wife, Diane, leaves him and quickly becomes aggressive. Seeking to understand why she left the marriage, he organizes to meet Diane and her lawyer at the Gotham Café. On arrival he notes something is not quite right with the maître d', Guy, but makes the mistake of ignoring the feeling and concentrating on what appear to be more important things.

The *Dark Love* version won the Bram Stoker Award from the Horror Writers Association for Superior Achievement in Long Fiction for 1995.

King links this tale to his other fiction by mention of Babylon, Alabama, which also appears in "Dedication" and **The Plant**.

Genesis: King says, "One day when I was in New York, I walked past a very nice-looking restaurant. Inside, the maître d' was showing a couple to their table. The couple was arguing. The maître d' caught my eye and tipped me what may have been the most cynical wink in the universe. I went to back to my hotel and wrote this story."

Movie: The 2005 **Dollar Baby** *Stephen King's Gotham Café* (or *Gotham Café*) was written by King expert Bev Vincent (*The Road to the Dark Tower*), Julie Sands and Peter Schink. King appears in a voice cameo only as Steve Davis' lawyer, Mr. Ring.

Maddie Pace

Just a month after telling her husband Jack in "**Home Delivery**" she's pregnant, he is lost at sea in while lobstering. She barely has the time to come to terms with her loss when people-eating zombies suddenly appear all over the world. Trapped on Gennesault Island, she and her neighbors must deal with the incredible.

The Man in Black

An important character in **The Dark Tower cycle**, he is an enemy of **Roland Deschain**. He is famously mentioned in the first line of **The Dark Tower: The Gunslinger**: "The Man in Black fled across the desert and the gunslinger followed." He is also known as **Walter**.

The Man in the Black Suit

This story won the 1996 O. Henry Award for Best American Short Story and the 1995 World Fantasy Award for Best Short Fiction. The O. Henry Awards are an annual collection of the year's best stories published in U.S. and Canadian magazines and written by U.S. or Canadian authors. King won first prize (in other words was judged to have been the best story written by a North American and published in a North American magazine). However, King found the result of his own retelling "humdrum" and was surprised by both critical and reader reaction: "This story is proof that writers are often the worst judges of what they have written."

The Man in the Black Suit was originally published in *The New Yorker* magazine for 31 October 1994, republished in **Six Stories** and collected in **Everything's Eventual**. Every King reader and certainly anyone who enjoys beautifully written, suspenseful tales must read it.

Gary, now 89 or 90 years of age, writes down an important part of his past in his diary. In the summer of 1914 he went down to the Castle Stream to fish and came across a strange man. This man, who was wearing a black suit, left no footprints, had eyes of fire, and claimed to have awful news for the young boy.

This is a chronologically early **Castle Rock** story and is also linked through mention of the town of Motton to stories such as *Lisey's Story*.

Genesis: King says this is his homage to Nathaniel Hawthorne's "Young Goodman Brown": "I think it's one of the best stories ever written by an American." King's tale was inspired when one of his friends who told him his Granpa truly believed he'd once met the Devil in the woods.

Movie: A **Dollar Baby** of the same name was produced in 2003.

The Man Who Loved Flowers

This derivate short story was originally published in *Gallery* magazine for August 1977 and is collected in **Night Shift**.

May 1963 is not a safe time for women to be alone in New York City. The Hammer Murderer has killed five women and the police seem to have no leads. A young man, obviously in love, walks slowly down Third Avenue, attracting the attention of all he passes.

Movie: A **Dollar Baby** titled *Flowers for Norma* was produced in 2010.

The Man Who Would Not Shake Hands

This story, collected in **Skeleton Crew**, is paired with "**The Breathing Method**," as both are presented as stories told in an unnamed New York gentlemen's club on East 35th Street, where elderly men gather to tell tales tall and true. It was originally published in the *Shadows 4* anthology (Doubleday, 1981) and King significantly revised it for *Skeleton Crew* (the original anthology can be found at second-hand booksellers).

Clint Tremain relates a strange tale to his friends at the club. After club member Henry Brower had been involved in the accidental death of a young boy in Bombay, he had been cursed by the boy's father. The consequences of the curse form the twist in his tale.

Man with a Belly

"Man with a Belly" is one of King's relatively rare crime stories. It was first published in the December 1978 *Cavalier* and was reprinted in *Gent* for November/December 1979. Copies of these two men's magazines are quite difficult to come by and buyers should note they contain graphic sexual content. Those seeking a copy should contact specialist King booksellers.

A 78-year-old Mafia boss offers a hit man $50,000 to rape his young wife as revenge for her gambling habits. Events turn on both the don and his hired hand and readers learn the meaning of the Sicilian term "man with a belly."

King has never allowed re-publication, either in a collection of his own or an anthology. The reasons are unknown but as the story was written very specifically for the men's magazine market and includes brutal sexual content, he may feel it would not reflect well upon his overall canon. Overall the story has some plot holes and is somewhat unsatisfying.

The Mangler

This story was originally published in *Cavalier* magazine in December 1972. King rewrote it before it was collected in **Night Shift** and **Stephen King Goes to the Movies**. Copies of the original magazine appear online from time to time at quite high prices (readers should also note *Cavalier* is a men's magazine, with graphic sexual content).

An ironing machine at the Blue Ribbon Laundry is responsible for the injury and death of a number of workers. The police investigate but are facing a problem far more serious than anyone suspects.

Genesis: In **On Writing** King describes his work at the New Franklin Laundry in Bangor (prior to his success, of course), including the fact that many of the tablecloths and napkins arrived for washing covered in live maggots—some of which would try to climb up his arms.

Movie: *The Mangler* (1994). Possibly the worst film ever made from a King story—avoid it.

Movie: *The Mangler 2* (2001). This has little or no connection with any King material and is worse than awful. Also known as *The Mangler 2: Graduation Day*.

Movie: *The Mangler Reborn* (2005). All this proves is that purchasing a story's name can lead to an eternal parade of mind-numbing and worthless screen material.

Margaret White

Margaret White is the religious fanatic mother of **Carrie White** in the novel *Carrie*. Born Margaret Brigham in Motton, Maine, her husband dies before their daughter is born. Originally a Baptist, her religious beliefs take a disturbing turn when she begins to worship from home. She insists her daughter conform to her views.

Genesis: King visited one of his classmates at her Durham home (she would form one of the inspirations for Carrie White) and was struck by a huge and "grisly" crucifix in their living room.

On the Screen: Piper Laurie is outstanding in the role in the 1976 film; and Patricia Clarkson more than competent in the 2002 TV remake.

On Stage: Barbara Cook and Betty Buckley played Margaret on stage in the 1988 musical; Patricia Catchouny appeared as Margaret in the 2009 musical. Kate Goerhing (2006) and Leah Walton (2010) appeared in a drag show version.

Mark Petrie

Mark Petrie is around 12 when **Kurt Barlow** comes to 'Salem's Lot, Maine. Probably the first to realize vampires are in town, he teams up with **Ben Mears**.

Mark is mentioned in **The Dark Tower V: Wolves of the Calla**, **The Dark Tower VI: Song of Susannah** and **The Dark Tower VII: The Dark Tower**.

On the Screen: Lance Kerwin plays the role in the 1979 TV movie; Dan Byrd reprises it in the 2004 version.

Marsh, Beverly "Bev" *see* Beverly "Bev" Marsh

Marty Coslaw

Ten-year-old wheelchair-bound Marty is the hero of *Cycle of the Werewolf*. When the town of Tarker's Mills, Maine, is threatened each month by an apparent werewolf, Marty is determined to uncover its human identity.

On the Screen: Corey Haim plays Marty in *Silver Bullet*.

Mattie Devore

Mattie Devore is a character in *Bag of Bones*. When her husband Lance dies, her father-in-law attempts to take custody of her only child, Kyra, but she is defended by successful local writer **Michael Noonan**.

Maximum Overdrive

King has written many screenplays, including for this original movie. But this is the only one he has directed and it is unlikely he will do so again, having commented publicly that he did not enjoy either the process or the work involved.

In the tale the Earth passes into the tail of a rogue comet and machines suddenly become sentient. Worse, they are aggressive towards humans (leading to some gory results in the early scenes). A group of people is trapped at the Dixie-Boy Truck Stop on Route 17 near Wilmington, North Carolina, by a group of trucks, which are attempting to wipe out our heroes. Can they survive, or even escape to somewhere out of the reach of humanity's now lethal technology?

This is another tale that illustrates King's thematic fascination with machines gone wild (**"The Mangler"** and *Christine* for example); it is not one of King's superior works.

The screenplay is difficult to find but copies do circulate in the King community and are sometimes available from King specialists. At various times before production it went under the titles *Trucks* and *Overdrive*.

Genesis: King took the basic premise from his short story "**Trucks**," but this screenplay is not an adaptation of that tale. The location and characters are entirely different.

Movie: *Maximum Overdrive* (1985), written and directed by King. Starring Emilio Estevez, Pat Hingle and featuring a cameo by Stephen King as "Man at Cashpoint." A heavy metal soundtrack from Australian band AC/DC may annoy some viewers. It is far from a great movie, or even a great "B" movie, but most King fans will at least appreciate the humor.

McFarland, Trisha *see* Trisha McFarland

McGee, Charlie *see* Charlie McGee

Mears, Ben *see* Ben Mears

Memory

This tale appeared in *Tin House* magazine (Issue 28, Vol. 7, No. 4). A significantly revised version appears as part of the novel **Duma Key**. Copies of the original magazine are generally available from resellers.

Merrill, Ace *see* Ace Merrill

Merrill, Reginald "Pop" *see* Reginald "Pop" Merrill

Michael Noonan

Michael Noonan is the protagonist of **Bag of Bones**. He'd been a reporter for the *Derry News* before becoming a successful novelist. When his wife Jo dies, he suffers writer's block and moves from their **Derry** home to their house on Dark Score Lake, Maine. There he is apparently haunted by both Jo and **Sara Tidwell**, as he defends **Mattie Devore** and her daughter Kyra from the rapacious wealthy Max Devore, Kyra's grandfather. He begins to fall in love with Mattie as events from the past threaten to overwhelm them all.

Genesis: Clearly Noonan's character has autobiographic overtones. He is a famous writer, has a lake home similar to that owned by King and his wife, and even attended the same college, the University of Maine.

Mid-World

Mid-World is part of **Roland Deschain**'s planet, **All-World**. It appears to have held out the longest against the rampages of the **Crimson King**'s minions. When **Gilead** in Mid-World fell, Roland set himself to the task of finding **The Dark Tower**. It is of Mid-World's civilization that Roland and readers alike most long for in **The Dark Tower Cycle**.

Mike Hanlon

Mike Hanlon lives all his life in **Derry, Maine**. In 1957–58 he and his friends, **Bill Denbrough, Benjamin Hanscom, Beverly Marsh, Richard Tozier, Stanley Uris** and **Eddie Kaspbrak**, form "the Losers Club" in the novel **It**, in an attempt to fight **Pennywise**. As an adult Mike is the librarian in Derry (**Insomnia**) and it is he who calls the Losers Club back to town. Photographs his father had owned feature in "**The Bird and the Album**."

On the Screen: Tim Reid played Mike in *It*.

Misery

One of King's most important and powerful novels, *Misery* won the Best Novel Bram Stoker Award for 1987 from the Horror Writers Association.

Paul Sheldon, a popular historical romance writer, crashes his car on Route 9 near Sidewinder, Colorado, during a snowstorm. **Annie Wilkes**, a registered nurse, comes upon the scene and takes the seriously injured Sheldon to her isolated farmhouse. Unfortunately for Sheldon, Annie is his "number one fan" and has a very special request.

All serious King readers will devour this novel, although it must be noted it does have very graphic content. King introduces clear and direct references to **Jack Torrance** and the events of *The Shining* at **The Overlook Hotel**, near Annie Wilkes' farm. Paul Sheldon is also mentioned in *Rose Madder*, "The Library Policeman" and *The Dark Tower VII: The Dark Tower*; and Sheldon's novels with the character Misery Chastain are mentioned in *Rose Madder*.

Genesis: King says he wrote *Misery* when he was having tough time with dope: "I knew what I was writing about. There was never any question. Annie was my drug problem, and she was my number-one fan. God, she never wanted to leave." Another inspiration was Evelyn Waugh's short story "The Man Who Loved Dickens."

Movie: *Misery* (1990). One of the best adaptations of a King tale, for which Kathy Bates won both Academy and Golden Globe Awards. The screenplay is by William Goldman (*Butch Cassidy and the Sundance Kid*). Rob Reiner (*Stand by Me*) directs and James Caan plays Sheldon. Available on DVD.

Stage: *Misery*. First performed professionally in 1992, this play has become a staple of smaller professional and local amateur groups worldwide. The play is by Simon Moore.

Trivia: King once claimed he "wrote most of *Misery* by hand, sitting at Kipling's desk in Brown's Hotel in London ... then I found out he died at that desk. That spooked me, so I quit the hotel." After *Misery* was published, a deranged fan, whose aunt was a nurse, broke into the King home and confronted **Tabitha King** late at night. Her husband was not at home but Tabitha was unharmed and the "fan" was arrested.

The Mist

This novella originally appeared in *Dark Forces* (Viking, 1980), edited by King's agent of the time, Kirby McCauley. The author substantially rewrote it for inclusion in **Skeleton Crew**. In the *Notes* to that book he writes, "I never liked it much until the rewrite." The anthology is available from resellers.

David Drayton, his wife and son live on Long Lake. After a severe storm damages the area a strange mist moves onto the lake. David and Billy leave to get supplies in nearby Bridgton, Maine, but they are trapped in a supermarket by the mist and what appear to be strange creatures hiding within it. Conflict opens between factions of the trapped townspeople and visitors (one led by religious bigot **Mrs. Carmody**), and Drayton is left to protect his son and somehow plan a return to his home and his wife.

Genesis: The novella was written specifically for the collection edited by his agent, Kirby McCauley, and was inspired by a storm ("much as described in the story ... there was indeed a waterspout") on Long Lake at Bridgton, Maine, when the King family lived there. In the notes to the collection, King also says he and his son were in a supermarket when he imagined shoppers trapped there by prehistoric animals.

Movie: *The Mist* (2007). The screenplay and direction are by Frank Darabont (*The Green Mile*, *The Shawshank Redemption*). This film is deliberately presented in the 1950s style and is best viewed in the black and white version. Available on DVD.

Computer Game: Mindscape released a computer game developed by Angelsoft, Inc., based on "The Mist" in 1985. It was later re-released by Thunder Mountain.

Mobius

This is an unpublished science fiction story King wrote in the late 1970s or early 1980s. The story is rather derivative, there being any number of science fiction and time travel tales along the same lines, and this may explain its lack of publication.

In the tale a scientist forces his student to travel through time and space in the Mobius machine. Aware of the risks involved in returning, Wayne Parsons initially decides to stay in the idyllic land he has been sent to, but the passing of the years may change his mind.

The story may be read at the Special Collections Unit of the University of Maine's **Raymond H. Fogler Library**. Ask for Box 1212.

Molly

King wrote a screenplay for an episode of the hit FOX television series *The X-Files* under the title "Molly." Chris Carter, the creator of the series, added and significantly changed material and both writers were credited with the new teleplay, "**Chinga**."

King's office has confirmed that "Molly" was not an early version of "Chinga" but a totally different teleplay. After King and Chris Carter discussed the changes Carter would want made to "Molly," King went in a different direction with "Chinga."

In "Molly," FBI Agent Dana Scully is staying with a friend in Ammas Beach, Maine, when she observes people suddenly attacking themselves inside a convenience store. A woman turns to her daughter and orders her to "stop it," but the girl cannot and we see her hate-filled doppelganger inside a frozen-food case. Agent Mulder flies in to help investigate the incident and the little girl's autism is revealed, along with video of the girl's duplicate. They visit the girl's home and discover a terrified mother and Polly playing with her doll, Chinga, and Molly the evil doppelganger. Events escalate as Mulder loses control of his hand, which grabs a sharp shell and tries to slit his throat. Can our heroes save themselves, let alone Polly and her mother from the other-worldly creature?

Copies of this screenplay exist but do not circulate. In this author's opinion it is a much more satisfying and interesting story than "Chinga," but certainly too long for a single TV episode.

Genesis: King originally approached Chris Carter to talk about writing an episode for *Millennium* but was convinced to write an episode of *The X-Files* instead. Another source has King becoming a fan of the program after meeting David Duchovny on *Jeopardy*.

The Monkey

This eerie tale was originally published in the November 1980 edition of *Gallery* magazine and was significantly rewritten for its inclusion in **Skeleton Crew**. Issues of *Gallery* appear for sale online, but readers should be aware it includes graphic sexual content.

In this short story, Hal Shelburn does not like the toy monkey his son Dennis found while looking through his recently deceased Aunt Ida's attic. Rightly — this toy has a nasty secret.

The Shelburn family had lived in Arnette, Texas, the same town where Stu Redman was resident when the superflu hit in **The Stand**. The same town is mentioned in **Desperation**.

Genesis: King was inspired by seeing a man selling wind-up toys on a New York street.

Graphic: An illustrated version is planned for in **Secretary of Dreams Volume 2** (Cemetery Dance), drawn by Maine artist Glenn Chadbourne.

Morality

Morality first appeared in the July 2009 edition of *Esquire* magazine and later as a bonus in the mass market version of the novella "**Blockade Billy**." That may be the easiest form of access for readers ahead of the inevitable inclusion in a future King collection.

In the tale a married couple is presented with a moral dilemma. Chad and Nora Callahan are struggling on his substitute teacher salary and her income home nursing the Rev. George Winston. Meanwhile the bills are piling up and Chad has the opportunity to complete a book of stories that just might get them out from under their creditors and off to a new life in Vermont. Out of the blue the patient offers Nora $200,000 cash, but of course this will come with strings.

This is a tale of morality, but King also captures the feeling of "ordinary"—how simple events might happen and how lives might unwind as a result of fateful decisions. King, of course, is a highly moral writer and this tale can be safely filed in that section of his work, but perhaps without being dusted off and read too often. It won the Shirley Jackson Award for Best Novelette of 2009.

Mordred Deschain

Mordred Deschain is the son of both **Roland Deschain** and **The Crimson King** and his mother, **Susannah Dean** and her alter ego, Mia. He first appears in **The Dark Tower VI: Song of Susannah** as Mia's "chap" (unborn child), in which Richard Sayre claimed he would be the most important child ever born. He is not human (in fact he is of the "Outer Dark") and his fate is resolved in **The Dark Tower VII: The Dark Tower**, along with that of all his parents.

Genesis: Inspired by Arthurian legend, in which Mordred is the illegitimate son of King Arthur and turns traitor to his father.

Morning Deliveries (Milkman #1)

In this **Skeleton Crew** tale, Spike Milligan, a milkman, makes morning deliveries in Devon, Pennsylvania. One morning he decides to leave a few surprises.

This story is closely linked to the *Skeleton Crew* version of "**Big Wheels (Milkman #2).**" Both stories come from an aborted King novel, The Milkman.

Mostly Old Men

This piece appeared in *Tin House* magazine No. 40 (August 2009) and was the first King poem published for fifteen years. It appears King may have been returning to poetry, as he published "**The Bone Church**" and "**Tommy**" the following year. *Tin House* had previously published "**Memory**," an early release segment of **Duma Key**.

In this short poem King builds a picture of largely elderly men traveling America's highways, allowing their mostly old dogs a chance to relieve themselves at rest stops, thereby forming a loose but anonymous coast-to-coast fellowship. It is a poignant piece in which King draws the reader instantly into everyday life.

Back copies of this issue of *Tin House* were available at the time of writing and should also be available from online sellers.

Movie Show

King keeps thoughts and stories in handwritten journals, some containing up to ten different pieces. Four incomplete stories are in a journal that is now kept at the **Raymond H. Fogler Library** of the University of Maine at Orono, and "Movie Show" is among them. For security reasons the journal has been moved to Box 1010 at the Special Collections Unit, meaning readers need King's written permission. Other partial stories in the journal indicate it was written in the 1989–91 time frame. The others are "**Muffe**," "**The Evaluation**," and "**Chip Coombs**," titles King provides in the journal.

This is the most interesting of the stories, as it has strong autobiographic undertones. In the 25-page fragment a boy heads to the movies. Jacky had been prepared to go strawberry picking in **Harlow**, Maine, one morning in June 1959 but the work is called off due to rain. He and his friends pick for H.A. "Frosty" Snowman, who owns a strawberry farm on Larkspur Road, on which Jacky and his mother lived. After the work is called off Jacky hitches a ride to nearby Lewiston with an old man driving an old farm truck.

Arriving on Lisbon Street in Lewiston, Jacky heads to the movie theater, the Ritz, and buys a ticket for the advertised double bill, *She Beast* and *The Black Scorpion*. Jacky observes the few other patrons and at this point the story fragment ends.

Jacky is writing the story at age 45 (it is unclear how old he was at the time he hitchhiked to the movies). He writes that he attended **Gates Falls** High five years later, in 1964, and that when he grew up he lived at 131 Elm Avenue, Utica (a town King mentions from time to time).

Harlow is sometimes used by King as a doppelganger for the small town of Durham, Maine, in which he grew up and in this piece King is reminiscing in the mode we are familiar with from "**The Body**." The nearby town of Gates Falls appears in many King works, including *Graveyard Shift*, *It Grows on You*, *Riding the Bullet* and "Sword in the Darkness." Even more clearly, the whole movie show experience reflects King's later dissertation in part 18 of the C.V. section of **On Writing**. There seems no prospect of King completing and publishing "Movie Show."

The Moving Finger

This rather strange short story first appeared in *The Magazine of Fantasy and Science Fiction* for December 1990 and was significantly revised and collected in **Nightmares and Dreamscapes**. Copies of the original magazine regularly appear for sale online.

A long finger suddenly protrudes from the drain in Howard Mitla's bathroom sink. Howard tries to tell himself the finger is just a hallucination but it continues to appear, although not when Howard's wife is at home. Howard decides to take aggressive measures.

Genesis: King says *The Moving Finger* is the type of fantasy short story that, unlike movies, do not have to explain why things happen and that the protagonist's efforts to deal with the finger forms "a perfectly valid metaphor for how we cope with the nasty surprises life holds in store for all of us.... In a tale of fantasy, this gloomy answer actually seems to satisfy us. In the end, it may be the genre's chief moral asset: at its best, it can open a window (or a confessional screen) on the existential aspects of our mortal lives."

Television: "The Moving Finger" (1991). A forgettable episode in the series *Monsters*; it is available on DVD.

Mrs. Carmody

Mrs. Carmody (her first name is never revealed) is exactly the sort of interfering, religious bigot busybody King describes so well. In **"The Mist"** she and others townspeople from Bridgton, Maine, are trapped in a supermarket by monsters. She forms a clique of fellow believers and claims the Last Times have arrived.

On the Screen: Marcia Gay Harden is superb in the movie.

Mrs. Todd's Shortcut

This amusing tale first appeared in *Redbook* magazine in May 1984 and is collected in ***Skeleton Crew***. **Ophelia Todd** loves driving, but not the time it takes to get from **Castle Rock** to Bangor, Maine. In fact, her compact Mercedes is full of maps of all sorts to help her find the shortest route. Using every road from the interstate to unmarked woods roads, Ophelia makes quite a game of this drive. However, some of the roads are not quite right; they are not on the map and are full of strange creatures.

Of this tale King says three women's magazines refused it for publication ("two because of the line about how a woman will pee down her own leg if she doesn't squat"). Four notable Maine towns from King's canon are mentioned — Castle Rock, **Derry, Gates Falls** and Haven (***The Tommyknockers***).

Genesis: Inspired by **Tabitha King**'s habits. King says, "The woman really is mad for a shortcut.... And Tabby really does seem to be getting younger sometimes."

Muffe

This is one of four incomplete tales in a handwritten a journal of King's thoughts and stories. Using King's titles, the stories have been dubbed "Muffe," **"The Evaluation,"** "**Movie Show**" and "**Chip Coombs**," and were probably written in the 1989–91 time frame.

King allowed the publication of a different snippet of "Muffe" in Bev Vincent's book *The Stephen King Illustrated Companion* (2009). These two pages come from a different journal, most likely written during the same time period, and encompass later events in the tale.

In the first fragment a man is trapped in a cage. Children are pelting Muffe of the Finger Kingdoms with clods of earth and rocks. His crime is that of laughing at the Palace of the Great One, Lord Vaggar. Vaggar's right hand man approaches and stops the children from pelting the prisoner, and at that point the first fragment ends.

In the second fragment Muffe is out of the cage, talking to the right-hand man, Mustus, initially about Clarissa, Vaggar's daughter, who had led the children pelting the caged man. Muffe and the man he thought of as the "barbarian" begin to feel each other out in conversation. Mustus tells him that very evening Vaggar will meet Muffe to learn more about his land and that if he wants to stay alive he should give Vaggar what he wants.

It seems these fragments were to be part of a fantasy tale, as the setting appears to be something like a Mongol town on the steppes. There is no indication King ever intended to publish the tale.

The journal is housed at the **Raymond H. Fogler Library** of the University of Maine at Orono, Box 1010 in the Special Collections Unit. King's written permission is needed for access.

Mute

This story first appeared in *Playboy* magazine in December 2007 and is collected in **Just After Sunset**. Monette, a traveling salesman, picks up an apparently deaf and mute hitchhiker. To relieve his boredom he relates the sordid tale of his embezzling wife and her lover to his uncomprehending fellow traveler. But the salesman is making a mistake when he bares his soul to this stranger.

Genesis: King read a story in a local newspaper about a woman who embezzled $65,000 in order to play the lottery. He wondered how her husband felt and wrote this story to work that question out.

My Pretty Pony

This delightful mainstream short story was originally published as a limited edition from the Whitney Museum in 1988. In October of that year it was released in a limited trade hardback (Alfred Knopf). Copies of each appear online from time to time but are expensive. King substantially revised the tale for inclusion in **Nightmares and Dreamscapes**.

George Banning takes his grandson Clive for a walk to explain the different types of time.

Genesis: Originally planned as a **Richard Bachman** novel, King junked the longer version and retained only this flashback scene. King has revealed Clive will grow up to become a contract hit man.

Movie: A **Dollar Baby** of the same name was produced in 2009.

N.

This weird novella was first publicly released as a set of 25 two-minute animated episodes to promote King's then-upcoming book, **Just After Sunset**, in which a text version is collected.

Dr. John Bonsaint has a patient who apparently suffers from obsessive-compulsive disorder and paranoid delusions—the doctor's notes identify him as "N." N is convinced a circle of stones in a field on the outskirts of Motton keeps changing and that he must somehow keep it in balance to prevent an apocalypse. But, is he really deluded?

The links to King's other fiction lie in the use of Motton, Maine, as a setting. The character "N" lives in Castle View, a suburb of **Castle Rock**; and certain characters went to school in **Harlow**.

Genesis: King says of the story's inspiration: "Not Lovecraft; it's a riff on Arthur

Machen's *The Great God Pan*, which is one of the best horror stories ever written. Maybe the best in the English language. Mine isn't anywhere near that good, but I loved the chance to put neurotic behavior — obsessive/compulsive disorder — together with the idea of a monster-filled macroverse."

Episodic Graphic Adaptation: *Stephen King's N.* (2008). Produced by Marvel Comics and initially released online and via mobile phone each weekday from 28 July to 29 August 2008, as 25 two minute episodes. Release on DVD (2008) as part of the *Just After Sunset* collector's set (certain editions of the book include the DVD — purchasers should ensure they are purchasing the correct edition and, if second-hand, that the DVDs are intact).

Comic: Marvel published a comic adaptation over four parts in 2010, as *Stephen King's N.*

Nadine Cross

Nadine Cross is orphaned at age 4½ years. When the superflu strikes in **The Stand**, she is a young woman and makes her way west, attracted to the Dark Man, **Randall Flagg**, in her dreams, but tries to avoid her fate by moving to the Boulder Free Zone and moving in with **Harold Lauder**. She has long, thick black hair with strong white streaks, and her hair whitens as she moves closer to Flagg. King is able to build reader empathy for Nadine, despite her ultimate affiliation.

On the Screen: Laura San Giacomo plays Nadine in *Stephen King's The Stand*.

Needful Things

One of King's longer novels, this story has the type of large cast many fans enjoyed in **The Stand** and, later, **Under the Dome**. It was originally billed as "the last **Castle Rock** novel," but King has in fact returned to that iconic town on numerous occasions. As a Castle Rock story, it is deeply linked with many other King fictions, and quite a few characters from earlier tales re-appear, including **Alan Pangborn, Ace Merrill** ("The Body"), Norris Ridgewick (**The Dark Half**) and there are mentions of events from tales such as *Cujo*, all providing a welcome home for King's "constant readers." It is ultimately a fast-paced tale of greed and passion, love and redemption.

Leland Gaunt is an outsider when he arrives in Castle Rock and sets up a shop he calls Needful Things. Eleven-year-old Brian Rusk is his first customer, and the first to find the thing he most wants. Soon, business is booming, as the each customer is able to satisfy his or her heart's desire. But there is a price. As events spiral out of control, Sheriff Alan Pangborn and his lover Polly Chalmers find themselves fighting a losing battle against desire, pain and morality.

Genesis: King notes he meant the novel to be satire about consumer culture and was surprised by the average critical reaction that it's an unsuccessful horror novel. He says it "is a black comedy about greed and obsession."

Movie: *Needful Things* (1993). A competent if forgettable adaptation. Ed Harris plays Alan Pangborn and Max von Sydow is Leland Gaunt. Available on DVD.

Never Look Behind You

This piece of juvenilia, in collaboration with King's childhood friend Chris Chesley, appears in **People, Places and Things**, along with six other King tales. Usurer George

Jacobs turns to face an approaching poor, old woman. After predicting he will never spend his ill-gotten gains, she raises her finger and he is struck dead.

This is a simple old-fashioned tale of revenge. There are hints of King's future efforts—revenge is a powerful motive in "**Dolan's Cadillac**" and *Dolores Claiborne*, for instance, and an older person raising their finger to dispense a curse is used to great effect in *Thinner*.

The New Lieutenant's Rap

Printed as a chapbook, the entire text of this story is in King's handwriting. It was provided to guests at a 1999 New York City party celebrating King's 25th anniversary in book publishing. His introduction to the chapbook states it's an early and very different version of a tale that would appear in his *Hearts in Atlantis* collection — that version is "**Why We're in Vietnam**."

The key characters are "Sully-John" Sullivan, who also appears in "**Low Men in Yellow Coats**," "**Blind Willie**" (but only in *Hearts in Atlantis* version), "**Heavenly Shades of Night Are Falling**," the "**Hearts in Atlantis**" short story and, of course, "Why We're in Vietnam," and Dieffenbaker (the "new lieutenant"), who also appears in "Why We're in Vietnam" and "Blind Willie" (but only in *Hearts in Atlantis* version). They recall a day in Vietnam that looks like it will escalate into something like the My Lai massacre (this includes a scene which is shocking even by King's standards). It's a compelling tale, at the heart of which is the Vietnam War and its lasting impact on both the characters and their entire generation.

It is very difficult to find a copy of this tale — of the 500 printed many were discarded and they rarely appear for sale on eBay. Photocopies sometimes circulate.

The New York Times at Special Bargain Rates

This tale first appeared in *The Magazine of Fantasy and Science Fiction* for October-November 2007 and is collected in *Just After Sunset*. A widow answers the phone and speaks to her husband — but he had died two days earlier in an airplane crash. In the short time he has to communicate he passes on some predictions and leaves her in shock.

Genesis: King wrote this story in Brisbane, Australia, after having arrived from San Francisco by plane. He slept for ten hours, awoke at 2 A.M. and wrote the story by dawn.

Nick Andros

Nick Andros is a much loved character from *The Stand*. When the superflu strikes, Nick is drifting from town to town and has just been viciously assaulted by some of the residents of Shoyo, Arkansas. Of course, he outlives them all and his dreams drive him to **Abagail Freemantle**, although he tells her he does not believe in God. Along the way he finds and befriends **Tom Cullen**. His role in the Boulder Free Zone will be critical to the resolution of the tale.

On the Screen: Rob Lowe (*The West Wing*) is superb as Nick in *Stephen King's The Stand*.

The Night Flier

This deeply scary tale was originally published in *Prime Evil: New Stories by the Masters of Modern Horror* (New American Library, 1988). King significantly revised it for collection in **Nightmares and Dreamscapes**. The original anthology may be purchased from booksellers.

Dwight Renfield cruises the night skies of the northeast United States, murdering his victims in and around small airfields. **Richard Dees**, a reporter for a scandal rag, *Inside View*, investigates the killings and is on what he thinks is a serial killer's trail. But Dees may well have underestimated his quarry.

Genesis: King sometimes discovers a supporting character who will not go away — in the case of Richard Dees (originally from **The Dead Zone**), his reprise is as intrepid reporter for a supermarket tabloid who gets more than he bargained for while chasing a vampire. He says Dees turned out to be a man of "profound alienation" who found the column of truth has a hole in it (*The Night Flier*). King also says, "Is this little boy's grandfather the same creature that demands Richard Dees open his camera and expose his film at the conclusion of *The Night Flier*? You know, I rather think he is" (**"Popsy"**).

The Night of the Tiger

This short story was first published in *The Magazine of Fantasy and Science Fiction* for February 1978 and later appeared in various anthologies, but has not been republished in English since 1992. It is likely King is unhappy with the tale. If this is the case, fans would benefit from a rewritten version.

It revolves around the dispute between a tiger tamer and another circus employee and is narrated by a young man who has joined the party as it tours the Midwest. Long simmering, the dispute comes to a head on a hot night as a tornado approaches the circus ground. In the confusion the tiger escapes and a mysterious confrontation ensues.

The story has the immediate feeling of King's response to Ray Bradbury's classic "circus visits small town" horror novel, **Something Wicked This Way Comes**, of which King later wrote an unproduced screenplay. Readers who access the tale will find the effort well spent in understanding the development of King the writer, this despite the feeling of many critics that the story fails in several aspects.

Genesis: King gives some background in **On Writing**, where he says he'd sent the tale as a teenager to the magazine that would later publish it but was rejected. Ten years later, after becoming successful, he rewrote the tale on a whim and (he speculates perhaps due to his fame) this time the editors accepted it for publication.

Back copies of the magazine are easily purchased online, and it appears in a number of anthologies.

Night Shift

Night Shift is King's first mass-market collection of short stories, released in 1978. Somewhat uneven, it does showcase King's early stories, which had originally been published between 1969 and 1977, with four original to the collection.

The tales are: **"Jerusalem's Lot,"** **"Graveyard Shift,"** **"Night Surf,"** **"The Mangler,"** **"The Boogeyman,"** **"Gray Matter,"** **"Battleground,"** **"Sometimes They Come Back,"** **"Trucks,"** **"Strawberry Spring,"** **"The Lawnmower Man,"** **"Quitters, Inc.,"** **"I Know What**

You Need," "Children of the Corn," "One for the Road" (horror), "The Last Rung on the Ladder" and "The Woman in the Room" (mainstream), "The Ledge," "The Man Who Loved Flowers" (crime) and "I Am the Doorway" (science fiction).

Night Shift (Unproduced Screenplay)

Around the end of the 1970s King wrote a screenplay based on three stories from his collection *Night Shift*. They are "**Strawberry Spring**," "**I Know What You Need**" and "**Battleground**," and the screenplay includes an original wrap-around tale set in the previously unknown town of Weathersfield, Maine, which is only eight miles from **Jerusalem's Lot** (one character even mentions the "Boogies" there).

Weathersfield was the only town that far north in the Massachusetts Colony to put supposed witches to death, and this fact plays an important role in the storyline, with the graves of three of these unfortunate women on the Town Common forming a central component linking King's three tales.

This is a very effective and interesting adaptation of King's own work and it is disappointing it was never produced.

Genesis: In *Danse Macabre*, King says NBC "optioned three stories from my 1978 collection, *Night Shift*, and invited me to do the screen-play. One of these stories was a piece called "Strawberry Spring," about a psychopathic Jack-the-Ripper–type killer."

This 88-page screenplay is held in the Special Collections Department of the **Raymond H. Fogler Library** at the University of Maine in Orono, the author's alma mater. Written permission from King is required to access this work and is generally only given to researchers.

Night Surf

One of King's earliest published short stories, it forms a prototype for his later masterpiece, *The Stand*, and therefore is very important to his canon. First published in *Ubris* magazine for Spring 1969, King substantially revised the tale for its appearance in *Cavalier* magazine's August 1974 issue and for collection in *Night Shift*. Copies of *Ubris* are effectively impossible to find but may be photocopied at the **Raymond H. Fogler Library** of the University of Maine, Orono.

In "Night Surf," the influenza epidemic wiping out humanity is colloquially known as "Captain Trips." This is also the popular name for the superflu in *The Stand*, as well as in the altered reality segment of *The Dark Tower IV: Wizard and Glass*. In *The Dark Tower VI: Song of Susannah*, character Susannah Dean notes her ka-tet had seen the results of a great plague — the superflu. Eddie Dean also recalls seeing a world that had been decimated by it. It is possible that the ka-tet saw the results of Captain Trips in the "Night Surf" reality, which is quite possibly different from *The Stand* reality. As no timeline is provided in this tale, both it and *The Stand* may also be tales from the same reality and timeline.

In the tale, a victim of a catastrophic flu epidemic comes across a small group of survivors living on Anson Beach, Maine. Alvin Sackheim is suffering from the effects of the A6 flu (or Captain Trips). The survivors on the beach decide to help him but not in the way he is expecting.

Movie: A **Dollar Baby** of the same name was produced in 2002.

Nightmares and Dreamscapes

Released in 1993, this important collection includes 22 stories, a poem ("**Brooklyn August**") and the only non-fiction piece King has included in one of his mass-market collections ("**Head Down**"). The stories are: "**Dolan's Cadillac**," "**The Fifth Quarter**," "**The Doctor's Case**" (crime); "**The End of the Whole Mess**," "**The House on Maple Street**" (science fiction); "**Suffer the Little Children**," "**The Night Flier**," "**Popsy**," "**It Grows on You**," "**Chattery Teeth**," "**Dedication**," "**The Moving Finger**," "**Sneakers**," "**You Know They Got a Hell of a Band**," "**Home Delivery**," "**Rainy Season**," "**Sorry, Right Number**," "**The Ten O'Clock People**," "**Crouch End**," "**Umney's Last Case**" (horror); "**The Beggar and the Diamond**" (fantasy); and "**My Pretty Pony**" (mainstream).

Television: The eight-episode mini-series *Nightmares and Dreamscapes: From the Stories of Stephen King* (2006) adapts five tales from the collection — "Crouch End," "Umney's Last Case," "The End of the Whole Mess," "The Fifth Quarter" and "You Know They Got a Hell of a Band." The other three tales are "**Battleground**," "**The Road Virus Heads North**" and "**Autopsy Room Four**." Available on DVD.

Nightmares in the Sky

Debate has raged in the King community about whether *Nightmares in the Sky* is actually "a King book," with many experts forming the view it is not, others adamant it is. This coffee table publication is a collection of photographs of gargoyles, mostly by photographer f-stop Fitzgerald, with text by Stephen King. Whether King's ten thousand word essay qualifies this volume as "a King book," it is one of his most important non-fiction pieces.

The essay is about the gargoyles that decorate many buildings in New York City. The book was originally published as a hardback in a U.S. printing of some 250,000 copies and is available from second hand booksellers.

Genesis: King was convinced to write the essay by an editor at Viking Penguin.

1922

This is a story from King's 2010 novella collection *Full Dark, No Stars*. According to his Web site, "The story opens with the confession of Wilfred James to the murder of his wife, Arlette, following their move to **Hemingford, Nebraska** onto land willed to Arlette by her father."

Hemingford is apparently the same town as Hemingford Home, where **Abagail Freemantle** ("Mother Abagail") lived all her life until the superflu struck in *The Stand*. The town is also mentioned in King's *Children of the Corn* (**Unproduced Screenplay**); as well as in "**Last Rung on the Ladder**" and *It*.

Nona

"Nona" was originally published in *Shadows* (Doubleday, 1978) as a Blainesville, Maine, story and was substantially revised for collection in *Skeleton Crew*. In that revision it became a **Castle Rock** tale. There are strong links to much of King's Maine fiction. An atmospheric and disturbing tale, it is not to be missed.

A college student failing his courses meets a mysterious woman in a bar while hitch-hiking. He sets out on a killing spree with the beautiful Nona at his side. Later, while sitting in a jail cell, he determines to write his story as preparation for an intended suicide.

Genesis: King once wrote that the best scene in the movie *Easy Rider* is the confrontation in the diner. King experts tend to see this scene as inspiration for a similar scene in *Nona*.

Graphic: A graphic novel version of the tale is planned for **Secretary of Dreams** (Volume Two) (Cemetery Dance), illustrated by Maine artist Glenn Chadbourne.

Stage: Adapted as part of *The Blood Brothers Present ... The Master of Horror* at the Gene Frankel Theater in New York (2008).

Noonan, Michael *see* Michael Noonan

The Old Dude's Ticker

This story originally appeared in the *NECON XX Commemorative Volume* (2000) and was later reprinted in *The Big Book of NECON* (Cemetery Dance, 2009). The latter publication should be accessible to most readers but the first is a valuable collector's item.

King rightly describes the tale as a pastiche, "a crazed revisionist telling of Poe's 'The Tell-Tale Heart.'" His original angle is to cast the narrator as a Vietnam veteran suffering from post-traumatic stress.

Genesis: King's introduction recalls he wrote the tale in the early 1970s, intending it for the men's magazine market, which had been consistently purchasing his stories. However, it did not sell and was rediscovered in his files in the late 1990s and he allowed its publication in the original format, giving readers another insight into his early style.

On Writing

This invaluable primer about the craft of writing was published in 2000 and won the Bram Stoker Award for Superior Achievement in Non-Fiction that year. It has probably been read by more writers who do not normally read King than regular King readers, as most fans would pass an apparent volume on "how to write" and move directly to King's next book of fiction. However, these fans miss a treat, as the book is delivered in major sections, and the "C.V." section delivers in spades for King aficionados—with lots of auto-biographical detail. And the "On Living: A Postscript" section briefly details King's 1999 near-death experience on a lonely Maine road and the loving support given by his wife and family during the long road to recovery.

The writing sections are recommended fare for writers at any level—from those starting out to professionals. It is not surprising the book is now a standard teaching tool for writing courses in schools and institutions of higher learning in the U.S. and many other countries.

Genesis: King explains that fellow author Amy Tan gave him the courage to write the book, which he dedicates to her: "One night ... I asked Amy if there was any one question she was never asked during the Q-and-A that follows almost every writer's talk.... Amy paused, thinking it over very carefully, and then said: 'No one ever asks about the language.' I owe an immense debt of gratitude to her for saying that. I had been playing with the idea of writing a little book about writing for a year or more at that time, but had held back because I didn't trust my own motivations—why did I want to write about writing? What made me think I had anything worth saying? ... What follows is an attempt to put down, briefly and simply, how I came to the craft, what I know about it now, and how it's done. It's about the day job; it's about the language."

One for the Road

This sequel to *'Salem's Lot* first appeared in *Maine* magazine for March-April 1977 (copies are difficult to secure). It is collected in **Night Shift**. It is also collected in *The Vampire Omnibus* (Orion, U.K., 1995) under the title "A Return to Salem's Lot" and was released as a stand-alone volume by PS Publishing of the United Kingdom in 2010.

Two men are having a quiet beer at Tookey's Bar when Gerard Lumley bursts in. Half frozen and suffering from frostbite, he had walked six miles from the turnoff to **Jerusalem's Lot, Maine**, all the way to Falmouth. His car had been caught in the snow and he wanted someone to help rescue his wife and daughter. However, the two drinkers know Jerusalem's Lot is no place to be after dark.

Graphic: A graphic novel version of the tale is planned for **Secretary of Dreams (Volume Two)** (Cemetery Dance), illustrated by Maine artist Glenn Chadbourne.

Ophelia Todd

Ophelia Todd loves driving, but not the time it takes to get from **Castle Rock** to Bangor, Maine, in the short story "**Mrs. Todd's Shortcut**."

The Other Side of the Fog

This piece of juvenilia appears in **People, Places and Things**, along with six other King tales. Pete Jacobs finds himself lost in time when surrounded by a fog outside his house. Stepping out of the fog, he finds himself in a futuristic city; frightened, he re-enters the fog, only to appear in the time of the dinosaurs. Again, he runs into the fog; it seems he is destined to be lost forever.

King would later use mist or fog elements to tremendous effect in both "**The Mist**" and "**Crouch End**."

Out-World

Out-World is part of **Roland Deschain's All-World** in The Dark Tower Cycle. It is only mentioned in **The Dark Tower III: The Wastelands**, "Calla Bryn Sturgis" (but not **The Dark Tower V: Wolves of the Calla**) and **The Dark Tower VII: The Dark Tower**. The term appears to best describe civilized parts of All-World farther away from **Mid-World** but not as far as the lands that border **End-World**.

The Overlook Hotel

The Overlook Hotel is the key location in **The Shining**. Apart from the extensive information provided in that novel, quite a bit of detail about its sordid past is provided in the short story "**Before the Play.**" There are also brief mentions in *Misery* and *The Regulators.*

Watching *The Shining Mini-Series* adds only a little to the hotel's history, but one can see King's image of the hotel in that presentation, which he wrote, starred in and spent a large proportion of the filming on set. King was unhappy with the Kubrick film of *The Shining* and was delighted to be able to film his version at the very hotel that had first inspired the tale.

According to King's mythology, the Overlook Hotel was built by Bob T. Watson between 1907 and 1909 and was to be the grandest resort hotel in America and, at nearly 12,000 feet above sea level, the highest. During the building phase, Watson's son, Boyd, was killed in a riding accident. The hotel is forty miles west of Sidewinder.

The first season was 1910, with the opening ceremony held on 1 June. A Congressman choked to death at the celebration dinner. By September 1914 Watson was bankrupt and in 1915 the Overlook was sold to James T. Parris, who died in 1922, after which it was sold to Clyde and Cecil Brandywine. In 1922 Woodrow Wilson stayed in the presidential suite. The hotel was resold in 1929 and 1936; Horace Derwent purchased it in 1945. Derwent sold out in 1952 and the hotel had a number of other owners before being bought in 1970 by Al Shockley and his associates, who refurbished it that year. In late 1977 **Jack Torrance** was the caretaker, staying at the isolated hotel with his family.

Genesis: Inspired by King's stay at the Hotel Stanley in Estes Park, Colorado. One of America's grand hotels, The Stanley still operates and has even hosted a Stephen King convention. King and his wife Tabitha famously stayed there at the end of the 1974 season, as the only guests. King wandered the halls and imagined scenes that would eventually become part of the novel. The Kings stayed in Room 217, which has an important role in the novel and second screen version (in Kubrick's adaptation Room 237 holds the dark surprise).

Oy

Oy is one of King's brilliantly drawn animal characters (other examples include Kojak from *The Stand* and **Cujo**). A billy-bumbler (a species that lives on **All-World**) he is the friend of **Jake Chambers** from *The Dark Tower III: The Wastelands* through *The Dark Tower VII: The Dark Tower* in **The Dark Tower Cycle.** He is so loyal he officially becomes part of **Roland Deschain's** "ka-tet," along with Jake, **Eddie Dean** and **Susannah Dean.**

He has a "foxy" face with gold-ringed eyes, a large number of teeth and a "cartoon squiggle of a tail" and is capable of speaking a few words (for instance he calls Jake "Ake" and Roland "Olan") and shedding genuine tears. Oy is a beloved figure among King fans.

Pace, Maddie *see* Maddie Pace

Pangborn, Alan *see* Alan Pangborn

Paranoid: A Chant

In this poem, collected in *Skeleton Crew*, everyone is engaged in spying on or trying to kill the narrator. A relatively minor piece, perhaps the only important note is that a "Dark Man" is mentioned, although this character may have no linkage with **Randall Flagg**.

Movie: A **Dollar Baby** of the same name was produced in 2002.

Stage: Adapted as part of *The Blood Brothers Present ... The Master of Horror* at the Gene Frankel Theater in New York in 2008. The entire presentation also included adaptations of "**In the Deathroom**," "**Quitters, Inc.**" along with vignettes from "**Survivor Type**" and "**Paranoid: A Chant.**"

Paul Edgecombe

Paul Edgecombe is jailer to **John Coffey** in *The Green Mile*. As E Block superintendent at Cold Mountain Penitentiary, it is his melancholy duty to supervise executions in the electric chair. A good man, he treats his prisoners and staff well for the time (the 1930s) and builds a friendship with John as many mysterious events surround that prisoner. He married Janice in 1911 and the end of John's story is not the end of Paul's, as readers discover in the novel and the movie.

On the Screen: Tom Hanks is superb as the younger Paul Edgecombe and Dabs Greer played the older Paul to perfection in *The Green Mile* (1999).

Paul Sheldon

Paul Sheldon is the protagonist in *Misery*. A successful novelist with the "Misery" series about heroine Misery Chastain, he crashes his car near Sidewinder, Colorado, in late February 1987. A former nurse who lives at an isolated nearby farm, **Annie Wilkes**, finds the wreck and takes the severely injured Sheldon home. A great fan of Misery Chastain, she holds him captive, insisting he write a new Misery novel just for her. Paul is tall, with sandy hair and blue eyes and had been a heavy smoker for two decades before the accident.

In "**The Library Policeman**," Sheldon is Naomi Higgins' favorite author, and he is also mentioned in *Rose Madder*.

On the Screen: James Caan is superb as Paul in *Misery*.

Paulson, Gary *see* Gary Paulson

Pennywise

Pennywise is one of the most feared characters in all of fiction. The name is but one carried by the ancient and feared creature that lives in the sewers under **Derry, Maine**, as recorded in the novel *It*. The name is normally used when the creature takes the appearance of a clown (hence the fear of clowns that has enveloped so many viewers). "He" is also known as "Bob Gray" or simply "It" and has terrorized Derry since at least 1715.

There is an apparent reference to Pennywise in *The Tommyknockers* (Tommy Jacklin saw a clown in the sewers there, and it is hard to believe that more than one clown lives in that city's drains) and a clear reference of great import to the creature in *Dreamcatcher*. In "**Gray Matter**," George Kelso once worked for the Bangor Public Works Department but quit after seeing what he thought was a large spider in the sewers.

People, Places and Things

People, Places and Things is a collection of eighteen short stories self-published by King and childhood friend Chris Chesley under the name Triad Publishing Company. First made available in 1960, it was reprinted in 1963. The two friends apparently wrote many stories together, and singly, for their amusement and that of their family and friends, and it is a small tragedy that most have been lost.

All in all the stories are best described as what they are — juvenilia. However, clear hints of the King to come appear in each story, and that is where they perhaps retain their greatest value.

Six King stories and another written with Chesley have survived the years: "**The Hotel at the End of the Road**," "**I've Got to Get Away!**" "**The Thing at the Bottom of the Well**," "**The Stranger**," "**The Cursed Expedition**," "**The Other Side of the Fog**" and "**Never Look Behind You.**"

Unfortunately, two of the King stories listed in the table of contents have been lost — no known copies of "The Dimension Warp" and "I'm Falling" exist.

King owns the sole known copy of the collection, which he rediscovered in his papers in 1985. Partial photocopies of the "Second Printing, 1963" version circulate freely in the King community. It is thought that fewer than a dozen original copies were ever printed.

Pet Sematary

A dark tale in the Bachman tradition, King finished writing this novel in 1979 but then put it away, refusing to offer it to his agent and publishers. He relented in 1983, partly to complete a Doubleday contract, and refused to participate in publicity. Despite this the book became King's biggest hardback seller to that time with over 750,000 copies sold. He had apparently warmed to the story enough by the late 1980s to write the *Pet Sematary* **Screenplay** and become deeply involved in the production when it was filmed in Maine.

Many critics describe this tale as a variation of the horror theme of unholy resurrection popularized by the W.W. Jacobs 1902 short story "The Monkey's Paw." As he has done with other stories, King took the theme contained in Jacobs' story, which ends with the father wishing his returned son away without being confronted, and added the stark and real multiple returns that Bill Baterman, **Jud Crandall** and **Louis Creed** suffer as his own powerful extension of the concept.

The Creed family moves to Ludlow, Maine, as Louis Creed takes up his job as a doctor at the University of Maine at Orono. On his first day at work Victor Pascow dies in the infirmary after being hit by a car. Before passing, Pascow warns Louis of the dangers of a Micmac burial ground, but Louis has no idea what he is talking about. Later, the family cat, Church, is killed on the road outside the house, which carries a constant flow of fast moving traffic. Concerned over his daughter's reaction, Louis buries the cat in a Micmac burial ground, which has the reputation of bringing back the dead, rather than in the local "Pet Sematary," as a child's sign had it. Church returns to life but is now a mean and unlovable animal. And even worse tragedy stalks the Creed family.

As a Maine tale there are many links to King's fiction, including that one of Gage Creed's sneakers was later found in Atropos' lair in *Insomnia*. The Gage Creed orchestra played at the masked ball to re-open **The Overlook Hotel** in King's screenplay for the mini-series version of *The Shining*. In that production King played Gage Creed on screen.

Genesis: King was inspired to write the story while living in a rented home on the real Route 15 in Orrington and commuting daily to the University of Maine at Orono as writer-in-residence. The initial inspiration for the story was prosaic — Naomi King's cat Smucky was killed on Route 15, with Tabitha and Stephen deciding they must confront her with the truth, rather than pretend the cat had run away. King says: "When ideas come they don't arrive with trumpets. They are quiet — there is no drama involved. I can remember crossing the road, and thinking that the cat had been killed in the road ... and [I thought] what if a kid died in that road? And we had had this experience with Owen running toward the road, where I had grabbed him and pulled him back. And the two things came together — on one side of this two-lane highway was the idea of what if the cat came back, and on the other side of the highway was what if the kid came back."

Movie: *Pet Sematary* (1989). With a screenplay by King (he also appears in a cameo role as a minister), this is an "edge of the seat" movie, guaranteed to terrify audiences. Available on DVD.

Movie: *Pet Sematary II* (1992). A sequel using Ludlow and the Pet Sematary as its links. Very poor, despite an appearance by Anthony Edwards (*ER*).

Radio: *Pet Sematary* (1997). A BBC Radio 4 (U.K.) dramatization, originally broadcast in six weekly parts. Available as a 180-minute tape compilation (BBC Radio Collection) and from Simon and Schuster Audio in the U.S. (1998) and (2001).

Computer Game: In 2009 an online computer game based on the movie, not the book, was developed by Last Legion Games and published by Paramount.

Pet Sematary (Screenplay)

Pet Sematary (1989) was the first movie ever produced from a screenplay in which King adapted one of his own novel-length works. It was filmed in Maine, a contractual requirement by King to assist his home state. The novel was published in 1983 and this script is remarkably faithful to the original. The author resisted changing details of the major characters, which seems to provide him with great entertainment in other screenplays.

The Special Collections Unit of the University of Maine's **Raymond H. Fogler Library** holds a copy of the screenplay. Ask for Box 2318. Copies of a different version circulate within the King community.

Movie: *Pet Sematary* (1989) is a genuinely frightening film and many a moviegoer was caught literally on the edge of their seats at screenings. Don't miss this one. It stars Dale Midkiff as **Louis Creed**. Fred Gwynne steals the show as **Jud Crandall**, Denise Crosby is Rachel Creed, and Miko Hughes is a suitably evil Gage Creed. Stephen King appeared in one of his cameos, this time as a minister.

Peter Riley

In the novella "**Hearts in Atlantis**," Peter Riley, a college freshman at the University of Maine in 1966, becomes addicted to the game of Hearts played in his dormitory. During this time he also dated **Carol Gerber**.

Genesis: Clearly based on one of King's fellow students at the University of Maine during the Vietnam era.

Petrie, Mark *see* Mark Petrie

The Plant

The Plant is perhaps the best known of the King stories not appearing in a collection. This is due to the intense publicity surrounding his decision to sell downloadable chapters on his Web site during the dot-com boom.

What is less well-known is that King has had not one, but two, failed attempts at finalizing this tale. The original was published by King's Philtrum Press as a signed, limited edition and provided as a Christmas gift from the Kings in 1982, 1983 and 1985. The author claims he stopped writing this first version after seeing the movie *Little Shop of Horrors* and realizing the storylines were too similar. Original copies of each part of this version are very difficult to find and run in the thousands of dollars. In fact, a complete set generally sells for over $6000. The best sources will be online King booksellers.

In 2000 King updated the story and released it on the Internet via his official Web site, but after six parts, *The Plant* folded its leaves again, the story still unfinished. The first five parts, issued from July through November 2000, were charged on an "honor" system, where the buyers downloaded the text and were expected to send in their payment. The last was given away as a Christmas gift to readers and, presumably, as a small apology for stopping the story mid-stream. It was announced the six installments had formed the first part of the novel, with that part to be known as "Zenith Rising." *The Plant* is no longer available from the Web site but copies do circulate in the King community.

Both versions are told in epistolary style, using letters, memos, newspaper articles and diary entries to provide the narrative. King also used this style for "**Jerusalem's Lot**" and "**The End of the Whole Mess**," and *Carrie* delves into a similar style with various quotes from news articles and books.

In the original version, Carlos Detweiller approaches Zenith House in New York to publish his manuscript, "True Tales of Demon Infestations." Editor John Kenton shows interest in the pitch and Detweiller sends the entire manuscript, including pictures of what appear to be actual human sacrifice. Disturbed, Kenton reports Detweiller to the police, but their investigation reveals the man "sacrificed" in the photos is apparently alive and well. Detweiller vows revenge on Kenton and soon after, the mysterious Roberta Solrac (we instantly understand this is "Carlos" in reverse) sends Kenton an ivy plant named Zenith. Kenton orders it destroyed but the janitor and internal mailman, Riddley Walker, decides to keep the plant in the office.

The storyline in the revised version is virtually identical until the new part four, where a deranged ex-soldier stakes out the publishing house, looking to take revenge on another employee. Meanwhile, Zenith the Ivy bides its time.

Disappointing though it is that the story finishes at less than mid-point, there are lots of references to other King tales, both obvious (a reference to the movie *Carrie*) and obscure (a character from ***Thinner***), and this provides some satisfaction to keen King readers.

The Pop of King

This is a regular column King wrote for *Entertainment Weekly* magazine from 2003 to 2011. There are over 120 of these columns, along with some other non-fiction King contributed to the magazine during the same period. They range across all forms of popular culture — music, books, television and film in particular, even some politics. Janet Maslin, in reviewing the nonfiction book **Faithful** for *The New York Times*, called *The Pop of King* "the savviest pop-cultural criticism this side of William Goldman's."

The columns can be accessed in any number of ways. Each is available on *Entertainment Weekly*'s Web site, if you are willing to spend time searching, as not all are easily accessible and many are even listed under different titles from that used in the magazine. To access them via this method one has to be a subscriber to the magazine, or input an America Online screen name and password. One could also subscribe to the magazine or buy it from the newsstands and read the newest installments, which appeared every three weeks or so. Older issues can be accessed at most large libraries, and copies can be purchased from used magazine dealers.

Popsy

This short story first appeared in an anthology *Masques II* (Maclay, 1987). It was substantially revised for collection in **Nightmares and Dreamscapes**. The original anthology appears for resale at online booksellers and the original version of the story was also anthologized in *The Best of Masques* (Berkley Books, 1988), *Karl Edward Wagner Presents the Year's Best Horror Stories XVI* (DAW Books, 1988) and *Dark Masques* (Pinnacle, 2001).

Briggs Sheridan has a gambling problem and to subsidize it he kidnaps children for "Mr. Wizard," who is willing to pay large sums for them. Sheridan identifies a new victim at a mall. The boy tells him he has lost his "Popsy," who had gone off to get him a drink. He kidnaps the surprisingly strong boy and takes him to his van. As they drive away the boy tells Sheridan his Popsy can fly and will be looking for him.

Genesis: King has indicated the title character is the same as the title character in "**The Night Flier**."

Movie: A **Dollar Baby** of the same name was produced in 2006; another in 2009.

Graphic: A comic book version of the story was published in *J.N. Williamson's Masques: An Anthology of Elegant Evil* (Innovation Books, 1992).

Premium Harmony

"Premium Harmony" first appeared in *The New Yorker* magazine for 9 November 2009. In this tale a couple arrives at the Quik-Pik in **Castle Rock, Maine**, on a hot summer day. Married for ten years, Ray and Mary Burkett now argue constantly. Ray thinks the deterioration in their relationship is connected to Mary's inability to have children, and to compensate he'd bought her a Jack Russell terrier, which she named Biznezz. The harsh economy has forced them to consider selling their house and cut back on cigarettes and other luxuries. As they drive through Castle Rock it is described as "pretty dead," also as a result of the economy. They stop and argue about money, including Mary's proclivity for sugary snacks, which has led her to weigh 200 pounds. She leaves Ray and the dog in the car and heads inside to buy her niece a ball, and a pack of the cheap cigarettes he's requested, the Premium Harmony brand. Mary takes some time and Ray sits impatiently in the air-conditioned car. A large woman rushes out to tell Ray his wife has collapsed. Locking the car, Ray rushes inside.

Premium Harmony is a simple and understated tale of tragedy, including the isolation that exacerbates failing marriages and illustrates King's skill in relating simple slices of life. As is often the case, King taps into the American zeitgeist — describing the Main

Street of Castle Rock as "dead" and the fact the couple are being forced to sell their home are both a reflection of the American economy at the time the tale was written.

The story seems to reflect earlier incidents in King's fiction. In **Cujo**, for instance, a dog traps a woman and her son in a hot car. More poignantly, Mary's sudden collapse seems eerily similar to that of Jo Noonan in the **Derry** heat (**Bag of Bones**).

All King's previous stories in *The New Yorker* have appeared in later collections, and there can be little doubt his next fiction collection will include this Castle Rock tale. In the meantime the magazine is held by many libraries and copies can easily be purchased on the Internet.

The Pulse

On 7 July 2005 amazon.com released this short piece, boosting it as "the chilling first chapter of a work in progress." While it forms part of the novel **Cell**, this initial version was heavily re-written and expanded in that form.

Quitters, Inc.

A very original story, it is collected in **Night Shift**. In the tale Richard Morrison decides to quit smoking but makes the mistake of signing up for the rather unorthodox service provided by Quitters, Inc.

Movie: *Cat's Eye* (1984). One of three segments in this movie, the screenplay is by Stephen King, and James Woods plays Dick Morrison. Also known as *Stephen King's Cat's Eye*.

Stage: Adapted as part of *The Blood Brothers Present ... The Master of Horror* at the Gene Frankel Theater in New York in 2008. The entire presentation also included adaptations of "**In the Deathroom**," "Quitters, Inc." along with vignettes from "**Survivor Type**" and "**Paranoid: A Chant**."

The Raft

This gruesome horror story was first published in *Gallery* magazine for November 1982 as a pull-out booklet. It was collected in **Skeleton Crew** with a number of changes, including the introduction of the term "Do you love?" and the correction of some earlier errors. The earlier version also appeared in *The Twilight Zone Magazine* for May-June 1983. Both magazines can be purchased online, although *Gallery* is very difficult to find (note also that it contains graphic sexual content).

Deke and his girlfriend Rachel, his roommate Randy and Randy's girlfriend LaVerne drive to Cascade Lake, where they decide to swim out to a raft. After they get there they are trapped by a deadly oil slick.

The tale is linked to "**Nona**" by the use of the term "Do you love?" and to stories such as "**The Crate**," *From a Buick 8* and **Christine** through the mention of Horlicks University.

Genesis: King wrote the story in 1968 as "The Float" and sold it in 1969 to *Adam* magazine, which never published it, despite making payment. King later lost the original manuscript and found himself re-writing the tale in 1981.

Movie: *Creepshow 2* was released in 1987. It included an adaptation of "The Raft," along with two new pieces, "Old Chief Wood'nhead" and "The Hitch-hiker." King did not write the latter stories. George Romero wrote the overall screenplay and King played a cameo role as a truck driver in "The Hitch-hiker" segment. Available on DVD.

Rage

This is the first of the novels King published under the pseudonym **Richard Bachman**. The original paperback novel is difficult to find, and expensive. It is collected in *The Bachman Books*.

Placerville High School student **Charles Decker** hears voices, whispering terrible instructions. One day Charlie listens, forcing his fellow students into a series of potentially lethal mind-games.

Due to the blight of school shootings, since 1998 King has not allowed the republication of *Rage* in the United States. As this book does indeed describe shootings in the context of educational establishments (although there is no evidence King's book has in any way been involved in inspiring these terrible events), care may be required when recommending the book to certain readers.

In an obvious link to fiction written by King and published under his own name, one student in Charles Decker's algebra class lives in **Gates Falls, Maine**. Another King town, **Harlow**, is also mentioned.

Genesis: King wrote the first 40 pages of this novel, originally titled "Getting It On," while still at Lisbon High School. He found it again in 1970 and completed it the following year.

Stage: *Rage*. First performed in 1989, it is a stage **Dollar Baby**. The script is by Robert B. Parker, Joan Parker and Dan Hurlin; originally directed by Dan Hurlin. Robert B. Parker is the author of Spenser detective series of books, from which the *Spenser for Hire* TV series sprang.

Rainbird, John *see* John Rainbird

Rainy Season

Originally published in *Midnight Graffiti* magazine for Spring 1989, King revised this horror tale for collection in **Nightmares and Dreamscapes**. The original version can be purchased from online resellers. King once described the story as "pretty gross."

Rainy season comes to Willow, Maine, every seven years and the Grahams make two mistakes—arriving on June 17 that seventh year and ignoring the locals.

Movie: A **Dollar Baby** of the same name was produced in 2002.

Graphic: A graphic novel version of the tale appeared in **Secretary of Dreams: Volume 1** (Cemetery Dance, 2006), illustrated by Maine artist Glenn Chadbourne.

Ralph Roberts

Ralph is the protagonist in the novel **Insomnia**. A resident of **Derry, Maine**, he begins to suffer from insomnia after his wife dies not long before his 70th birthday. He starts to see auras and forms a romantic relationship with Lois Chasse. His actions will be important to the future of all worlds. Ralph is also mentioned in *Bag of Bones* and *The Dark Tower VII: The Dark Tower*.

Randall Flagg

Randall Flagg is probably the villain most King readers love to love (if that is possible). He is supremely arrogant and this flaw will determine his fate.

Flagg first appeared by name in *The Stand* (1978), but King has indicated he is "the Dark Man" in his 1969 poem "**The Dark Man.**" He also appears as "Flagg" (The Dark Man, or Flagg the Hooded) in *Eyes of the Dragon* and plays a crucial role in **The Dark Tower cycle.** He is mentioned in *The Dark Tower II: The Drawing of the Three*, and **Walter** mentions him to **Roland Deschain** in *The Dark Tower III: The Wastelands*—this latter turns out to be important, if misleading. By *The Dark Tower IV: Wizard and Glass* it is revealed that under another alias, he has played an important role in Roland's past, and this is further explored in *The Dark Tower VI: Song of Susannah*. All is revealed in *The Dark Tower VII: The Dark Tower*.

Flagg is able to make himself "dim" so that he cannot be seen, and this skill can apparently be taught. As a result he may have some involvement with Carole Gerber (the *Hearts in Atlantis* collection). He often uses aliases with the initials "R.F." (for instance, Rudin Filaro, Richard Fannin) and is known under a variety of nicknames, including "the Walking Dude" and "the Man in Black." Despite speculation, most experts have concluded he is not John Farson, the "Good Man" (*Wizard and Glass*).

Genesis: This author speculates King chose the name after seeing the R.M. Flagg premises on State Street, Bangor, near the iconic Mt. Hope Cemetery. There is also a Flagg Street in nearby Veazie, Maine—in *The Dead Zone* Sarah Bracknell had an apartment there. The R.M. Flagg Company had its beginnings in the 1930s as a heating and ventilation business founded by Roscoe M. Flagg—it's possible King took the "R" from R.M. Flagg to create "Randall."

On the Screen: Jamey Sheridan plays Flagg in *Stephen King's The Stand* (1994). It is not a perfect portrayal but he *is* scary.

Ray Garraty

Ray is the central character in *The Long Walk*. Sixteen-year-old Ray from Porterville, Maine, enters The Long Walk, an annual event where 100 teenage boys begin at the United States–Canada border and keep walking south through Maine and New Hampshire until only one walker remains alive.

Raymond H. Fogler Library

The Raymond H. Fogler Library is the campus library at the University of Maine in Orono and is also the largest research library in the state. Stephen and Tabitha King met in the library's stacks when both were students.

The Special Collections Department holds the papers of Stephen Edwin King (along with other luminaries such as Civil War hero General Joshua Lawrence Chamberlain). The papers were gifted by King over a period beginning in 1976, but little new material has been added in the past decade. Visitors may inspect the material in most boxes in the collection when visiting but written permission from King is required to access certain material.

Another valuable resource at the Fogler is their extensive microfiche collection of newspapers and magazines, including *The Maine Campus* (which published *King's Garbage Truck*), *Ubris* and the *Bangor Daily News* — making it one of the few resources for finding and printing obscure King material.

The Reach

This beautiful and haunting tale is one of the few King pieces of fiction for which the title was changed. It was originally published as "**Do the Dead Sing?**" in *Yankee* magazine for November 1981; King substantially revised the short story and collected it in *Skeleton Crew* as "The Reach." While the core tale does not change, the original tale lacked the term "Do you love?"

Stella Godlin has lived her entire life on Goat Island, Maine. She has never ventured to the mainland, a short distance across the Reach, as in her nearly 96 years she has never found the need. But now she begins to see her long dead friends and they have a proposal for her.

An illustrated edition of the tale appears in *Secretary of Dreams* (Volume One) (Cemetery Dance, 2006), brilliantly drawn by Maine artist Glenn Chadbourne.

Genesis: King's brother-in-law, once in the Coast Guard, told him the story of a real woman named Stella Flanders who never wanted to visit the mainland.

The Reaper's Image

Originally published in *Startling Mystery Stories* magazine for Spring 1969, this derivative horror tale is collected (with minor wording changes) in *Skeleton Crew*. King wrote the story in the summer of 1966 and it was the second he sold professionally, receiving $35 in payment. It provides an excellent rear-view mirror to his writing maturity at the age of eighteen.

Jonathan Spangler is very interested in the DeIver looking glass, held in the Samuel Claggert Memorial Private Museum. He is not interested in the rumors that the DeIver could make people disappear but wants to prove the authenticity of the very rare mirror, as there are reportedly only five in existence. There is more to this mirror than initially meets the eye.

Genesis: King says he wrote the story "when I was eighteen, in the summer before I started college" and had the idea "when I was out in the back yard of our house in West Durham, Maine, shooting baskets with my brother."

Redman, Stu *see* Stu Redman

Reginald "Pop" Merrill

"Pop" Merrill is a key character in the novella "**The Sun Dog**" and is mentioned in *Needful Things*. Thoroughly dislikable, he is a moneylender and con man and runs a shop in **Castle Rock, Maine**. He is **Ace Merrill**'s uncle.

The Regulators

This novel of the fantastic, published as by **Richard Bachman**, is paired with ***Desperation***, with which it shares many character names and something of an altered reality. Quite a few readers found the two novels confusing when read in conjunction and it may be better to leave some months before reading the second. At the time of publication it was claimed that this would be the last of the Bachman novels (and was said, tongue-in-cheek, to have been published after his "death"), but a subsequent novel published under King's Bachman pseudonym has since appeared — ***Blaze***.

Seth Garin, an autistic boy, has been living with his aunt since his family were killed in a drive-by shooting five days after they visited the Deep Earth Mining Corporation site near the town of Desperation, Nevada. Two years later and back in Audrey's home town of Wentworth, strange vehicles sprouting equally strange weapons suddenly attack the residents of Poplar Street.

This harrowing, violent and surreal novel is one of King's strangest — no quarter is given, mayhem reigns and the trapped victims must not only fight for survival, but find their way back to normality. Apart from links to *Desperation*, King also links ***The Shining*** and ***Thinner***.

Genesis: See "The Shotgunners"

The Reploids

"The Reploids" is one of King's least satisfying short stories, mostly due to an unsatisfactory and inconclusive ending that does not even leave the readers with particularly interesting questions to ponder. King has only allowed publication in one anthology (although that has appeared in three different guises) and a magazine, and has not included it in a collection. It is clear he is unhappy with this story and possibly regrets allowing publication.

In 1988 King biographer Douglas E. Winter edited an anthology, *Night Visions 5*, which included three King stories, the most ever released in one volume outside King's own collections. These were "The Reploids," "**Dedication**" and "**Sneakers.**" King completely rewrote the latter two, which further indicates he felt the first could not be recovered.

In this tale the normal world takes a strange and very visible twist. On 29 November 1989, the filming of *The Tonight Show* is disrupted as Johnny Carson disappears and is mysteriously replaced by Edward Paladin. Paladin claims he, not Carson, is the host of the show, that everyone should know him and treat him as a star. The reader quickly understands that something strange, in the tradition of *The Twilight Zone* and the later series *The X-Files*, is going on. Escorted protesting from the set, Paladin's conviction that he is the star of the late night show only begins to crack when his lawyer is shown not to exist, and both he and his interrogators are presented with further weird evidence. As noted the story ends inconclusively and the piece actually has the feel of the opening scenes from a novel.

Readers should be able to find second-hand copies of *Night Visions 5* (Dark Harvest, 1988); alternatively, the anthology also appeared as *Dark Visions* (Victor Gollancz, 1989) and *The Skin Trade* (Berkley Books, 1990). It also later appeared in a slightly abridged version in a short-lived British magazine, *Skeleton Crew* (July 1990).

Rest Stop

This short story is a very important comment on domestic violence (and not King's first, see **Rose Madder**), a mainstream piece of high quality powerful prose. First published in *Esquire* magazine for December 2003, it is collected in **Just After Sunset**.

Author John Dykstra is alone at a highway rest stop when another man begins abusing his pregnant partner. Dykstra, who writes under the pseudonym Rick Hardin, must decide what action, if any, to take.

Genesis: King stopped at a rest stop in Florida and heard a couple arguing and on the verge of getting physical: "I wondered what in the world I'd do if that happened, and thought: *I'll have to summon by inner **Richard Bachman**, because he's tougher than me.*"

The Revelations of 'Becka Paulson

This imaginative short story first appeared in *Rolling Stone* magazine for 19 July and 2 August 1984. It was substantially revised to become part of **The Tommyknockers**. The original version appears in the limited edition of **Skeleton Crew** (but not the mass-market version) and was also republished in *I Shudder at Your Touch* (New American Library, 1991).

In the original version, strange events follow a gunshot wound. While spring cleaning, Rebecca (Becka) Paulson finds her husband's .22-caliber target pistol. Falling while holding the gun, Becka accidentally shoots herself in the head, just above the left eye. When she wakes she is shocked to find a hole in her head that turns out to be five inches deep when she measures it with an eyebrow pencil inserted into the wound. She cannot remember what happened and a few days later the picture of Jesus atop her television begins telling her secret things.

Television: "The Revelations of 'Becka Paulson" (1997) is an episode of *The Outer Limits* (the revival series). Steven Weber (**The Shining** mini-series) appears. DVD: *The Outer Limits: The New Series*, Season 3.

The Revenge of Lard Ass Hogan

This funny and gross story was originally published in *Maine Review* magazine for July 1975. King later updated it and included it (changing some character names) in his novella, "**The Body**." The story is set in **Gates Falls, Maine**, one of King's favored towns.

David "Lard Ass" Hogan suffers from a glandular problem, which makes him appear fat. Ace Carmody, Eyeball Chambers and Billy Norcross chase him down and force him to enter the local annual pie-eating contest. But "Lard Ass" has developed a plan of revenge.

Movie: *Stand by Me* (1986). A portion of this film is an adaptation of the story. Andy Lindberg plays "Lard Ass."

Richard Bachman

On February 9, 1985, Stephen King admitted what had become obvious to insiders— he was also publishing under a pseudonym — Richard Bachman. The first Bachman novel had been published in 1977 and the story included two fictional towns King had made up. **Gates Falls** had already appeared in King's "**Graveyard Shift**," published in 1970 but not collected until **Night Shift** in 1978. From then on the clues were available to those who looked hard enough — in the last of the paperback originals Bachman even mentions **Derry, Maine**.

King would publish a total of five novels under the pseudonym before he was forced to admit the truth, but his denials had been quite precise, for instance, "The rumor has gotten around that I am Richard Bachman, but it's not true. I know him and I believe he lives in Connecticut — as I recall, he was a surly fellow" (1981); "I'm not Richard Bachman, but I know who he is, and I can't tell" (1982); "Bachman is indeed a pen-name, for a superannuated hippie-type who lives in New Hampshire. I know who he is, and tell you with no qualms at all that he is authentically crazy" (1983).

The four Bachman novels in original paperback were: *Rage* (1977), *The Long Walk* (1979), *Roadwork* (1981) and *The Running Man* (1982). The only hardback issued as Bachman before the secret was revealed was *Thinner* (first published in November 1984). The first four novels were collected as *The Bachman Books* in 1985 and, as King has taken *Rage* out of print, that is now the only practical way to read that story. That same year King declared Bachman dead, of "cancer of the pseudonym."

King has returned to using the Bachman pseudonym twice — *The Regulators*, a new novel written specifically to be published as Bachman; and *Blaze*, an older, previously unpublished novel resurrected as "by" Bachman. Of course, the events of *The Dark Half* partly work out King's frustration about the whole Bachman affair ("I'm indebted to the late Richard Bachman for his help and inspiration. This novel could not have been written without him."), and *Misery* was originally intended as a Bachman original. Those interested in King's own final word on the matter should read "The Importance of Being Bachman," King's introduction to editions of *The Bachman Books* published from 1996: "The importance of being Bachman was always the importance of finding a good voice and a valid point of view that were a little different from my own. I wonder if there are any other good manuscripts, at or near completion, in that box found by the widowed Mrs. Bachman in the cellar of their New Hampshire farmhouse. Sometimes I wonder about that a lot." He updated that in 1997 with this tongue-in-cheek comment on his official Web site, claiming the widow had found more manuscripts: "I really haven't looked through them, so I don't know how good they are or how bad they are. I see that one of them is a novel about a sexual vampire, actually, which looks sort of interesting. But I got a lot to read so I haven't been up to Bachman's stuff yet."

Apart from "voice," why publish under a pseudonym at all? The answer is simply that King and his publisher were worried about over publishing under his own name (something that, while a problem early in his career, would not be an issue today).

According to the *Castle Rock* newsletter for April 1985, the man whose photograph appears on the dust jacket of *Thinner* as "Richard Bachman" is in fact Richard Manuel, a real estate broker from St. Paul, Minnesota. "As for where the name Richard Bachman came from, as Steve tells it when the publisher called to ask what pseudonym he wanted to use, a book by Richard Matheson was on his desk and Bachman-Turner Overdrive was playing on the radio, so he chose Richard Bachman." Bachman's "death notice" in the *Castle Rock* newsletter for May 1985 reported that **John Swithen**, another of King's pseudonyms, was Bachman's half-brother.

King even invented a "wife" for the author: Claudia Bachman (credited with taking the author's photo) or Claudia Inez Bachman (to whom *Thinner* is dedicated). This lady has yet another life — a "Claudia y Inez Bachman" wrote the *Charlie the Choo-Choo* book that features in **The Dark Tower V: Wolves of the Calla** and **The Dark Tower VI: Song of**

Susannah. In *Song of Susannah* the character Stephen King calls Bachman "Dicky" and claimed he had beaten adult-onset leukemia and, in **The Dark Tower VII: The Dark Tower** it is noted that Bachman had written *The Long Walk*.

Those with a deeper fascination for Bachman should read *Stephen King is Richard Bachman* by Dr. Michael Collings (Overlook Connection Press, 2008), a noted King scholar.

Trivia: King appeared on an episode of the TV series *Sons of Anarchy* in 2010. As homage his character is called Richard Bachman.

Richard Dees

Richard Dees is a reporter for the scandal rag *Inside View* in "**The Night Flier**," in which he is tracking what he believes is a serial killer. He had appeared earlier as a reporter for the same periodical in **The Dead Zone**. There, **Johnny Smith** threw him out of his house.

On the Screen: Miguel Ferrer is tremendous as Dees in the movie *The Night Flier*.

Richard Kinnell

Kinnell is the protagonist of "**The Road Virus Heads North**." A moderately successful horror author from **Derry, Maine**, he makes the mistake of buying a disturbing picture at a yard sale.

On the Screen: Tom Berenger plays Kinnell in "The Road Virus Heads North" episode of *TNT's Nightmares and Dreamscapes: From the Stories of Stephen King*.

Richard "Richie" Tozier

Richard Tozier (also known as "Trashmouth") is living in **Derry, Maine**, in 1957–58 when he and his friends, **Bill Denbrough, Ben Hanscom, Beverly Marsh, Mike Hanlon, Stanley Uris** and **Eddie Kaspbrak** form "the Losers Club" in the novel **It**, in an attempt to fight **Pennywise**. As an adult his ability to make up annoying voices helps him become a DJ. He returns to Derry in 1985 when Mike Hanlon calls the Losers Club back.

Richards, Ben *see* Ben Richards

Riding the Bullet

King released this particularly scary story as an electronic book at the height of the Internet bubble. Originally released just after midnight on 14 March 2000 at a download cost of $2.50, servers crashed worldwide and it was claimed that as many as 500,000 downloads were made. A number of King's favored towns are mentioned, including **Gates Falls**. It is collected in **Everything's Eventual**.

Jean Parker suffers a stroke and her son Alan hitchhikes from Orono, where he attends the University of Maine, to her hospital in Lewiston. One driver takes him to Gates Falls, where he then has trouble getting another ride. Walking out of town, he passes through a graveyard and sees George Staub's gravestone. Despite the very late hour he secures another ride on the dark and lonely country road, but soon realizes he has made a very serious mistake.

Genesis: King says, "Like an earlier story of mine ('**The Woman in the Room**'), it's an attempt to talk about how my own mother's approaching death made me feel. This is probably the single great subject of horror fiction: our need to cope with a mystery [death] that can be understood only with the aid of a hopeful imagination."

Bullet was the name of one of Bryan Smith's dogs—Bryan Smith was the driver of the van that hit and nearly killed King in 1999. In the story Jean Parker was admitted to the Central Maine Medical Center, the name of the hospital King was taken to after the accident.

Movie: *Stephen King's Riding the Bullet* (2004). Screenplay and direction by King aficionado Mick Garris. A respectful adaptation and well worth viewing.

Riley, Peter *see* Peter Riley

Rita Hayworth and Shawshank Redemption

One of King's best-loved stories in both print and the film adaptation, this important novella is a story of loss, love, hope, betrayal and redemption. No King reader, indeed no reader, should miss this tale. It is collected in *Different Seasons*. In one interesting link Andy Dufresne did bookwork for Arthur Denker in "**Apt Pupil**." Partly because of the movie many people accidentally and wrongly call this tale "Rita Hayworth and *the* Shawshank Redemption."

Banker **Andy Dufresne**, wrongly convicted of the murder of his wife and her lover, is sent to **Shawshank Prison** in Maine. He meets "Red," a fellow inmate who is able to get almost anything for prisoners, at a price. As the years pass Red and Andy become friends but Andy never forgets his hope of a life outside the prison walls.

Movie: *The Shawshank Redemption* (1994). In the top few favorite movies of almost every movie lover, it was heavily nominated but was finally bereft of major awards. The screenplay and direction is by Frank Darabont (*The Green Mile*, *The Mist*). Tim Robbins plays Andy Dufresne, Morgan Freeman is "Red" Redding, and James Whitmore is superb as Brooks Hatlen.

Stage: *The Shawshank Redemption* is by Owen O'Neill and Dave Johns. It was first performed in Ireland in 2009.

Genesis: Shawshank Prison is based on the Maine State Penitentiary in Thomaston, which has since been demolished. Shawshank is mentioned in many stories, including "The Sun Dog," *Bag of Bones*, "The Body," *Dolores Claiborne*, *Dreamcatcher*, *It* and *Needful Things*. King wrote the tale immediately after completing *The Dead Zone*.

Trivia: Red's name is never given in the novella, but in the movie he is formally Ellis Boyd Redding.

The Road Virus Heads North

This eerie and compelling horror story first appeared in an anthology, *999*, in 1999 (hence the title), and was revised for collection in *Everything's Eventual*. The original anthology is still in print.

Richard Kinnell, a moderately successful horror author, buys a painting of a man in a sports car at a yard sale on his way home to **Derry, Maine**. As he travels he realizes that the painting is changing and shows the car and driver moving ever closer.

Genesis: King actually owns the picture described in this story, given to him as a present by wife Tabitha, who thought he might like, "or at least react to it." When he hung it in his office their children claimed the eyes followed them as they crossed the room.

Television: "The Road Virus Heads North" (2006) is a chilling series episode from *TNT's Nightmares and Dreamscapes: From the Stories of Stephen King*. Tom Berenger plays Richard Kinnell and Marsha Mason is Aunt Trudy.

Movie: A **Dollar Baby** of the same name was produced in 2004.

Graphic: A graphic novel version of the tale appeared in *Secretary of Dreams* (Volume One) (Cemetery Dance, 2006), brilliantly illustrated by Maine artist Glenn Chadbourne.

Roadwork

First published as a **Richard Bachman** paperback original, this fairly insignificant mainstream novel is collected in *The Bachman Books* and has also been re-released in a stand-alone edition (Signet, 1999). The original 1981 Signet edition appears for sale from time to time and may command on the order of $100.

Forty-year-old Barton Dawes is to be forced from both his home and his workplace after a decision to extend a freeway. But Dawes does not intend to lie down and let a faceless bureaucracy achieve its goals with ease.

Roberts, Ralph *see* Ralph Roberts

Roland Deschain

Roland Deschain is the son of Steven and Gabrielle and was born in **Gilead** in **Mid-World**. The youngest ever to earn the title "gunslinger," his adventures, which are crucial to all worlds and realities, are chronicled in **The Dark Tower cycle**. Indeed, he is the last Gunslinger and the descendant of the legendary Arthur Eld, founder of civilization in **All-World**, of which Mid-World is an important part.

In *The Dark Tower I: The Gunslinger*, he is on the trail of the Man in Black, while also searching for **The Dark Tower**, and meets **Jake Chambers**. Roland's adventures previous to this are chronicled in "**The Little Sisters of Eluria**" and a significant part of *The Dark Tower IV: Wizard and Glass* (in which he uses the pseudonym Will Dearborn and falls in love). In *The Dark Tower II: The Drawing of the Three*, he meets other members of his future "ka tet" — **Eddie Dean** and **Susannah Dean**, and in *The Dark Tower III: The Wastelands*, they all face great risks. The last three novels in the cycle — *The Dark Tower V: Wolves of the Calla, The Dark Tower VI: Song of Susannah* and *The Dark Tower VII: The Dark Tower* — resolve his fate and that of his friends and enemies, such as **The Crimson King**. In the meantime he meets his creator.

Roland is a knight warrior of sorts, set on a quest by fate, and is likely to be one of King's most enduring and important characters. Initially cold, readers grow to know a man who "has not forgotten the face of his father" as the cycle passes and quickly become totally invested in his fate. A flawed man, his heart is in the right place and, after all, the pressure of having the fate of everything, everywhere in one's hands must be close to unbearable, even for a great hero. One day, Roland may prevail and, if he does, all will be well with the Universe.

In *Insomnia*, Patrick Danville draws and describes Roland, and he is mentioned in **Black House** as the last gunslinger. Although not mentioned by name, he is clearly described in "**Low Men in Yellow Coats**." **The Dark Tower Graphic Novels** adapt occurrences from Roland's life in King's canon but also expand on them (for instance, detail around the Fall of **Gilead** and the Battle of Jericho Hill, which are referred to but not described in King's written works).

Genesis: The character is partly inspired by Robert Browning's 1855 epic poem, "Childe Roland to the Dark Tower Came," and by Clint Eastwood's character Blondie (or "The Man with No Name") in the movie *The Good, The Bad and The Ugly* (1966).

Roland LeBay

Roland LeBay is the disgusting original owner of a 1958 Plymouth Fury in the novel *Christine*. When he sells the car to **Arnie Cunningham** he fails to divulge that his daughter had choked to death in the vehicle and that his wife had committed suicide in it.

On the Screen: Roberts Blossom plays the character (renamed as George LeBay) in the 1983 film.

Rose Daniels

In *Rose Madder*, Rose Daniels is married to wife-beater Norman Daniels. After she finally decides to leave him she tries to start a new life, but Norman does not give up easily.

Rose Madder

This important King novel deals with the issue of domestic violence, in particular violence within a marriage. Many women have found in this book the courage to leave abusive relationships and this alone marks it apart from most of his fiction. It is a cross-genre novel of both fantasy and the mainstream.

In an interview King said, "I've had bad books. I think *Rose Madder* fits in that category, because it never really took off [King means in the sense of a story that went where *it* wanted to go]. I felt like I had to force that one."

Rose Daniels plucks up the courage to leave her abusive husband, who is also a policeman. Rose begins to get her life back on track and one afternoon purchases a painting titled "Rose Madder." But Norman Daniels has not forgotten his wife or reconciled himself to their separation. King links a number of other works, including *Insomnia*, *Misery* and *Desperation*.

Rose Red

Rose Red was a carefully staged major media event in 2002, with both television and book connections. On release of the prequel novel, *The Diary of Ellen Rimbauer*, using major characters from *Rose Red* prior to the mini-series airing, there was much speculation as to whether Stephen King or **Tabitha King** had written the book. The original paperback purported to be by Joyce Reardon, herself a character in the mini-series. Some time after the original screening it was revealed Ridley Pearson had actually written the novel.

In the story, a professor begins recruiting for an expedition aimed at awakening a house in Seattle she believes is possessed. Ellen Rimbauer, the original owner of the house known as Rose Red, was convinced that as long as it was under construction she would not die. She continually made additions to the house after it was occupied early in the 20th century and, after she disappeared in 1950, the house continued to build itself. Her closest friend was her servant, **Sukeena**.

Professor Joyce Reardon of the University of Washington is obsessed with Rose Red and related psychic events at the site. In its almost 100 year history many people had died there or simply vanished. While the house had grown quiet, Reardon believes the right people can bring it to life and provide her with hard evidence of paranormal phenomena. She gathers a group with different psychic abilities, including **Annie Wheaton**, 15 years old, autistic and who also has telekinetic powers. The group enters Rose Red, which has been waiting patiently.

The teleplay includes links or allusions to *Carrie*, *Storm of the Century*, "The Glass Floor" and *It Grows on You. The Dark Tower VI: Song of Susannah* even refers to Rose Red.

Television: *Stephen King's Rose Red* debuted on the ABC-TV network in 2002. It suffers from poor casting, some strange editing, questionable special effects, and outrageous overacting by Nancy Travis, playing Dr. Joyce Reardon. Craig R. Baxley directed. In another of his many screen cameos, Stephen King plays a pizza delivery guy. It was released on DVD in 2002.

The actual screenplay has not been published. However, there are a very few copies in circulation. Some, signed by King, were sold to benefit the Wavedancer Foundation, an organization dedicated to helping disabled performers, writers, and members of the production community.

Television: *The Diary of Ellen Rimbauer* (2003), using characters King created as part of *Rose Red*. Disappointing.

Genesis: In November 1999 King noted he'd begun work on *Rose Red*, which "is an expansion of a screenplay I wrote some years ago" for Steven Spielberg. When King submitted the haunted house story script, Spielberg kept asking for changes, and after three drafts King felt the project was no longer his. He later pitched it to producer Mark Carliner, who accepted days before King's near fatal accident on 19 June 1999. It would be four months before he could actually begin to write the new teleplay.

The members of the expedition were chosen for a variety of psychic skills and this concept will remind horror fans of Shirley Jackson's classic 1959 novel *The Haunting of Hill House*. King has often acknowledged Jackson's influence on his writing, so there is little doubt that *Rose Red* is both homage and King's take on the "wake-up the haunted house expedition" sub-genre.

Rowsmith, Edie see Edie Rowsmith

Ruiz, Sheemie see Sheemie Ruiz

Runaround Pond

Johnny Smith fell and struck his head at Runaround Pond in Durham, Maine, in *The Dead Zone*. He was around five at the time and the blow may have been part of the reason he later had psychic abilities. The leeches' scene in *Stand by Me* is supposedly also inspired by the original Runaround Pond.

Genesis: The real Runaround Pond is in Durham, Maine, only a few hundred feet from the house in which King lived during his teenage years.

The Running Man

This was the last of the **Richard Bachman** novels to be published as a paperback original (1982). It is collected in **The Bachman Books** and was later released in a stand-alone edition (Signet, 1988). King says this may be the best of his first four Bachman novels. It was written in seventy-two hours and published virtually unchanged.

In 2025 everyone watches Free-Vee game shows. **Ben Richards** decides to try out in the hope of winning money to buy medicine for his sick baby. He is accepted for *The Running Man*, the big money game show where contestants are hunted to their deaths and now must fight the network for his life and that of his family.

In an interesting link to King's unpublished work, Harding, the city in which Richards lived, appears to be the same city as features in **Sword in the Darkness**. **Derry, Maine**, is also mentioned.

Movie: *The Running Man* (1987). This has little connection to King's book, other than the title, but the film does make acceptable viewing. Perhaps the most interesting aspects is an eclectic group of actors: Arnold Schwarzenegger as Ben Richards, Jesse Ventura, Mick Fleetwood and Dweezil Zappa. Available on DVD.

Computer Game: Grandslam Entertainment released a computer game with the same title in 1989, but it was based on the movie, not the book.

Rush Call

"Rush Call" and "**Jumper**" were originally published in a neighborhood newspaper, *Dave's Rag*, published by King's older brother David in Durham, Maine. This story was published in 1960, when King was only 12.

Both stories were re-published in the Book of the Month Club's collection of miscellaneous King writings, **Secret Windows: Essays and Fiction on the Craft of Writing**, in 2000. The stories were re-published as originally written, with only the spelling corrected.

In "Rush Call," a young boy is trapped after a Christmas Eve car accident. A grouchy, bitter old doctor volunteers to take out his appendix while he is still trapped in the car. Dr. Thorpe, "one of the best in his day," climbs into the car and begins the dangerous operation. This tale is heavy on sentiment with predictable results, but after all we are talking about a 12-year-old writer's story in his brother's free local newspaper.

'Salem's Lot

This is King's second novel and the first to appear on *The New York Times* bestseller list. Despite tanking in hardback, the paperback first appeared at number 9 on 5 September

1976, before hitting number 1 on 19 September, the author's first number one bestseller. This is King's famous "vampire comes to America" novel, long before tales such as *Interview with the Vampire* and *True Blood*, let alone **American Vampire**, were conceived.

The novel features some of the scariest scenes King has ever written, including some set in the Marsten House (inspired by a nearby house when King was growing up), and the scene in which **Mark Petrie** thinks, "Death is when the monsters get you." It has a wonderful cast of characters (some of whom form what in the **Dark Tower cycle** would be called a "ka-tet") and contains some of King's most descriptive prose. No King fan and no fan of true horror can miss reading this masterpiece.

In 2004 an edition that includes 49 pages of "Deleted Scenes" from the original manuscript was released (this version is in print, so readers can easily access it). The scenes are included in a separate section after the text of the original novel, making the examination of the excised material a simple matter. This gives a fascinating insight into King's early writing and some interesting facts, including that the king vampire once had a different name (Sarlinov). The town name is different and important changes were made to events involving **Father Donald Callahan**.

Writer **Ben Mears** returns to **Jerusalem's Lot, Maine**, to find something not quite right in the town. His new friend Susan Norton agrees and soon a little boy is abducted while walking through the woods. Meanwhile, a mysterious man and his partner no one ever sees moves into the old Marsten House, which had a history of murder and suicide. Townspeople begin to disappear or die, but some of the dead are seen around town by the living. Mears and Norton bring Dr. Cody and Father Callahan into their confidence, and they are accompanied by schoolboy Mark Petrie and teacher Matt Burke as they struggle to understand the events engulfing their town.

The book and Father Donald Callahan serve critical roles in the last three novels of the Dark Tower cycle. The short story "**Jerusalem's Lot**" is something of a prequel to this novel and "**One for the Road**" is definitely a sequel.

Television: *Salem's Lot* (1979). David Soul plays Ben Mears and James Mason is Straker in this four hour mini-series. On DVD seek the longest version possible; the shorter the version the lesser the final product in this case. Among the titles for various releases of this miniseries on TV or DVD are: *Blood Thirst*, *Salem's Lot: The Miniseries* and *Salem's Lot: The Movie*.

Movie: *A Return to Salem's Lot* (1987). The only link to the original in the so-called sequel is the name of the town. Avoid.

Television: *Salem's Lot* (2004). Departs considerably from the original tale but is nevertheless watchable. Rob Lowe plays Ben Mears, Donald Sutherland appears as Richard Straker, Rutger Hauer portrays **Kurt Barlow**, and James Cromwell plays Father Donald Callahan. The DVD was released as *Salem's Lot — The Miniseries*.

Radio: *Stephen King's Salem's Lot* (1994). BBC Radio 4 (U.K.) dramatization originally broadcast in seven weekly parts in 1994 and 1995.

Genesis: This is King's take on the vampire comes to small-town America (a rare literary breed at the time), with the obvious inspiration Bram Stoker's legendary *Dracula*. It resulted directly from his musing, what if Count Dracula had come to the America of the 1970s, and wife **Tabitha King**'s response, "What if he came here, to Maine?" The Marsten House is inspired by a real family home that lay abandoned but fully furnished near King's home in Durham, Maine, during his teen years (King describes this in **Danse Macabre**). Another inspiration was a dream. In 1969, years before the novel was published, he described in a *King's Garbage Truck* column a dream in which he saw a friend's body hanging from a gibbet the night before the friend died. In *Danse Macabre* he describes the same dream, acknowledging he'd used it as inspiration for a well-known scene in *Salem's Lot*.

Trivia: King revealed the novel's original title was changed to *'Salem's Lot* "because my wife, Tabby, said that *Second Coming* sounded like a sex manual." At one point it was also to be called *Jerusalem's Lot* (a short story was later given that title).

Sara Tidwell

Sara Tidwell is a key character in **Bag of Bones**, and her tale is critical to the future of many in the book, including **Michael Noonan, Mattie Devore** and Mattie's daughter, Kyra. An African American blues singer, she and her clan arrive in 1900 at Dark Score Lake in Maine. Local white men are unhappy with Sara's activities as a musician and as a strong black woman in their rural community and plan to bring her down. This will set off a series of events that will not be resolved for nearly a century. Among her songs are "I Regret You, Baby," "Walk Me Baby" and "Fishin' Blues."

Sawyer, Jack *see* Jack Sawyer

Scott Landon

Scott Landon is the tortured best-selling author married to Lisey Landon in **Lisey's Story**. They live in the Castle View section of **Castle Rock, Maine**. From childhood he had been tormented by hereditary psychological issues (his insane father had killed Scott's brother, and Scott had been forced to kill his own father). But he has an even greater secret, around a place he calls Boo'ya Moon and a creature he called "the Long Boy."

Secret Window, Secret Garden

This novella is collected in **Four Past Midnight**. Strangely compelling, it is linked to King's fiction through mentions of **Derry, Maine**.

Mort Rainey, a successful writer, has recently divorced and is depressed when John Shooter suddenly arrives in his life, pointing an accusing finger. Shooter claims Rainey has stolen a story that he himself had written many years previously. Provided with a copy of the story, Rainey sees there is a striking resemblance between his story, "Sowing Season" and Shooter's "Secret Window, Secret Garden." Rainey's was published two years before Shooter claims to have written his, but events suddenly spiral out of control.

Genesis: King says the tale is "about writers and writing and the strange no-man's land which exists between what's real and what's make believe." He had begun to consider writing "a secret act — as secret as dreaming" and discovered a previously unnoticed view from his laundry room into a small internal garden, hence the story's title.

Movie: *Secret Window* (2004). An ordinary and slightly confusing movie, starring Johnny Depp.

Radio: *Secret Window, Secret Garden* (1999). A BBC Radio 4 (U.K.) dramatization, originally broadcast in three weekly parts, it is available as a 115-minute compilation (BBC Radio Collection), plus an interview with King.

Secret Windows: Essays and Fiction on the Craft of Writing

This is a Book of the Month Club–only collection of short stories, essays, speeches, and book excerpts. It can be purchased by joining the Stephen King Library section of the Book of the Month Club, or through second-hand resellers. Despite the title, it has no connection with the tale "**Secret Window, Secret Garden**." Among important pieces are an introduction by Peter Straub (co-author of *The Talisman* and *Black House*); two stories from King's childhood ("**Jumper**" and "**Rush Call**"); and a significant amount of non-fiction.

The Secretary of Dreams (Volume One)

Published by Cemetery Dance and magnificently illustrated by Glenn Chadbourne (*Horrors! Great Tales of Fear and Their Creators*— McFarland, 2010) this is a collection of graphically presented tales ("**The Road Virus Heads North**," "**Uncle Otto's Truck**" and "**Rainy Season**") and others which are only illustrated ("**Home Delivery**," "**Jerusalem's Lot**" and "**The Reach**"). The book is out of print but can be purchased from resellers.

The Secretary of Dreams (Volume Two)

Due to be published by Cemetery Dance and magnificently illustrated by Glenn Chadbourne, this will be a collection of graphically presented tales ("**Gray Matter**," "**One for the Road**" and "**Nona**") and others which are only illustrated ("**The Monkey**," "**Strawberry Spring**" and "**In the Deathroom**").

Seth Garin

Young Seth Garin, an autistic boy, has been living with his aunt since his family was killed in a drive-by shooting five days after they visited the Deep Earth Mining Corporation site near the town of Desperation, Nevada. Two years later, back in Audrey's home town of Wentworth, strange vehicles sprouting strange weapons suddenly attack the residents of Poplar Street. Appears in *The Regulators*.

Shawshank Prison

The fictional Shawshank Prison in Maine has been in existence since at least 1901 (Jared Devore mentioned it in *Bag of Bones*). It is most famous as the place at which **Andy Dufresne** and Red are imprisoned in "**Rita Hayworth and Shawshank Redemption**" and is portrayed in the movie *The Shawshank Redemption*.

Among its many other occupants are George Footman (*Bag of Bones*), Richard Macklin (*It*), Nat Copeland (*Needful Things*), and Ace Merrill ("The Sun Dog"). King constantly mentions this institution, including in *Dolores Claiborne*, *Dreamcatcher* and "The Body."

Shearman, Bill *see* Bill Shearman

Sheemie Ruiz

Sheemie is an important character in **The Dark Tower cycle**. His first name (actually a nickname) comes from his mother (Dolores Sheemer)—his real first name is the same as his father, Stanley. Although he is barely mentioned in *The Dark Tower I: The Gunslinger*, he is of great importance to events in both *The Dark Tower IV: Wizard and Glass* and *The Dark Tower VII: The Dark Tower*.

He is a little retarded (but this conceals other talents) and follows **Roland Deschain**'s first "ka-tet" back to **Gilead** from Hambry (these events are likely to be portrayed in **The Dark Tower Graphic Novel** comic, *The Dark Tower: The Gunslinger—Sheemie's Tale*).

Trivia: In the final Dark Tower novel it is revealed that Sheemie looks exactly like the fictional version of Bryan Smith, the driver of the van that struck and nearly killed Stephen King.

Sheldon, Paul *see* Paul Sheldon

The Shining

One of King most famous and popular novels, this haunted hotel tale is familiar across popular culture. It features perhaps the most terrifying scene in King's fiction (certain action in Room 217). The writing is clear and crisp and readers are able to build empathy with most of the major characters.

Jack Torrance, a failed teacher and struggling writer with a drinking problem, takes a caretaking job for the winter at **The Overlook Hotel** deep in the Colorado mountains. Jack's wife, Wendy, and son, **Danny Torrance**, also settle into the hotel, hoping for a better turn in their lives after Jack's alcoholism led to both the loss of his teaching job and his breaking Danny's arm in a drunken rage. Danny has an ability that hotel employee **Dick Hallorann** tells him is called "the shine" or "shining."

Jack becomes fascinated by the sordid history of the Overlook Hotel and spends more time looking into that than working. The deepening winter snow cuts the family off from nearby Sidewinder. Danny and Jack begin to see strange things—a masked ball, topiary creatures that move, and a bartender in an empty and alcohol free hotel. Events are rushing to a head as Wendy finds it harder and harder to communicate with her obsessed husband.

There are links to King's other fiction through locations such as Stovington, Vermont (*The Talisman*, *The Stand* and "Everything's Eventual" story), **Derry, Maine** (*It*), Sidewinder, Colorado (*Misery*, *American Vampire*) and minor references to certain characters.

The short story "**Before the Play**" is the novel's deleted prologue and can be read either before or after the novel. King also wrote an epilogue, "**After the Play**," but it was lost after the publisher excised it from the original manuscript.

Both screen adaptations (see below) somehow fail to capture the psychological power of the novel. *The Shining* is one of King's greatest novels and will certainly be on the reading list for students of the American novel for decades to come.

Genesis: The novel was inspired by Ray Bradbury's short story "The Veldt" and was originally to be titled *Darkshine*. The draft of that story, to be set in an amusement park, was on the back burner when the Kings went to visit the Hotel Stanley in Estes Park,

Colorado, on 30 October 1974, where they are said to have stayed in Room 217. Inspired by the eerie atmosphere of the end-of-season hotel, King began working again on the manuscript, now known as *The Shine*. At publication the book was given its final title. King's own battle with alcohol also served as inspiration and, perhaps, motivation.

King has written of the dream that set him writing (it was of his son running, screaming through the hotel's corridors), the decision (a "lucky accident") to make Jack Torrance an alcoholic child-beater, King's feeling of pressure and inadequacy in his "early-marriage doldrums" prior to the success of **Carrie**, and of the use of *The Shining* as "ritual burning of hate and pain" from those times.

Movie: Stanley Kubrick's classic movie adaptation, *The Shining*, starring Jack Nicholson as Jack Torrance, was released in 1980. Kubrick's adaptation is the subject of much controversy within the King community. Despite its obvious brilliance as a movie and Nicholson's outstanding acting, many King fans cannot bring themselves to fully appreciate the movie due to the many changes Kubrick made to the storyline and the way he presented Jack Torrance's character. Instead of the slow decline into insanity portrayed in the novel, moviegoers understood that Jack was quite mad to begin with (this was perhaps further influenced by Nicholson's Academy Award winning role as an asylum inmate in *One Flew Over the Cuckoo's Nest*, released only five years earlier). King himself did not particularly enjoy the adaptation. However, anyone who enjoys a good horror movie or indeed, a great movie, should not miss this outstanding piece of film making, which includes one of the most famous movie quotes of all time—"Here's Johnny!"

Television: *Stephen King's The Shining* (1997). A mini-series available on DVD. The teleplay is by King and the director is Mick Garris. It is close to King's original story and very viewable.

The Shining (Mini-Series Screenplay)

King's screenplay for the mini-series of **The Shining** has never been published and it is most unlikely that it ever will be, as readers have the novel and viewers the DVD or video to enjoy. Copies of the telescript do, however, circulate freely in the King community, and readers should have no great difficulty in finding one.

King never enjoyed Kubrick's movie adaptation of the novel, as it is both too far from his own imagining and he felt Jack Nicholson as Torrance appears mad from the get-go. He described the movie as "cold and disappointingly loveless—but chilling." The author always harbored a strong desire to remake the movie in the manner in which he would have preferred and got his chance with the 1997 mini-series, appropriately named *Stephen King's The Shining* (as compared to Stanley Kubrick's). While that newer adaptation is faithful to the core storyline and motivations of the novel, it lacks the dramatic punch of the movie. To be allowed to produce the mini-series, Warner Bros. had to make a payment described as "rather enormous" to Kubrick, who held the sequel and remake rights from the original movie.

There are subtle changes from the novel to the screenplay but the only major alteration is the addition of an epilogue (perhaps what King had intended with the now lost "After the Play"?). A further addition to the original storyline is the Gage Creed Band and its bandleader, the definitely *not* one and only **Gage Creed**, played by King himself, wonderfully camping the role. Of course, Gage Creed is the name of a major character in **Pet Sematary**, whose sneaker was found in Atropos' lair in **Insomnia**. This is a nice little in-joke for King's faithful fans, to go with his enjoyable acting cameo.

Television: A superb piece of television, genuinely frightening and a faithful adaptation of the material, and containing an element of fun lacking in both the book and the movie. It debuted on the ABC-TV network in 1997. Mick Garris directed, having earlier helmed **Sleepwalkers**, the mini-series of **The Stand** and *Quicksilver Highway* (which includes an adaptation of "**Chattery Teeth**"). The actors include Steven Weber as **Jack Torrance**, Rebecca De Mornay portraying Wendy Torrance, Courtland Mead as **Danny Torrance**, Melvin Van Peebles in the role of Dick Hallorann, and Elliott Gould, Pat Hingle, and Cynthia Garris (the wife of the director, in fantastic makeup) as the Woman in Room 217. King played Gage Creed. The production won two Emmys; the DVD was released in 2003.

The Shining (Unproduced Screenplay)

King has effectively created three versions of the tale with which even non–King fans associate him, **The Shining**. Most fans would immediately identify both the novel and many the mini-series screenplay, but few know King also wrote a movie length screenplay that, of course, was never produced. The 132 page, 369 scene screenplay was originally written for Stanley Kubrick.

Unsurprisingly, this screenplay is very faithful to the original story. Although the script would have adequately served a movie adaptation, it lacks the power and passion of Kubrick's interpretation, and it is fortunate that the King screenplay actually produced was that for the mini-series, written nearly two decades later, allowing more maturity to his scriptwriting, and the valuable extra length allowed in the television format. All in all, the second script is the richer and more expressive of the two.

It will never been published; however, it may be read at the Special Collections Unit of the **Raymond H. Fogler Library** at the University of Maine in Orono. Ask for Box 2318.

Genesis: It was written before Stanley Kubrick and novelist Diane Johnson developed their version, which was used in Kubrick's film (one version is dated October 1977). Kubrick declined King's version because he did not want to be influenced by anyone else's view of the book (not even King's).

Shooter, John *see* John Shooter

The Shop

The Department of Scientific Intelligence, also known as "The Shop," is a highly secretive U.S. government organization.

They ran the Lot Six experiments on **Charlie McGee**'s parents, which resulted in her talents. In **Firestarter**, psychopathic agent **John Rainbird** chases her down and brings her back to headquarters, to unexpected consequences.

In **Golden Years**, they were the sponsors of the experiments that lead Harlan Williams to begin to age backwards and sent a highly trained killer, Jude Andrews, to eliminate him. Andrews was said to be an even better operative than Rainbird.

They are also mentioned in "The Langoliers" and in the revised edition of **The Stand**.

It is interesting that King has not returned to this shadowy and unprincipled government agency since *Golden Years* was written in 1991.

The Shotgunners

"The Shotgunners" is an unproduced screenplay and is clearly the forerunner of *The Regulators*, the **Richard Bachman** credited companion volume to *Desperation*. While the premise is the same, the characters are completely different. It appears that this screenplay actually developed into *The Regulators* novel.

In the screenplay, shootings begin without warning late one afternoon on a quiet suburban street. Cars cruise onto Maple Street, shotguns protruding from the windows, shooting randomly at people and houses. Survivors gather together as the victims mount and they soon realize something is very wrong — no police arrive, indeed there is no apparent reaction from the outside world. When three of the trapped locals attempt to leave the block they find the mystery deepens.

The theme and storyline of the this screenplay and *The Regulators* are similar, but in the screenplay the cause of all the mayhem is supernatural, while in the novel it's the power of a strange creature, Tak, operating through an autistic boy.

Genesis: According to various sources, the legendary film director Sam Peckinpah died while pre-producing this script. Peckinpah made *Straw Dogs*, *The Wild Bunch* and was famed for the violence portrayed in his later films, long before the emergence of Quentin Tarantino in the 1990s. If Peckinpah was indeed working on pre-production for this screenplay when he died in 1984, it was over a decade until it appeared reworked as *The Regulators* in 1996. Bachman/King's dedication in the book, "Thinking of Jim Thompson and Sam Peckinpah: legendary shadows," would seem to confirm the story.

The good news for potential readers is the screenplay is held in Box 2318 of the Special Collections Unit of the **Raymond H. Fogler Library** at the University of Maine, Orono, and may be read by the general public.

Silence

This 12-line poem appeared in a University of Maine literary magazine, *Moth*, in 1970 along with two other King poems ("**The Dark Man**" and "**Donovan's Brain**"). It's never been included in one of King's books but can be found in a collection of horror poems, *The Devil's Wine* (Cemetery Dance, 2003).

Relatively unimportant, the poem describes the narrator listening to nothing but the fridge.

Silver Bullet

This is King's screenplay adaptation of *Cycle of the Werewolf*. Signet published a tie-in book to that movie, also titled *Silver Bullet* (1985). That edition included *Cycle of the Werewolf*, the original shooting script for the film and a new foreword by King. As it is King's final shooting script, the text differs from the release print of the film.

A werewolf stalks the small town of Tarker's Mills and only local boy **Marty Coslaw** seems to be able to identify the monster's human form.

Movie: *Silver Bullet* (also known as *Stephen King's Silver Bullet*). This is a competent, viewable King adaptation and is unsurprisingly faithful to the original story. Corey Haim starred as Marty Coslaw and Gary Busey as Uncle Red. Released on DVD in 2003.

Six Stories

This is a collection of King's fiction issued as a limited edition of 1100 copies by his own imprint, Philtrum Press. Copies are difficult to secure and buyers should expect to pay over $600. All the stories have now been published in mass-market King books. They are "**Lunch at the Gotham Café**," "**L.T.'s Theory of Pets**," "**Luckey Quarter**," "**Autopsy Room Four**," "**Blind Willie**" and "**The Man in the Black Suit.**"

Skeleton Crew

Skeleton Crew is a collection of short stories, released in 1985. It includes many of King's early stories, the best of which is "**The Mist.**" "**Morning Deliveries (Milkman #1)**" and two poems, "**Paranoid: A Chant**" and "**For Owen,**" are original to the book, all the others had been previously published. Readers can therefore get a feel of the short fiction King was publishing as early as 1968 and through 1984. The overall quality is quite high with outstanding stories such as "**Nona,**" "**The Reach**" and "**Mrs. Todd's Shortcut.**"

Other tales included are: "**Here There Be Tygers,**" "**The Monkey,**" "**Cain Rose Up,**" "**The Jaunt,**" "**The Wedding Gig,**" "**The Raft,**" "**Word Processor of the Gods,**" "**The Man Who Would Not Shake Hands,**" "**Beachworld,**" "**The Reaper's Image,**" "**Survivor Type,**" "**Uncle Otto's Truck,**" "**Big Wheels: A Tale of the Laundry Game (Milkman #2),**" "**Gramma**" and "**The Ballad of the Flexible Bullet.**"

Skybar

In 1982 the Doubleday imprint Dolphin Books published a paperback for budding writers, *The Do-It-Yourself Bestseller: A Workbook*. A number of well-known authors were convinced to contribute the opening paragraphs and closing paragraph of a story, and "Skybar" was King's. Empty lined pages were provided between the opening and closing sections and the reader was to "complete" the story. This was actually the second time King had contributed a partial story for writers to complete. The March 1977 issue of *Cavalier* magazine contained the first section of "**The Cat from Hell.**" He later provided the opening lines of "**The Furnace.**"

The story opens in classic fashion: "There were twelve of us when we went in that night, but only two of us came out — my friend Kirby and me. And Kirby was insane." The setting is an amusement park and all we know about the lost 10 children is that they were murdered. King's closing lines indicate twelve years have passed and Kirby still sits in a psych ward, with the narrator still concerned for his welfare.

This partial story displays King's trademark style, quickly establishing atmosphere, and reminds readers of the carnival segment of *The Dead Zone*, portions of *It* and even "The Body."

Copies of the workbook appear at second-hand bookselling venues from time to time.

Slade

"Slade," one of King's earliest public works, is best described as a satirical western. It was published as a serial (the author would later publish *The Plant* and *The Green Mile* this way) in *The Maine Summer Campus* just before and after his 1970 graduation. King had earlier written a series of 47 non-fiction columns, **King's Garbage Truck**, for the newspaper.

Slade, a cowboy with a difference, lost his one true love, Polly Peachtree of Paduka, Illinois, in a tragic accident in which a Montgolfier hot air balloon crashed on the barn where she was milking her cows. Saddened and lost, he takes the job of helping Sandra Dawson save her ranch from the evil Sam Columbine. In the process he shoots some innocent people and even some of Columbine's men. Things get stranger as Columbine strikes back.

The story is spread over eight chapters, most ending in the cliff-hangers that are typical of this mode. While derivative, King clearly understood this and delighted in humor and the chance to run outrageous story twists. Here, readers have a chance to observe the young adult author indulging in pure fun.

Generally, the only way to secure a copy is from the microfiche at the **Raymond H. Fogler Library** of the University of Maine. Unfortunately, the originals have been stolen.

Sleepwalkers

Sleepwalkers was the first production of a wholly original King movie screenplay. The tale features wholly original monsters— ancient and incestuous creatures, called Sleepwalkers, who have evolved from cats; in their true form they have reptilian and feline features but are able to appear human. They feed upon the life force of humans, but modern cats are their mortal enemies.

Carl and Martha Brodie live in Bodega Bay, California (apparently the same setting as Alfred Hitchcock's classic *The Birds*), but are attacked by local cats, which have discovered the Sleepwalkers in their midst. The mother and son barely escape with their lives and move on, to Travis, Indiana. Settling into this new town as the Bradys, Charles enrolls at the local high school and set his sights on attractive, 17-year-old Tanya Robertson, who is now at risk.

In an interesting twist, King names a nearby town as Castle Rock, Indiana (apparently more than homage to **Castle Rock, Maine**, as both towns share a Sheriff Pangborn). King has never returned to these creatures, which have the same ability to make themselves "dim," as does **Randall Flagg**. In another fun link, the movie theater at which Tanya works is showing **Misery**.

The screenplay has not been published but copies circulate in the King community.

Movie: *Sleepwalkers* (1992) (aka *Stephen King's Sleepwalkers*). Mick Garris directed, the first time he had done so for a King production. He would go on to helm the miniseries of **The Stand** and of **The Shining**, as well as *Quicksilver Highway*, **Riding the Bullet** and **Desperation**. Madchen Amick appears as Tanya Robertson, and Alice Krige as Mary Brady. There are many cameos, including the director's wife, Cynthia Garris, as Laurie Travis; *Animal House* director John Landis as a lab tech; *Gremlins* director Joe Dante as a lab assistant; Stephen King as a cemetery caretaker; along with horror writer Clive Barker and *The Texas Chain Saw Massacre* director Tobe Hooper as forensic techs. The movie was first released on DVD in 2000.

Genesis: **Joe King**, the author's son (who now publishes as **Joe Hill**), had a crush on the popcorn girl at the local cinema. One night, watching the two talk, King thought of "a guy wanting to ask the popcorn girl out for all the wrong reasons, and the story just followed that burst of inspiration."

Trivia: At one point King's title for the tale was *Tania's Suitor.*

Smith, Johnny *see* Johnny Smith

Sneakers

First published in *Night Visions 5* (Dark Harvest, 1988) King completely re-wrote this ghost story for collection in **Nightmares and Dreamscapes**. Unusually, this tale is not linked to any other King fiction. Not one of King's best, it is still competent and interesting, with a nice twist.

John Tell has been hired to help mix music at Tabori Studios. Each time he goes to the third floor men's room he sees the same set of old sneakers in the same toilet stall. When someone else is in the stall he can see both sets of shoes but the other men in the toilets do not notice anything unusual.

Something to Tide You Over

This humorous tale of revenge is collected in the graphic novel **Creepshow**. Richard Vickers discovers his wife is having an affair with Harry Wentworth. Despite his plans, he may discover revenge works both ways.

Movie: *Creepshow* (1982), the "Something to Tide You Over" segment starred Leslie Nielsen and Ted Danson.

Graphic Novel: The "Something to Tide You Over" segment of *Creepshow* (New American Library, 1982).

Something Wicked This Way Comes

This screenplay is an adaptation of Ray Bradbury's classic novel of the same name, published in 1962 and regarded as a classic in both the fantasy and horror genres. In an interview, King says: "I felt more divorced from the source material. I loved the book, and I think that of all the screenplays I've done, that was the best. But in spite of loving it I was a little divorced from it, where I wasn't with my own book." The date of this interview indicates the script was completed no later than 1978. It appears King wrote the piece for practice rather than to be produced, as Bradbury himself wrote the screenplay for the movie, released in 1983.

Largely faithful as the script is to the novel, a detailed description of the story is not required. Suffice to say as the carnival arrives in Green Town, Illinois, adventure awaits 13-year-old Jim Nightshade and his friend Will Halloway.

King's screenplay is held in the Special Collections Department of the **Raymond H. Fogler Library** at the University of Maine in Orono, the author's alma mater. Written permission from King is required to access this work and is generally only given to researchers. Those who have not read Bradbury's novel should, as well as King's in-depth analysis in **Danse Macabre**.

Trivia: In *Danse Macabre* King writes, "My first experience with real horror came at the hands of Ray Bradbury — it was an adaptation of his story 'Mars is Heaven!' on *Dimension X*. This would have been broadcast about 1951, which would have made me four at the time. I asked to listen, and was denied permission by my mother ... I crept down to the door to listen anyway, and she was right it was plenty upsetting."

Sometimes They Come Back

This horror short story originally appeared in *Cavalier* magazine for March 1974 and is collected in **Night Shift**.

When Jim Norman was nine, his 12-year-old brother Wayne had been brutally murdered by four boys. Many years later, after Jim begins teaching at Harold Davis High School, two students die mysteriously and a third goes missing. Very strange individuals replace them in class and Jim begins to realize he and his wife are in mortal danger.

Television: *Sometimes They Come Back* (1991). Definitely a "B-grade" horror flick, it is available on DVD. It is also known as *Stephen King's Sometimes They Come Back*.

Movies: *Sometimes They Come Back ... Again* (1996). A sequel to the first movie with little connection to it or the story. Avoid. *Stephen King's Sometimes They Come Back 2. Sometimes They Come Back for More* (1999) is another execrable sequel, available on DVD. Also known as *Frozen* and *Ice Station Erebus*.

Trivia: In **On Writing** King explains his daughter was ill and he had no money to pay for medicine when a check for $500 arrived for this story. He says he hadn't believed the story would sell, let alone for this amount, which was the most he had ever received at that time.

Sorry, Right Number

This teleplay is collected in **Nightmares and Dreamscapes**. A woman briefly hears an anguished caller when she picks up the phone. She and her husband try to find the source of the call but events later that night cause Katie Weiderman to forget the incident, which will come back to haunt her.

When Katie Weiderman calls Polly at the dorm, the person answering says that if the caller is Arnie, Christine is not in (a reference, however obscure, to **Christine** and its key characters).

Genesis: King says he wrote this screenplay "pretty much as it appears here [*Nightmares and Dreamscapes*] in two sittings." After writing the telescript, King relates, "My West Coast agent — the one who does film deals — had it by the end of the week. Early the following week, Steven Spielberg read it for *Amazing Stories*, a TV series which he then had in production ... Spielberg rejected it — they were looking for *Amazing Stories* that were a little more upbeat he said — and so I took it to my long-time collaborator and good friend, Richard Rubinstein, who then had a series called *Tales from the Darkside* in syndication. Richard bought "Sorry" the day he read it and had it in production a week or two later." King continues, "This version, by the way, is my first draft, which is longer and a little more textured than the final shooting script, which for budgetary reasons specified just two sets." The title is possibly homage to Richard Matheson's tale "Sorry, Right Number."

Television: "Sorry, Right Number" on *Tales from the Darkside* (season four, 1987). The episode is available on video as part of Volume 4 of a compilation set from the series, but not yet on DVD. The production itself suffers from a lack of suspense.

Sorry, Right Number (The Shooting Script)

The published screenplay for a series episode of the horror anthology series *Tales from the Darkside* appears in the 1993 collection **Nightmares and Dreamscapes**. Most fans would be forgiven for believing this was the telescript actually used for the program. However, it varies significantly from the actual shooting script, which is held at the Special Collections Unit of the **Raymond H. Fogler Library** at the University of Maine, Orono. Ask for Box 1012, which is available to the public.

Genesis: King explains the background in the notes to *Nightmares and Dreamscapes* (see **Sorry, Right Number** above). There are numerous differences between the two telescripts but no major change to the storyline.

Television: *Sorry, Right Number* on *Tales from the Darkside* (Season Four, 1987). The episode is available on video as part of Volume 4 of a compilation set from the series, but not yet on DVD. The production itself suffers from a lack of real suspense.

Trivia: King's **The Word Processor of the Gods** was also adapted for this anthology TV series.

Squad D

Squad D was written in the late 1970s for a Harlan Ellison edited anthology, *Last Dangerous Visions*. Ellison later said: "Stephen sent me a story for *Last Dangerous Visions* that needs to be rewritten.... I was sent this short story, and I think there's a lot more in it than Stephen had time to develop. The story deserves better, the work deserves better, and Stephen's reputation deserves better." The anthology itself never appeared and, as King has not otherwise published the story, it cannot be read, except in photocopies of the manuscript that circulate quite freely in the King community. Interestingly, two different versions of the manuscript have appeared — one in which the events occur three years after Squad D is attacked in Vietnam and another set eleven years later.

Josh Bortman from **Castle Rock, Maine**, is the only survivor of his army unit, Squad D. In 1974 the Viet Cong killed the other nine squad members as they crossed a bridge over the Ky River in Vietnam.

Remorseful, Bortman sends a framed photograph showing all nine dead members of Squad D to each of their parents. Some years later relatives of the dead men begin to call the Bortman household after noticing that a tenth soldier appears in their photos. The twist in the tale, of course, is why this new soldier now appears in every photo.

A fairly short story (around 2000 words), this is one of the best of King's unpublished works. The story is full of angst, pain, remorse and possibly redemption and speaks to the horrors the survivors of Vietnam experience. The power of King's writing is illustrated by the opening sentences, "Billy Clewson died all at once, with nine of the ten other members of D Squad on April 8, 1974. It took his mother two years, but she got started right away, on the afternoon the telegram came announcing her son's death, in fact."

If rewritten to avoid certain flaws, which are not as serious as Ellison implies, the tale would make a welcome addition to any future collection.

The Stand (Mini-Series Screenplay)

King wrote a screenplay for the ABC-TV mini-series version of his iconic novel. As it was written after **The Stand: The Complete and Uncut Edition**, it is fair to assume it adapts that later version of the book.

Television: *Stephen King's The Stand* (1994) was shown over four nights with the parts titled "The Plague," "The Dreams," "The Betrayal" and "The Stand." One casting decision upset hard-core fans, with Molly Ringwald totally mishandling the role of **Fran Gold-smith**. Mick Garris also helmed *Sleepwalkers*, the mini-series of *The Shining*, *Quicksil-ver Highway*, *Desperation* and *Riding the Bullet*. The production won an Emmy for Best Achievement in Make-up. Issued on DVD in 1999, this is a superior production of King's work and will be enjoyed by fans of the books and viewers in general.

The actors include Gary Sinise as **Stu Redman**, Molly Ringwald as Fran Goldsmith, Jamey Sheridan as **Randall Flagg**, Laura San Giacomo as **Nadine Cross**, Ruby Dee as **Abagail Freemantle**, Miguel Ferrer as Lloyd Henreid, Ray Walston as **Glen Bateman**, Rob Lowe as **Nick Andros**, Kathy Bates as Rae Flowers, Ed Harris as Starkey, and Cynthia Garris (the wife of the director) as Susan Stern.

King plays the role of Teddy Weizak — and this is no cameo — he has quite a few speaking lines throughout the production. It is interesting to note that the character survives this version, whereas he dies in both books. It is clear that the power of the author to give life or death can come into stark focus when that same author is playing the character!

King is very true in this screenplay to the book versions, making few substantive changes to the storyline. He does change the sex of Fran Goldsmith's baby from a boy, Peter, in each of the earlier versions, to the very sentimentally named girl, Abagail, in this offering. To allow for Kathy Bates' appearance as the DJ at KLFT during the epidemic, the final screenplay includes a sex change for the character and a change of the name from Ray to Rae Flowers.

King took the opportunity in this script to make some subtle links to his other fictions that had not appeared in the books. Here **Tom Cullen** is sent west from the Stanley Hotel in Estes Park, Colorado. This is, of course, the hotel at which King conceived *The Shining* and at which that mini-series was filmed. When seen in Mother Abagail Freemantle's cornfield, Randall Flagg is described as being "dim." This is a skill Raymond Fiegler (most serious King students believe this is a pseudonym for Randall Flagg) taught **Carol Gerber** in the *Hearts in Atlantis* version of "**Blind Willie**."

The Stand (Novel)

One of King's most loved novels, the tale of good men and women making their stand in a post-apocalyptic America is likely to stand the test of time as a classic of 20th Century American dark fiction. It is impossible to be a true fan of King's work without reading this book, first published in 1978 and updated as *The Stand: The Complete and Uncut Edition* in 1990. It has the largest cast of characters he has ever created, many of whom are loved by fans (**Stu Redman, Fran Goldsmith, Nick Andros, Glen Bateman, Larry Underwood,** "Mother" **Abagail Freemantle,** Kojak); others loathed (**Randall Flagg, Harold Lauder**); yet others for whom we have strong empathy (**Donald Merwin Elbert,** aka "The Trashcan Man," **Tom Cullen**); and a host of fully-formed minor characters (Ray Flowers, the Monster Shouter, Judge Farris, The Kid).

A superflu virus is released from a government facility and devastates the world, leading to an apocalyptic confrontation between good and evil. The virus escapes into the general populace when Charles Campion and his family flee the Project Blue Base after an accident. Three days later Campion crashes into a gas station in Arnette, Texas, at which Stu Redman and his cronies are drinking and shooting the breeze. The flu, quickly dubbed Captain Trips, has 99.4 percent communicability and 99.4 percent excess mortality and quickly engulfs the world. Within two weeks America lies devastated with the few survivors in shock. As the survivors slowly began to regroup, most suffer vivid dreams of an old black woman or of a Dark Man and are drawn to the presence of one or the other.

As one of King's major "worlds" or realities, *The Stand* is linked with much of his other significant fiction. Characters who appear or are mentioned in other King fiction include Randall Flagg, Abagail Freemantle, The Trashcan Man and **Bobbi Anderson** (of **The Tommyknockers**). King also links the story to others through the towns of Arnette, **Castle Rock**, **Hemingford Home** and Stovington.

Genesis: King says this novel is about how difficult it is — perhaps impossible — to close Pandora's technobox once it's open. He also describes it as a "long tale of dark Christianity" and notes he has been writing for most of his career about God and the consequences for humanity if he exists. In **Danse Macabre**, he notes, "I wrote 'A dark man with no face' and then glanced up and saw that grisly little motto again: 'Once in every generation a plague will fall among them.' And that was that."

Television: Technically, the mini-series *Stephen King's The Stand* is an adaptation of *The Stand: The Complete and Uncut Edition*. Very accurate to the tale in the book, with some casting questions. Teleplay by Stephen King; directed by Mick Garris. Gary Sinise is brilliant as Stu Redman; Molly Ringwald awful as Fran Goldsmith; Jamey Sheridan outstanding as Randall Flagg; Ruby Dee near perfect as Abagail Freemantle; as is Rob Lowe as Nick Andros. Excellent contributions from Miguel Ferrer (Lloyd Henreid); Ray Walston (Glen Bateman); Kathy Bates (Rae Flowers); Stephen King (Teddy Weizak); Ed Harris (Starkey); and Kareem Abdul-Jabbar (the Monster Shouter). Available on DVD.

Graphic Novel: In 2008 Marvel began a series of graphic novel arcs that will cover the entire tale. The four arcs to the time of writing were *The Stand: Captain Trips*; *The Stand: American Nightmares*; *The Stand: Soul Survivors* and *The Stand: Hardcases*.

Trivia: In section 10 of the "On Writing" section of **On Writing**, King says he suffered writer's block on the direction of the story after five hundred or so pages and was nearly incapable of completing it. In fact, it was the only published book length work from that time until *On Writing* itself to suffer being laid away in a drawer, perhaps never to be completed. He once wrote of the fan base's high opinion of *The Stand*, "There's something a little depressing about such a united opinion that you did your best work twenty years ago, but we won't go into that just now, thanks."

King has effectively created five versions of his seminal work *The Stand*. This will surprise most readers, who would immediately identify two or three versions but would struggle to identify the remainder. Regarded by many as the author's masterpiece, *The Stand* was first published as a novel in 1978. Subsequent paperback editions used the original hardcover text, in which the tale is set in 1980. U.S. paperback editions published after 1980 moved the events to a new timeline of 1985, providing a second version of the tale. However, most, if not all, overseas paperback editions stayed with the original text. Then, in 1990, King famously republished the book as he had originally intended, as *The Stand: The Complete and Uncut Edition*, the third version. He also wrote a movie script, which has never been produced (see below) and forms the fourth version. Finally, in 1992, King wrote the screenplay for the ABC mini-series and that forms the fifth and, to date, final version (also below).

The Stand (Unproduced Movie Screenplay)

King wrote a screenplay of his classic novel, which was intended for a movie length production. It was never produced or published but a mini-series version of the tale was produced (see entry above). A copy is held in Box 2318A at the Special Collections Unit of the **Raymond H. Fogler Library** at the University of Maine, Orono, and readers can access it there.

Considering the varying timelines for the different versions of **The Stand**, it is interesting that King chose to set this particular script in 1985. This may indicate that the version of the script held at the Fogler was written about 1984, considering King's penchant for setting storylines one or two years in the future. Various sources note that King began writing scripts for a movie version of **The Stand** as early as 1979.

Here, the author is very true to the storyline in the original, 1978 book version. Of the changes made the most notable is the combining of Glenn Bateman's character with Judge Richard Farris. The new character, Judge Glen Farris, is the owner of Kojak, a dog whose importance to the tale cannot be exaggerated.

The Stand: The Complete and Uncut Edition

In 1990 King famously republished **The Stand** as he had originally intended, complete and uncut. In the second part of the preface King states, "I am republishing 'The Stand' as it was originally written," although he also comments that certain parts originally cut stayed on the cutting room floor. In fact, indications are that some 150,000 words were added, whereas it appears 100,000 had originally been removed. King clarified this matter in his foreword to the revised and expanded edition of *The Gunslinger*: "What I reinstated in the late eighties were revised sections of the pre-existing manuscript. I also revised the work as a whole, mostly to acknowledge the AIDS epidemic."

Television: See other entries for *The Stand* for full details.

Graphic Novel: In 2008 Marvel began a series of graphic novel arcs that will cover the entire tale. The four arcs to the time of writing were *The Stand: Captain Trips*; *The Stand: American Nightmares*; *The Stand: Soul Survivors* and *The Stand: Hardcases*.

Stanley Uris

Stanley (Stan) Uris was living in **Derry, Maine**, in 1957–58. He and his friends—**Bill Denbrough, Ben Hanscom, Beverly Marsh, Richard Tozier, Mike Hanlon** and **Eddie Kaspbrak**—form "the Losers Club" in the novel *It*, in an attempt to fight **Pennywise**. As an adult he moves to Atlanta, Georgia. He also appears in "**The Bird and the Album**."

The Star Invaders

King self-published this short story in 1964 — only a few researchers are known to have read it and the author apparently owns the only copy. It was clearly written under the heavy, and heady, influence of King's beloved 1950s science-fiction films and television episodes, radio drama and graphic comic books, most particularly the classic 1956 movie *Earth vs. the Flying Saucers*. In the story individual heroes deal with hostile aliens as they try to take over out planet.

It may well be this same publication is the tale King calls "The Invasion of the Star-Creatures" in the CV section of *On Writing*.

Stark, George *see* George Stark

Stationary Bike

This long and fascinating tale was first published in an anthology, *Borderlands 5* (Borderlands Press, 2003), and collected in *Just After Sunset*. The editors introduced it: "This is one of those stories that should make a lot of English professors salivate. It would allow them to use phrases like 'fraught with symbolism,' 'trenchant metaphors,' and 'penetrating subtext.' We just took it for what it was— one hell of a ride." Fans of King's early fiction will particularly enjoy this very original short story, which takes a number of interesting twists.

Freelance artist Richard Sifkitz is advised by his doctor to do something about his health. The doctor likens Richard's metabolism to a work crew, so Sifkitz returns home and paints a magnificent mural of a work crew on a country road. He sets up a stationary exercise bike in front on the mural and as he rides each day he begins to fantasize about the workers, giving them names and lives. As time goes by he even imagines he is riding in the countryside he has painted for the work crew and then begins to believe his own fantasy.

Genesis: King says, "This story came out of my hate/hate relationship not just with stationary bikes but with every treadmill I ever trudged."

Staub, George *see* George Staub

Stella Flanders

Stella Flanders has lived her entire life on Goat Island, Maine. Born Stella Godlin, she has never ventured to the mainland, a short distance across the Reach, as in her nearly 96 years she has never found the need. But she begins to see her long dead friends and they have a proposal for her, in "**The Reach**" (also known as "**Do the Dead Sing?**").

Stephen King Goes to the Movies

A largely irrelevant collection of five tales that had previously been included in other King collections. Some fans felt this publication was nothing more than a commercial exercise by the publishers. Even a short new introductory note explicating King's feelings about the movies made from each tale fails to justify the purchase price. The stories are: "**1408**," "**The Mangler**," "**Low Men in Yellow Coats**," "**Rita Hayworth and Shawshank Redemption**" and "**Children of the Corn**."

Stillson, Greg see Greg Stillson

Stokely Jones

Stokely Jones III is one of the incredibly well-drawn characters King creates from time to time, in this case for the story "**Hearts in Atlantis.**" Disabled in a car accident, he moved about on crutches and was a quiet dissenter about the Vietnam War.

Storm of the Century

This is the only instance of King publishing a screenplay in stand-alone form (other collected screenplays include *Sorry, Right Number* and *Silver Bullet*).

A storm strikes **Little Tall Island, Maine**, cutting it off from the mainland, just after the first murder in 70-odd years. A stranger, Andre Linoge, admits to the killing, yet other residents die while he sits in his jail cell. Linoge demands that a child be freely given to him as his heir or everyone on the island will die.

The tale is linked through Little Tall Island to *Dolores Claiborne* and the screenplay includes references to *Rose Red* and *The Shining*. **Derry** is also mentioned.

Genesis: King says this story gave him "a chance to say some interesting and provocative things about the very nature of community ... because there is no community in America as tightly knit as the island communities off the coast of Maine." And that in "*Storm of the Century* ... I tried to express the belief that sometimes good people do not win. Sometimes good people are corrupted."

Genesis: King conceived this project as a mini-series screenplay but has noted that if it had not been picked up for production he would have turned the tale into a novel.

Television: *Storm of the Century* (1999). With the screenplay by Stephen King, this is a genuinely intriguing and scary production. Colm Feore is brilliant as Andrew Linoge. Available on DVD. Also known as *Stephen King's Storm of the Century*.

The Stranger

This piece of juvenilia appears in *People, Places and Things*, along with six other King tales.

Kelso Black kills a guard during a robbery. While toasting his takings he hears footsteps. A stranger enters and tells Black it's time to come, as they have a long way to go. Looking into the stranger's face, Black apparently recognizes the devil, for he begins to scream. The two disappear, leaving nothing but the smell of brimstone in the room.

Readers will know that King uses a similar artifice in *The Stand*, where looking into the face of **Randall Flagg** at certain times can drive the viewer insane.

Strawberry Spring

This short horror story was originally published in the Fall 1968 edition of *Ubris* magazine. It was substantially rewritten for publication in *Cavalier* magazine for November 1975 and *Gent* magazine for February 1977. That version is collected in **Night Shift**. While the two "Strawberry Spring" stories are simply versions of the same story, the setting is completely different, moving from Wiscasset College in Maine in the *Ubris* version to the New Sharon Teachers' College in an unnamed but probably New England state in the *Night Shift* version. It is effectively impossible to secure a copy of *Ubris*, but it may be photocopied at the **Raymond H. Fogler Library** at the University of Maine, Orono.

In March 1968 the weather starts to warm, although everyone knows it is too early for spring. This was a rare strawberry spring but unlike any they have seen before. At the small New Sharon Teachers' College, four young girls are murdered within a few days. Who is the strawberry spring killer?

Movie: A **Dollar Baby** of the same name was produced in 2001.

Graphic: An illustrated version is planned for **Secretary of Dreams** (Volume Two) (Cemetery Dance), drawn by Maine artist Glenn Chadbourne.

Stu Redman

Stu Redman is one of the key characters in **The Stand**. At the beginning of the tale he is living in East Arnette, Texas, when a superflu virus hits and wipes out most of the world's population. He meets **Fran Goldsmith** and they travel to meet **Abagail Freemantle** in Boulder, where she taps Stu as one of those who must stand against **Randall Flagg**. Many male readers identify with Stu as the hero they hope they might be if required and many women simply adore the concept of a partner like him.

On the Screen: Gary Sinise is perfect as Stu Redman in *The Stand*.

Stud City

"Stud City" was one of King's earliest published stories, appearing in the University of Maine literary magazine *Ubris* for Fall, 1969. He heavily revised it to appear as a story written by Gordie Lachance in the 1982 **Different Seasons** novella, "**The Body**" (the same technique he applied to "**The Revenge of Lard Ass Hogan**").

In this tale 16-year-old Edward "Chico" May begins his journey to manhood. He makes love to his 16-year-old girlfriend, Jane, for the first time, and drives home to tell his father he intends to join the Marines. A classic confrontation between father and rebellious son results, and some of the forces that have brought Chico to this point are revealed.

This story is not at all in the classic King horror mold displayed in most of his early published stories, and is more like *The New Yorker* stories of his later career. When rewriting it for "**The Body**," the author made numerous changes. For instance, in the short story Chico's older brother Johnny had joined the Marines, but in the novella he had been killed when a runaway car hit him while he was changing a tire at the Oxford Plains Speedway. In other changes a controversial sexual encounter is deleted; Chico's natural mother Cathy is no longer mentioned; nor is her death in childbirth.

Copies of *Ubris* are almost impossible to find, although the story can be photocopied at the **Raymond H. Fogler Library** of the University of Maine in Orono. Those seeking an original copy should check online King booksellers but can expect a long wait and a hefty price tag if one appears for sale.

Suffer the Little Children

This short horror tale was first published in *Cavalier* magazine for February 1972 and is one of King's earliest commercially published stories. He heavily revised it for collection in **Nightmares and Dreamscapes**. *Cavalier* appears for sale online but buyers should note it contains graphic sexual content.

Emily Sidley is a respected but feared teacher. She knows what her students are doing even with her back turned, as she observes their reflections in her own thick glasses. One day, Robert, a student, seems to change into a monster and then return to human form. Emily must decide what action to take.

Movies: Two **Dollar Baby** short movies have been made from this tale — *Suffer the Little Children: The Bathroom Scene* (2005) and *Suffer the Little Children* (2006).

Genesis: King wrote of the tale, "I like it quite a lot — it feels a little like the Bradbury of the late forties and early fifties to me.... Put another way [it] is a ghastly sick-joke with no redeeming social merit whatever. I like that in a story."

Sukeena

Ellen Rimbauer's servant in *Rose Red*, Sukeena came to America with Ellen and her husband, John, when they returned from Africa. A strong-willed woman, fiercely loyal to Ellen, she poses great danger to Joyce Reardon and her team.

On the Screen: Tsidii Leloka plays Sukeena in both *Rose Red* and the prequel TV movie (which is not based on King's work), *The Diary of Ellen Rimbauer*.

Sullivan, John *see* John Sullivan

The Sun Dog

This novella is collected in *Four Past Midnight*. As a **Castle Rock** tale, it is linked to much of King's fiction, and many characters reappear here, including **Alan Pangborn**, Norris Ridgewick (*Lisey's Story*), Polly Chalmers and **Reginald "Pop" Merrill** (*Needful Things*).

Kevin Delevan is given a Sun 660 Polaroid camera for his fifteenth birthday. However, it seems to be faulty — no matter what Kevin takes a picture of the photo that comes out of the camera is of the same thing, a dog by a fence. On closer examination, Kevin notices there is a difference in each photo, as the dog seems to be getting closer and is preparing to attack.

Survivor Type

This short and rather nasty horror tale first appeared in an anthology, *Terrors* (Playboy Press, 1982), and is collected in **Skeleton Crew**. Originally, no one would publish the story and it sat unsold for five years.

Richard Pine had been an accomplished surgeon with a practice on Park Avenue but also had a dark side — he'd sold blank prescription pads and stolen drugs from the hospital — and eventually lost his medical license. He agrees to carry 2kg of drugs on a cruise liner but the ship sinks and he is stranded on a deserted island with little water and no food.

Genesis: "Survivor Type" came about when King was mulling cannibalism one day, "because that's the sort of thing guys like me sometimes think about ... anyway, I started to wonder if a person could eat himself." The author discussed it with a retired doctor as part of his research.

Stage: Adapted as part of *The Blood Brothers Present ... The Master of Horror* at the

Gene Frankel Theater in New York in 2008. The entire presentation also included adaptations of "**In the Deathroom**," "**Quitters, Inc.**" and vignettes from "Survivor Type" and "**Paranoid: A Chant.**"

Susannah Dean

Susannah Dean is the name taken by Odetta Susannah Holmes when she merged with another personality living deep in her psyche — Detta Walker. She was in a coma for three weeks after being hit on the head by a brick when she was five years old; when she was about 21 she lost both her legs when she was pushed in front of a train. Five years later **Roland Deschain** took her into his world as part of his "ka-tet." She is the de facto wife of **Eddie Dean** and a close friend of **Jake Chambers** and his pet, **Oy**.

She is first mentioned in *The Dark Tower I: The Gunslinger*, but first actually appears as a character in *The Dark Tower II: The Drawing of the Three*. She is a significant figure in the balance of **The Dark Tower** cycle, particularly in *The Dark Tower VI: The Song of Susannah*.

Swithen, John *see* John Swithen

Sword in the Darkness (Novel)

The manuscript of this unpublished novel is held in Box 1010 at the Special Collections Unit of the **Raymond H. Fogler Library** at the University of Maine, Orono. In 2006 King allowed the publication of Chapter 71 of the novel (see below) and that excerpt represents by far the best part of the manuscript. A criminal gang plans a race riot in the Midwestern city of Harding (probably the same city as features in *The Running Man*) as cover for a string of robberies they intend to commit. A complex series of personal conflicts (which melodramatically result in rape, suicide and murder) are portrayed in what is very obviously a young writer's early novel. It was rejected for publication a dozen or so times.

Genesis: King wrote the novel in his senior year at the University of Maine: "Back in my dorm room was my dirty little secret: the half-completed manuscript of a novel about a teenage gang's plan to start a race riot. They would use this for cover while ripping off two dozen loan-sharking operations and illegal drug-rings in the city of Harding, my fictional version of Detroit (I had never been within six hundred miles of Detroit, but I didn't let that stop me or even slow me down). This novel, *Sword in the Darkness*, seemed very tawdry to me when compared to what my fellow students were trying to achieve; which is why, I suppose, I never brought any of it to class for a critique. The fact that it was also better and somehow truer than all my poems about sexual yearning and post-adolescent angst only made things worse. The result was a four-month period in which I could write almost nothing at all."

Sword in the Darkness (Story)

In 2006 King allowed the publication of Chapter 71 from his unpublished novel *Sword in the Darkness* in *Stephen King: Uncollected, Unpublished* by Rocky Wood, et al. (Cemetery

Dance Publications). The book is currently out of print but appears from time to time for resale online.

This long excerpt from the novel is effectively a standalone horror tale, set in pre-war **Gates Falls, Maine**. In some of King's best early writing, **Edie Rowsmith** relates a dark incident from her past to a fellow teacher.

Tad Trenton

Tad is a little boy who believes there is a monster in his closet in *Cujo*. He is about four years old and living with his parents in **Castle Rock, Maine**, when he and his mother, Donna, travel to the Camber property to have her car serviced. No one is there and the car breaks down, leaving them trapped and at the mercy of a rabid St. Bernard, **Cujo**.

Trivia: King updates Tad's story in **Cujo** (**Unproduced Screenplay**).

On the Screen: Danny Pintauro plays Tad in the movie.

The Tale of Gray Dick

"The Tale of Gray Dick" is a version of the chapter of the same name in *The Dark Tower V: Wolves of the Calla*, published in November 2003. The stand-alone short story was first published in a magazine, *Timothy McSweeney's Quarterly Concern*, on 25 February 2003, and in an anthology, *McSweeney's Mammoth Treasury of Thrilling Tales*, published by Vintage Books, the following month.

There are some variations between this publication and the chapter in the full-length novel, the changes clearly made to avoid giving away plotlines in the novel ahead of its publication.

Copies of the magazine and book can be purchased on the secondary market.

The Talisman

This is King's first novel written in collaboration with another writer, Peter Straub. Many fans have a deep affection for this work and many of its characters, particularly **Jack Sawyer** and **Wolf**. *Black House* is the sequel to *The Talisman*. On the likelihood of a third book in this series, Straub had this to say: "Given the tendency of fantasy novels to parcel themselves out in units of three, it would be entirely reasonable to propose a third part to the *Talisman* series. After all, the first book is set more or less equally in this world and the Territories; the present book takes place mainly in this world; and the third could be set mostly in the Territories. There's a nice balance in that structure."

One of King's more important novels, it has a magical flow created by having the two authors write different parts of the novel as it continues. With a significant cast of fully created characters, this is a quest tale, as is **The Dark Tower cycle**.

Jack Sawyer is 12 years old when his mother, star of many B-grade movies, is stricken with cancer. His father is long dead. Jack makes a friend in retired blues musician Speedy Parker, who teaches him how to "flip" between our world and an alternate reality, The Territories, and tells him about the Talisman that can save his mother's life. Jack begins an epic journey to find the Talisman. He faces awful dangers in both worlds and begins to realize his quest may have greater importance than even his desire to save his mother.

Movie: A **Dollar Baby**, *Stephen King's The Talisman* was released on YouTube in 2008.

Comic: Del Rey began publishing a comic book adaptation from 2010. The script is by Robin Furth (former research assistant for King, who also wrote **The Dark Tower Graphic Novel** adaptations for Marvel). The first arc of six comics is subtitled "The Road of Trials" (also collected as a graphic novel); the second arc is subtitled "A Collision of Worlds."

Trivia: The book is dedicated to the authors' mothers, Ruth King (see **King, Ruth**) and Elvena Straub.

Ted Brautigan

Ted Brautigan is a much-loved character, who first appeared in "Low Men in Yellow Coats" as **Bobby Garfield**'s friend and mentor. Readers receive updates on Ted's life after Bobby in "**Heavenly Shades of Night Are Falling**," **Black House** and **The Dark Tower VII: The Dark Tower**.

Ted was in his sixties when he lived near the Garfields. A telepath, he had drifted around the U.S. until he came to the attention of **The Crimson King** and his minions, who forced him to work as a "Breaker," trying to bring down **The Dark Tower**. Brautigan is crucial to **The Dark Tower cycle**.

On the Screen: Academy Award winner Anthony Hopkins plays Ted in "Hearts in Atlantis."

The Ten O'clock People

This short horror story is collected in **Nightmares and Dreamscapes**. Brandon Pearson gives up smoking but goes back to the habit and, while outside his office building on a cigarette break, sees a hideous monster wearing a suit. Before he can scream, Duke Rhinemann stops him and explains he has seen a real creature. For some reason they can only be seen by people who had been smokers and given up, but had then taken it up again on a lesser scale. A group has been formed to secretly fight the "bat people."

Genesis: King noted the "odd pockets of sociological behavior" that are working smokers, forced out of their buildings and onto the streets to get their fix.

The Territories

This is a world parallel to our own. Residents of each can sometimes "flip" between the worlds and often have a "twinner" in the opposite world. The population is quite small. It is apparently smaller than our world, for instance when Jack Sawyer travels 150 feet in the Territories it equates to one half mile in our world. The Territories is an agrarian monarchy which uses magic instead of science. It is a key location in **The Talisman** and is important in **Black House**, from which readers know they are linked to **Roland Deschain**'s **Mid-World**.

Thad Beaumont

Thad Beaumont is the protagonist of **The Dark Half** and lives in both **Castle Rock** and Ludlow, Maine.

In 1960 Dr. Hugh Pritchard removes a growth in eleven-year-old Thad's brain. It contains an eye, part of a nostril, three fingernails and two teeth (one with a cavity). As an adult Thad is a successful writer, both in his own name and using the pseudonym **George Stark**. After one bestseller, he decides to "bury" George Stark in a media performance and reveal the pen name to the public. Stark is "buried" but soon the gravesite has been dug up and tracks lead away. Thad realizes he, his wife and children are at mortal risk.

King updates Beaumont's life in *Needful Things* and *Bag of Bones*.

On the Screen: Timothy Hutton plays both Beaumont and Stark in the 1992 movie.

That Feeling, You Can Only Say What It Is in French

This mesmerizing story first appeared in *The New Yorker* magazine editions of 22 and 29 June 1998. It is collected in *Everything's Eventual*.

Carol and Bill Shelton have been married for 25 years and are flying to Florida for a second honeymoon. On the trip Carol begins to sense things are repeating themselves. She remembers what she is about to see but each time events are slightly different.

Genesis: King says the story is about Hell, "a version of it where you are condemned to do the same thing over and over again... My idea is that [Hell] might be repetition." A note on an original typescript reads: "Written ... very much under the influence of Don De Lillo's 'Underworld.'"

They're Creeping Up on You

This nifty horror tale is collected in the graphic novel *Creepshow*. Reclusive millionaire Upson Pratt is a fanatic about cleanliness and hates cockroaches most of all, spending any amount of money to exterminate them. A blackout offers his enemy a chance to get their own back.

Movie: *Creepshow* (1982), in the "They're Creeping Up on You" segment, starring E.G. Marshall.

Graphic Novel: "They're Creeping Up on You" segment of *Creepshow* (New American Library, 1982).

The Thing at the Bottom of the Well

This piece of juvenilia appears in *People, Places and Things* along with six other King tales, and is the least derivative of this group of stories.

Oglethorpe Crater, a nasty little child readers can easily dislike (a nice touch by the young King), enjoys hurting people and animals. From tying a rope across the stairs to trip a servant to poking pins into his pet dog, nothing is beyond his wretched ways. One day he hears a voice in a well, inviting him in. He goes down and is found a month later, tortured and dead.

For readers so inclined, the creature in the well presents as an early prototype of **Pennywise**, the evil from *It*.

The Things They Left Behind

This beautiful and mystic tale was originally published in the anthology *Transgressions* (Forge Books, 2005) and is collected in *Just After Sunset*. Anyone who loves America and anyone who loves beautifully written fiction must read this story.

Scott Staley recalls the first time the "things I want to tell you about — the ones they left behind" showed up in his New York apartment, "not quite a year after a piece of the sky fell down and everything changed for all of us." These things evince raw emotional power and appear in his apartment without explanation. Their very impossibility causes Staley to question his sanity. Each of the items belonged to one of Staley's dead co-workers from an insurance company in the Twin Towers. And why was Staley was not at his desk that fateful day?

Genesis: This is clearly King's elegy for those killed in the September 11, 2001, attacks on the United States. It is also a story about the power of memory. Scott Staley's character grew up in southern Maine: "My father put an egg in his shoe and beat it when I was two and my sister four." Staley's mother died of cancer in middle age. If we delete sister and add brother we have King's own backstory.

Thinner

This was the last **Richard Bachman** novel to be published prior to the revelation that Bachman is, in fact, Stephen King, and the only Bachman novel published in hardback prior to that revelation. As soon as the connection to King was made sales soared (28,000 as Bachman; 280,000 as King) and the book reached number 1 on the *New York Times* hardcover and paperback bestseller lists. A particularly insightful study in psychology and revenge, the book was originally to be titled *Gypsy Pie*.

Grossly overweight lawyer **Billy Halleck** knocks down and kills an old gypsy woman while driving but is cleared by contacts in the legal community. As he leaves court an elderly gypsy man touches him and mutters one word — "thinner." From that day on, Halleck starts to lose weight at a startling rate. At first he's happy, but as time passed he realizes the weight loss is not going to stop. Convinced he's under a curse, he must track the gypsies down. Reversing the curse may bring its own risks.

In links to King's other fiction, Richard Ginelli appears to be the same character as in **The Plant** and, in an alternate reality, **The Dark Tower: The Drawing of the Three**.

According to the *Castle Rock* newsletter for April 1985, the man whose photograph appears on the dust jacket of **Thinner** as "Richard Bachman" is in fact Richard Manuel, a real estate broker from St. Paul, Minnesota.

Genesis: On a planned weight loss program of his own, the author began to wonder what would happen if someone trying lose weight found they couldn't stop.

Movie: *Thinner* (1996). A very ordinary movie, in which King appears in a cameo as Dr. Bangor. Available on DVD.

Also known as *Stephen King's Thinner*.

Throttle

"Throttle" is the first published collaboration between King and his author son, **Joe Hill**. So far it has only appeared in print in *He Is Legend: An Anthology Celebrating Richard Matheson*, edited by Christopher Conlon (Gauntlet Publications, 2009).

It also appears on the audio book *Road Rage* (Harper Audio), which includes both "Throttle" and the story which inspired it, "Duel." It is unclear when, or if, the short story will be included in either a Stephen King or Joe Hill collection.

In the tale an apparently rogue trucker begins to run down members of a motorcycle gang who are returning from an aborted robbery that had turned into "a slaughterhouse." Vince is the leader and finds himself desperately trying to save his son from the implacable attack. Another inherently moral tale, this is one of the better short fiction efforts by both King and Hill.

Genesis: The story is inspired by Richard Matheson's short story "Duel" (filmed by Stephen Spielberg early in his career to great acclaim). The anthology for which it was written includes many fine stories riffing Matheson's outstanding canon, including "I Am Legend Too" by Mick Garris, director of many King films and TV adaptations.

Tidwell, Sara *see* Sara Tidwell

Todd Bowden

Thirteen-year-old Todd is one of two major characters in the novella "**Apt Pupil**." He discovers the terrible past of his neighbor **Arthur Denker** and uses it to blackmail him.

On the Screen: Brad Renfro appears a Todd in the 1998 film. Rick Schroder played the role in an earlier unreleased film version.

Todd, Ophelia *see* Ophelia Todd

Tom Cullen

Slightly retarded Tom Cullen is living in May, Oklahoma, when the superflu strikes in *The Stand*. A big, blond man of about 45, **Nick Andros** finds him and takes him under his care as they travel to the Boulder Free Zone, where he will be asked to undertake a very important task. Tom is a much loved character and something of a counterpoint to **Donald Merwin Elbert** ("The Trashcan Man").

On the Screen: Bill Fagerbakke is convincing as Tom in *Stephen King's The Stand*.

Tommy

This poem is a love letter to King's own past. In this accessible piece of some beauty and nostalgia, the narrator reminisces over the events surrounding the funeral of a hippie friend, Tommy. Other hippies also died in those years around 1969, and forty years later they are "asleep under the earth." It was published in *Playboy* magazine for March 2010 and is, as yet, uncollected. Copies of the magazine are easily secured online.

Genesis: Clearly inspired by King's memories of his time at the University of Maine during the "flower power" and anti–Vietnam War protest era. Indeed, King once lived at 110 North Main Street in Orono, the same address as the apartment the narrator and his friends repair to after Tommy's funeral and reception. It was there King began writing **The Dark Tower cycle**. **Johnny Smith** lived at the same address (but in Cleaves Mills, Maine) in *The Dead Zone*.

The Tommyknockers

The schizophrenic nature of this long science fiction novel has left it with a poor reputation. With the distance of time it is a better novel than first thought, but still not one of King's best. In some ways it now feels like a trial run for *Needful Things*.

Bobbi Anderson discovers processed metal buried in the woods near her home in Haven, Maine. She begins to dig it out and, as she does, is compelled to construct strange devices. As more and more of the metal is exposed, the townspeople also begin to construct strange inventions, many of which are harmful. **Jim Gardener**, an alcoholic and Anderson's lover, helps her dig and is immune to the strange side effects, possibly because of the metal plate in his head from a childhood accident. The end-game approaches as the townspeople become welded to a greater force and the authorities seem powerless to intervene.

As a Maine novel, it is linked with much of King's fiction through locations such as **Derry** and **Juniper Hill Asylum**, entities such as **The Shop** (*Firestarter*), books (one of Bobbi Anderson's novels is mentioned in *The Stand*), and characters (**Pennywise** is mentioned, along with **Greg Stillson** from *The Dead Zone*). King's story "**The Revelations of 'Becka Paulson**" was significantly revised and included as part of the storyline of this novel.

Genesis: King says the first verse of a ditty about Tommyknockers is "common enough for my wife and myself to have heard it as children, although we were raised in different towns, different faiths, and came from different descendants—hers primarily French, mine Scots-Irish." He also incorporated some of the thoughts of Stephen Jay Gould, that famed historian of science, about "dumb evolution." He says the belief expressed underneath the story is that technology is a "blown horse" (the dangers of rampant technology feature in many King tales).

Television: *The Tommyknockers* (1993). This mini-series was largely filmed in New Zealand, about as far from Maine as it is possible to travel. Despite prominent actors, including Jimmy Smits (playing Jim Gardener) and Marg Helgenberger (Bobbi Anderson), this is a poor adaptation and difficult to watch. Available on DVD. Also known as *Stephen King's The Tommyknockers*.

Torrance, Danny *see* Danny Torrance

Torrance, Jack *see* Jack Torrance

Tozier, Richard "Richie" *see* Richard "Richie" Tozier

Trenton, Tad *see* Tad Trenton

Trisha McFarland

In *The Girl Who Loved Tom Gordon*, Patricia "Trisha" McFarland becomes lost while trekking part of the Appalachian Trail with her mother and brother. Disoriented, the nine-year-old walks deep into the uninhabited Maine woods. She has very little food and each night listens to her Sony Walkman in hopes that her hero, Tom Gordon, will be pitching in a broadcast Boston Red Sox game. As she grows delirious, "Tom Gordon" becomes her traveling companion, helping her overcome her fears. Then she realizes she is being followed — by "The God of the Lost."

Trucks

This science fiction tale originally appeared in *Cavalier* magazine for June 1973 and is collected in **Night Shift**.

King took the basic premise of the story to create the movie **Maximum Overdrive**.

A small group of people are trapped at Conant's Truck Stop and Diner after vehicles suddenly become sentient. Escape is not an option, as the trucks simply run down anyone who tries to leave.

Genesis: It is thought King was partly inspired by a truck stop just off the interstate in Bangor, Maine — Dysart's Truck Stop and Restaurant. King fans often stop there for a meal.

Umney's Last Case

This detective and science fiction short story is collected in **Nightmares and Dreamscapes**, and King once claimed it's the story he likes best from the entire collection.

Detective Clyde Umney, who runs a successful practice in 1930s Los Angeles, notices some very unusual things happening around him. His blind paperboy's mother wins the lottery in Tijuana. Shops are closed without notice and the elevator operator suddenly retires. His finely tuned nose says something major is out of kilter. One day he meets his landlord, Samuel Landry, who knows far too much about Umney and appears to be his almost identical twin, albeit they are 10 or 15 years different in age. Umney is about to find himself in a new and unwanted career.

Genesis: King describes "Umney's Last Case" as an ambitious pastiche: "I have loved Raymond Chandler and Ross Macdonald passionately since I discovered them in college ... and I think it is the language of these novels which so fired my imagination; it opened a whole new way of seeing, one that appealed fiercely to the heart and mind of the lonely young man I was at that time."

Television: "Umney's Last Case" (2006). A series episode from *Nightmares and Dreamscapes: From the Stories of Stephen King*, it is available on DVD. William H. Macy plays Sam Landry/Clyde Umney.

Movie: A **Dollar Baby** of the same name was produced in 2006.

Uncle Otto's Truck

This amusing and creepy short story originally appeared in the October 1983 edition of *Yankee* magazine. King substantially rewrote that version for collection in **Skeleton Crew**. The original magazine is difficult to find but does appear for sale online from time to time. A **Castle Rock** story, it is linked to other King fiction — **Derry** and **Harlow** are also mentioned.

After Otto Schenck arranges for rival George McCutcheon to be deliberately crushed under his derelict truck, the murderer becomes fixated on the vehicle, abandoned in a nearby field. He even insists it is not only moving of its own accord but actually coming to kill him.

Genesis: King has said the story is based on a real house and a real truck.

Graphic: A graphic novel version of the tale appeared in *Secretary of Dreams* (Volume One) (Cemetery Dance, 2006), brilliantly illustrated by Maine artist Glenn Chadbourne.

Under the Dome

One of King's longest novels, *Under the Dome* also represented King's return to the fictional ground of western Maine when it appeared in 2009.

The setting, Chester's Mill, which neighbors **Castle Rock**, may as well be Lisbon Falls, where King attended high school and readers of the novel get to enjoy a constant stream of references to such familiar locations as **Harlow**, the TR-90 and **Derry**.

The novel was King's third attempt at this tale — he lost the original manuscript in 1978 and failed to make the second attempt ("**The Cannibals**," unpublished under that title) work to his satisfaction in 1981. However, "The Cannibals" is a very different tale, set in an apartment building as compared to this novel, the setting of which is an entire town.

Without warning an invisible dome (it's not actually a "dome," as the borders follow the town line exactly) descends on Chester's Mill, separating it from America and civilization, and setting off a series of human interplays that may destroy the town and all those unlucky enough to have been trapped there. Indeed, it is the choices the characters make under pressure, and the way they respond to others, that present the true horror. The source of the Dome, although it is part of the tale, is largely irrelevant. The total isolation it imposes — which releases the worst impulses of the town megalomaniac, his psychotic son, and their all too willing followers — is not.

Here King manipulates a huge cast of characters, ranging from the short-order cook living with his Iraq-tour-of-duty-guilt, through the local newspaper editor, to a host of dour Yankees — a near archetype the author always portrays realistically. The antagonist, used car lot owner and petty politician Big Jim Rennie, is crooked, a manipulative and egomaniac Christian. A group of locals must stand against his not-so-petty dictatorship, but find themselves caught in a series of moral dilemmas ordinary enough to be totally believable, yet dangerous enough to build the reader's commitment to their cause.

Most reminiscent of **Needful Things** and "**The Mist**," this tale demonstrates how thin the veneer of civilization can be. Readers are not disappointed in this tale by the author's uncanny ability to put them in the mindset of young teenagers (similar to "**The Body**" or *It*) and canine characters (**The Dark Tower**, *Cujo*).

Genesis: See "The Cannibals." King says he felt not delivering on "The Cannibals" was like a baseball player missing a really fat pitch, but that during a plane trip to Australia in 2009 the inspiration to revisit the concept returned: "The image that caught my mind was the idea of these people giving a press conference to the outside world ... and from what you see there's nothing between them and the cameras until somebody reaches out and knocks on, you know, thin air." He also said the environment was a key factor: "I saw it as a chance to write about the serious ecological problems that we face in the world today ... the fact is we all live under the dome. We have this little blue world we've all seen from outer space, and it appears that's all there is."

Underwood, Larry *see* Larry Underwood

Untitled (The Huffman Story)

This partial untitled manuscript is held in Box 2702 in King's papers at the **Raymond H. Fogler Library** of the University of Maine in Orono, and the public may read it. The tone and events are hauntingly reminiscent of the **Castle Rock** murders in the classic *The Dead Zone,* and it may that this caused King to abandon the story, or possibly that this story was a first attempt at a section of that novel. Well laid out, it is just reaching an interesting turning point when the manuscript ends. It is a typical King tale in which the readers become deeply engrossed in the people, history and ambience (good and bad) of small town Maine within a few short pages. The characters leap off the page and the town itself seems fully realized as the storyline unfolds.

The story opens as five-year-old Tansy Dolgun arrives at her mother's shop in Huffman, Maine (hence the tale is known in the King community as "The Huffman Story"). In a nearby park a man offers candy to another five-year-old, Frances Tho. After Frances is reported missing, a Huffman police officer finds her body in the park's pond. The tale quickly moves into the back-story of Huffman and its inhabitants as, in the way of King small towns, blame is laid and fear spreads even faster than gossip.

Fans of Castle Rock will be interested to know that Huffman is apparently in the same county as that town, which is mentioned.

Untitled (She Has Gone to Sleep While...)

This poem was first published in a magazine, *Contraband,* No. 1, for 31 October 1971 (Halloween), along with "**Woman with Child.**" The 28-line poem has never been republished. The easiest way for readers to access it is to acquire a photocopy at the **Raymond H. Fogler Library** of the University of Maine at Orono. King did not allow this poem to be reprinted along with six other poems from the 1960s and 1970s in *The Devil's Wine.*

The narrator drives while a female, presumably his wife, sleeps. He thinks about what his life will become as he grows older. In one interesting point the narrator thinks of his inner thoughts as "the Library of Me." This could just as easily describe the mind of Gary Jones in *Dreamcatcher.*

Untitled Screenplay (Radio Station)

This untitled partial screenplay is held in Box 1011 at the **Raymond H. Fogler Library** at the University of Maine, Orono. It was never produced but may be read at the library.

It was apparently written in the late 1970s; in a 1979 interview King talks about the screenplay, saying he is working on it "now, off and on."

In the story a rural radio station in western Maine is to be converted from manned to automated operation, with changeover at midnight. That night the owner, Roger Lathrop confronts the last DJ on shift, a drunken Bob Randall, who later returns to his apartment and hangs himself. The script ends after a funeral scene.

Another of the DJs, Chester Robichaud, is reminiscent of Henry Leyden, the DJ of many characters in *Black House.*

UR

UR was first published on 12 February 2009 as a download for Amazon's Kindle 2 e-reader. While it has yet to see a print publication, the audio book was released in February 2010. It can be safely assumed the story will see a mass-market print version at some point, although it was not included in King's 2010 collection, **Full Dark, No Stars**, possibly due to contractual obligations with Amazon.

The tale is critically important to *The Dark Tower* reality. In it, college English instructor Wesley Smith receives a strange pink Kindle that gives him access to books and newspapers in over a million other realities. When he makes the mistake of accessing a future edition of his local newspaper a series of events is put into play that may risk the entire universe.

Genesis: King's agent, Ralph Vicinanza, had originally approached King to write a story for e-book release to "create some excitement" (as King's **Riding the Bullet** had done in 2000) at a time when the publishing industry was in the doldrums. As the story deal was with Amazon, it was obvious that it be written with the Kindle as a feature.

Uris, Stanley *see* Stanley Uris

Verrill, Jordy *see* Jordy Verrill

A Very Tight Place

This gross but grimly amusing story first appeared in *McSweeney's* magazine (No. 27 for 28 May 2008) and is collected in **Just After Sunset**.

In the novella, Curtis Johnson and Tim Grunwald are involved in an increasingly bitter legal dispute. Grunwald lures Johnson to an isolated construction site, forces him into a portable toilet and tips it over, leaving a trapped Johnson to die in the heat of a Florida day. Johnson is in a very tight place, indeed.

Genesis: King says he has never used a portable toilet without thinking of Edgar Allan Poe's short story "The Premature Burial" and wondering what would happen if he became trapped in one. He says, "I cannot close without telling you what childish fun this tale was. I even grossed myself out."

The Village Vomit

Sometime in the school year of 1963–64, King edited a satirical take-off of the high school newspaper he later edited, *The Drum* (two of his stories from that newspaper, "**Code Name: Mousetrap**" and "**The 43rd Dream**" came to light more than three decades later). The satire was titled *The Village Vomit* and King tells its sordid story in section 19 of the "C.V." part of **On Writing**: "One night — sick to death of Class Reports, Cheerleading Updates, and some lamebrain's efforts to write a school poem — I created a satiric high school newspaper of my own when I should have been captioning photographs for *The Drum*. What resulted was a four-sheet which I called *The Village Vomit*. The boxed motto in the upper lefthand corner was not "All the News That's Fit to Print" but "All the Shit

That Will Stick." That piece of dimwit humor got me into the only real trouble of my high school career."

Taking the paper to school for his friends to "bust a collective gut" over, King was caught when a copy was confiscated by one of the teachers lampooned in the paper, on which King had, "either out of over-weening pride or almost unbelievable naiveté, put my name as Editor in Chief & Grand High Poobah, and at the close of school I was for the second time in my student career summoned to the office on account of something I had written." One teacher took enormous offense at her description and demanded King be disciplined. "In the end, Miss Margitan settled for a formal apology and two weeks of detention for the bad boy who had dared call her Maggot in print. If it makes any difference, my apology was heartfelt. Miss Margitan really had been hurt by what I wrote, and that much I could understand. I doubt that she hated me — she was probably too busy — but she was the National Honor Society advisor at LHS, and when my name showed up on the candidate list two years later, she vetoed me. The Honor Society did not need boys "of his type," she said. I have come to believe she was right. A boy who once wiped his ass with poison ivy probably doesn't belong in a smart people's club. I haven't trucked much with satire since then." No known copies of *The Village Vomit* exist.

Walter

An important character in **The Dark Tower cycle**, he is an enemy of **Roland Deschain**. He is also known as **The Man in Black**.

The Wedding Gig

This crime caper was originally published in *Ellery Queen's Mystery Magazine* in December 1980 and reprinted in the same magazine for June 2004. King revised the short story for collection *Skeleton Crew*. Copies of the original magazine appear for sale online.

Small time hood Mike Scollay hires a jazz band to play at his sister's wedding. Maureen weighs 300 pounds and her new husband, Rico Romano, is short and weighs only 90 pounds. Scollay knows people are laughing at the grossly mismatched pair but ignores them until a stranger deliberately insults the bride.

Genesis: King says, "It isn't the sort of tale I ordinarily tell, and maybe that's why I like it so much."

Weeds

"Weeds" was originally published in *Cavalier* (a men's magazine) for May 1976 and reprinted in *Nugget* (another men's magazine) for April 1979. It is a far better story than some of the pulp fiction stories that appear in **Night Shift**, published in 1978, but it has never been collected in text form.

In the short story a meteor falls on **Jordy Verrill**'s farm near Cleaves Mills, New Hampshire. As it has set off a grass fire, poor, simple Jordy dowses the meteor with water, causing it to split and infect him with an alien substance. The tale revolves around his attempt to deal with the infestation.

The tale is part of an aborted novel, but the author says, "Once the weeds started to grow beyond that closed world and toward the town, I couldn't find any more to say."

It was adapted for both the film and graphic novel *Creepshow* (1982) as "**The Lonesome Death of Jordy Verrill**," with the farm in those versions located near **Castle Rock, Maine.**

Original copies of the magazines are difficult to secure, even via Internet sellers.

Movie: *Creepshow* (1982), in "The Lonesome Death of Jordy Verrill" segment, starring Stephen King as the title character.

Graphic Novel: "The Lonesome Death of Jordy Verrill" segment of *Creepshow* (New American Library, 1982).

Wharton, William *see* William Wharton

Wheaton, Annie *see* Annie Wheaton

White, Carrie *see* Carrie White

White, Margaret *see* Margaret White

Why We're in Vietnam

This elegiac tale is a later and revised version of "**The New Lieutenant's Rap**" and is collected in ***Hearts in Atlantis***. This is an important story, reflecting as it does much of the angst at the heart of America's Vietnam experience. The novella can be read stand-alone but is also part of the broader storyline of the collection. Further, there is a very important **Dark Tower cycle** connection.

John Sullivan is badly wounded in Vietnam and, even though he begs to die, eventually makes an almost complete recovery. By 1999 his Sullivan Chevrolet is a highly successful business. However, he's never been able shake the image of an old woman he thought of as "mamasan," murdered during the war by another soldier. She appears to him at various times throughout his post-war life, yet he sees nothing abnormal in this. On his way to another vet's funeral, he remembers the war, those he fought with and his life afterward. At the funeral Sullivan sits with yet another vet, Dieffenbaker, and discusses how their lives have turned out. On his way home he starts to see very strange things.

Wilkes, Annie *see* Annie Wilkes

Willa

This passionate ghost story first appeared in *Playboy* magazine for December 2006 and is collected in ***Just After Sunset***.

A group of travelers are left at an isolated railway station after their train derails. David Sanderson realizes his fiancée, Willa Stuart, has headed into the nearby town on foot, without him. He follows her into a crowded live music bar where she tries to tell him something he doesn't want to hear.

Genesis: King says, "I hold to the main idea [of organized religion], which is that we survive death in some fashion or other. What that survival might be like, though ... my best guess is we might be confused, and not very willing to accept our new state. My best hope is that love survives death."

William Wharton

William Wharton is an important character in **The Green Mile**. Thoroughly unlikable, he puts **John Coffey** at risk and will end Percy Wetmore's career as a death row guard. He'd been in trouble with the law most of his life before finally being arrested for killing three people and a police officer during a holdup. He likes to be known as "Wild Bill" or "Billy the Kid."

On the Screen: Sam Rockwell is perfect as Wild Bill in the 1999 film.

Wimsey

"Wimsey" is a story fragment from the Lord Peter Wimsey novel King worked on in late 1977. Although it has never been published, copies of this fourteen-page fragment circulate in the King community.

The attempted novel was the result of both the King family's abortive move to England and a discussion between the author and his editor of the time, Bill Thompson. That discussion revolved around the writing of a novel using Wimsey, a fictional detective created by Dorothy L. Sayers.

The King family moved to England in the fall of 1977. King said he wanted to write a book "with an English setting." His U.S. paperback publisher issued a press release stating the author had moved to England to write "a novel even more bloodcurdling than the previous ones." Of course, this does not sound much like a genteel British detective novel.

Once in England, King did not find the inspiration required for an English novel, perhaps explaining the fragmentary nature of Wimsey, but he did begin **Cujo** during the three months the family remained there. One short story based in England did result from the trip—"**Crouch End**."

In what is available of this aborted novel, Lord Peter Wimsey and his servant Bunter are on their way by car to a party at Sir Patrick Wayne's estate. After they cross "an alarmingly rickety plank bridge which spanned a swollen stream," Wimsey calls for a toilet stop and finds the bridge's supports have been cut almost through. And so the mystery begins.

The author adopts a style that is indeed very English in tone, including a rather dry exchange between Bunter and the title character. During an interview for *The Waldenbook Report* in late 1997, King listed Wimsey's creator, Dorothy L. Sayers, as one of the authors he most admired. Sayers' character was immensely popular in the 1920s and 1930s and the books are still read avidly today.

Stephen King has presented "constant readers" with a limited but quality selection of other crime and detective stories, including "**The Fifth Quarter**," "**Man with a Belly**," "**The Wedding Gig**," "**The Doctor's Case**," "**Umney's Last Case**" and **The Colorado Kid**.

Wolf

A secondary character in **The Talisman**, this 6' 5" tall werewolf is **Jack Sawyer**'s friend as they are both held prisoner at the Sunlight Gardener Scripture Home for Wayward Boys. Wolf is one of the most loved minor characters in King's fiction.

The Woman in the Room

This very important short story is collected in **Night Shift**. John and Kevin's mother is in hospital dying of cancer and without hope. Although doctors recommend a massively invasive operation, John ponders another alternative.

Genesis: The story is autobiographical in tone, stemming from the death of King's own mother from cancer. The direct connection with the story is made very clear in King's discussion of the real events in **On Writing**.

Trivia: There were two previous titles for the story in draft — "The Last of Her" and "Time in a Glass That Ran."

Movie: Stephen King's The Woman in the Room (1983). This outstanding **Dollar Baby** was written and directed by Frank Darabont, some years before his later and more famous efforts with *The Shawshank Redemption* and **The Green Mile**. This is the only Dollar Baby commercially available — on video (not DVD) — as part of *Stephen's King's Night Shift Collection*, also known as *Stephen's King's Nightshift Collection Volume One: The Woman in the Room*.

Movie: La Femme Dans La Chambre (2005). This is a thirteen minute French short film. Frank Darabont holds the commercial rights to this tale and granted them in this case in a manner effectively replicating King's Dollar Baby system.

Woman with Child

This poem was first published in a magazine, *Contraband*, No. 1, for 31 October 1971 (Halloween), along with "**Untitled (She Has Gone to Sleep While...)**." The 17-line poem has never been republished. The easiest way for readers to access it is to acquire a photocopy at the **Raymond H. Fogler Library** of the University of Maine at Orono. King did not permit this poem to be reprinted along with six others from the 1960s and 1970s in *The Devil's Wine*.

In it a pregnant woman gets out of the bath and feels her unborn child moving. It is without horror or undertones, simply a mainstream reflection of a moment in time in a pregnant woman's daily life.

The Word Processor

Originally published in *Playboy* magazine for January 1983 as "The Word Processor," King substantially revised and retitled this story as "**Word Processor of the Gods**" for collection in **Skeleton Crew**.

Word Processor of the Gods

This is a revised and retitled version of "The Word Processor," which was published in the January 1983 issue of *Playboy* magazine. The revision "Word Processor of the Gods" appeared in **Skeleton Crew**.

Richard Hagstrom's wife is a fat, nasty woman who spends her time running him down, and his son is far from ideal. Roger, his older brother, is a drunk and a wife beater, but *his* wife and son are close to Richard's image of the perfect family members. After a family tragedy Richard is presented with the opportunity to change his world.

Television: "The Word Processor of the Gods" (1984). A series episode of *Tales from the Darkside*, it is available on DVD on *Tales from the Darkside: The First Season*.

You Know They Got a Hell of a Band

Originally published in an anthology, *Shock Rock* (Pocket Books, 1992), King substantially rewrote this darkly humorous tale, which is collected in **Nightmares and Dreamscapes**. One of King's most entertaining short stories it is not to be missed.

On a driving holiday, Mary and Clark Willingham take a diversion to see the countryside and get lost. Driving miles on poor quality back roads, they come upon the quaint town of Rock and Roll Heaven, Oregon.

Genesis: This short story is clearly inspired by the Righteous Brothers song "Rock and Roll Heaven" (the name of the town in Oregon that features in the tale). King says it's part of a sub-genre — the "peculiar little town story" that he also visited in **Children of the Corn** and "**Rainy Season**."

Television: "You Know They Got a Hell of a Band" (2006). An excellent episode from *Nightmares and Dreamscapes: From the Stories of Stephen King*, it is well worth watching. Available on DVD.

Zimmer, Alfie *see* Alfie Zimmer

Stephen King Bibliography

This bibliography is limited to King's fiction, poetry and book length non-fiction. The works are listed in order of publication.

Books

Carrie. Garden City, NY: Doubleday, 1974.

'Salem's Lot. Garden City, NY: Doubleday, 1975.

The Shining. Garden City, NY: Doubleday, 1977.

The Stand. Garden City, NY: Doubleday, 1978.

Night Shift. Garden City, NY: Doubleday, 1978.

The Dead Zone. New York: Viking Press, 1979.

The Long Walk. New York: Signet, 1979.

Firestarter. New York: Viking, 1980.

Roadwork. New York: Signet, 1981.

Danse Macabre. New York: Everest House, 1981.

Cujo. New York: Viking, 1981.

The Running Man. New York: Signet, 1982.

Creepshow. New York: Plume, 1982.

Different Seasons. New York: Viking, 1982.

The Dark Tower: The Gunslinger. West Kingston, RI: Donald M. Grant, 1982.

Christine. New York: Viking, 1983.

Cycle of the Werewolf. Westland, MI: Land of Enchantment, 1983.

Pet Sematary. Garden City, NY: Doubleday, 1983.

The Eyes of the Dragon. Bangor, ME: Philtrum, 1984.

The Talisman, with Peter Straub. New York: Viking, G.P. Putnam's Sons, 1984.

Thinner. New York: New American Library, 1984.

Skeleton Crew. New York: G.P. Putnam's Sons, 1985.

Silver Bullet. New York: Signet Book, 1985.

The Bachman Books. New York: New American Library, 1985.

It. London, England: Hodder and Stoughton, 1986.

The Dark Tower II: The Drawing of the Three. West Kingston, RI: Donald M. Grant, 1987.

Misery. New York: Viking, 1987.

The Tommyknockers. New York: G.P. Putnam's Sons, 1987.

Nightmares in the Sky. New York: Viking Studio Books, 1988.

My Pretty Pony. New York: Library Fellows of the Whitney Museum, Whitney Museum of Art, Artists and Writers Series, 1988.

Dolan's Cadillac. Northridge, CA: Lord John Press, 1989.

The Dark Half. New York: Viking, 1989.

The Stand: The Complete and Uncut Edition. New York: Doubleday, 1990.

Four Past Midnight. New York: Viking, 1990.

The Dark Tower III: The Waste Lands. Hampton Falls, NH: Donald M. Grant, 1991.

Needful Things. New York: Viking, 1991.

Gerald's Game. New York: Viking, 1992.

Dolores Claiborne. New York: Viking, 1993.

Nightmares and Dreamscapes. New York: Viking, 1993.

Insomnia. New York: Viking, 1994.

Rose Madder. New York: Viking, 1995.

The Green Mile Part 1: The Two Dead Girls. New York: Signet, March 1996.

The Green Mile Part 2: The Mouse on the Mile. New York: Signet, April 1996.

The Green Mile Part 3: Coffey's Hands. New York: Signet, May 1996.

The Green Mile Part 4: The Bad Death of Eduard Delacroix. New York: A Signet Book, June 1996.

The Green Mile Part 5: Night Journey. New York: Signet, July 1996.

The Green Mile Part 6: Coffey on the Mile. New York: Signet, August 1996.

Desperation. New York: Viking, 1996.

The Regulators. New York: Dutton, 1996.

The Dark Tower IV: Wizard and Glass. Hampton Falls, NH: Donald M. Grant, 1997.

The Green Mile: The Complete Serial Novel. New York: Plume, 1997.

Six Stories. Bangor, ME: Philtrum, 1997.

Bag of Bones. New York: Scribner, 1998.

Storm of the Century. New York: Pocket Books, 1999.

The Girl Who Loved Tom Gordon. New York: Scribner, 1999.

The New Lieutenant's Rap. Bangor, ME: Philtrum Press, 1999.

Hearts in Atlantis. New York: Scribner, 1999.

Blood and Smoke. New York: Simon and Schuster Audioworks, 2000 (audio book only).

Riding the Bullet. New York: Scribner/Philtrum Press, 2000 (electronic book). Released in a print edition: *Riding the Bullet: The Deluxe Special Edition Double,* by Mick Garris and Stephen King. Baltimore, MD: Lonely Road Books, 2010.

On Writing: A Memoir of the Craft. New York: Scribner, 2000.

Secret Windows: Essays and Fiction on the Craft of Writing. New York: Book of the Month Club, 2000.

Dreamcatcher. New York: Scribner, 2001.

Black House. New York: Random House, 2001.

Everything's Eventual: 14 Dark Tales. New York: Scribner, 2002.

From a Buick 8. New York: Scribner, 2002.

The Dark Tower: The Gunslinger (Revised and Expanded Edition). New York: Viking, 2003.

The Dark Tower V: Wolves of the Calla. Hampton Falls, NH: Donald M. Grant, 2003.

The Dark Tower VI: Song of Susannah. Hampton Falls, NH: Donald M. Grant, 2004.

The Dark Tower VII: The Dark Tower. Hampton Falls, NH: Donald M. Grant, 2004.

Faithful: Two Diehard Boston Red Sox Fans Chronicle the 2004 Season. New York: Scribner, 2004.

The Colorado Kid. New York: Hard Case Crime Book, 2005.

Cell. New York: Scribner, 2006.

The Secretary of Dreams, Volume I. Baltimore, MD: Cemetery Dance, 2006.

Lisey's Story. New York: Scribner, 2006.

Blaze: A Posthumous Novel. New York: Scribner, 2007.

Duma Key. New York: Scribner, 2008.

Just After Sunset. New York: Scribner, 2008.

Stephen King Goes to the Movies. New York: Pocket Books, 2009.

UR. Electronic book (for Amazon's Kindle device), February 12, 2009. Audio book, New York: Simon and Schuster Audio, [February] 2010.

Under the Dome. New York: Scribner, 2009.

Blockade Billy. Baltimore, MD: Cemetery Dance Publications, 2010.

Full Dark, No Stars. New York: Scribner, 2010.

The Secretary of Dreams, Volume II. Baltimore, MD: Cemetery Dance, 2010.

Short Fiction and Poetry

Where pieces were first published other than in a King collection, the first publication is noted, along with the King volume in which it was later collected or adapted.

"Jumper." *Dave's Rag.* Published by King and his brother, David, in Durham, Maine. Part 1, December 29, 1959. Part 2 and 3, Unknown. Collected in *Secret Windows.*

"Rush Call." *Dave's Rag.* Published by King and his brother, David, in Durham, Maine, 1960. Collected in *Secret Windows.*

"The Hotel at the End of the Road." *People, Places, and Things.* Self-published by King and Chris Chesley under the name Triad Publishing Company, 1960. Also in *Market Guide for Young Writers,* 4th Edition, edited by Kathy Henderson. Cincinnati: Writer's Digest Books, 1993.

"I've Got to Get Away!" *People, Places, and Things.* Self-published by King and Chris Chesley under the name Triad Publishing Company, 1960.

"The Thing at the Bottom of the Well." *People, Places, and Things.* Self-published by King and Chris Chesley under the name Triad Publishing Company, 1960.

"The Stranger." *People, Places, and Things.* Self-published by King and Chris Chesley under the name Triad Publishing Company, 1960.

"The Cursed Expedition." *People, Places, and Things.* Self-published by King and Chris Chesley under the name Triad Publishing Company, 1960.

"The Other Side of the Fog." *People, Places, and Things.* Self-published by King and Chris Chesley under the name Triad Publishing Company, 1960.

"Never Look Behind You." *People, Places, and Things.* Self-published by King and Chris Chesley under the name Triad Publishing Company, 1960.

"The Star Invaders." Self-published, June 1964.

"Code Name: Mousetrap." *The Drum,* Lisbon High School newspaper, Lisbon, Maine. Vol. 3, No. 1 (October 27, 1965).

"I Was a Teen-age Grave Robber." *Comics Review.* Chapters 1 and 2, No. 1 ([May] 1965). Chapters 3 and 4, Vol. 1, No. 2 (June 1965). Chapters 5 and 6, No. 3 (1965). Chapters 7, 8 and 9, No. 4 (1965).

"In a Half-World of Terror." *Stories of Suspense,* MW Publications, No. 2 (1966).

"The 43rd Dream." *The Drum,* Lisbon High

School newspaper, Lisbon, Maine. Vol. 3, No. 4 (January 29, 1966).

"The Glass Floor." *Startling Mystery Stories*. Vol. 1, No. 6 (Fall 1967).

"Here There Be Tygers." *Ubris*, University of Maine, Orono, literary magazine (Spring 1968). Collected in *Skeleton Crew*.

"Cain Rose Up." *Ubris*, University of Maine, Orono, literary magazine (Spring 1968). Collected in *Skeleton Crew*.

"Strawberry Spring." *Ubris*, University of Maine, Orono, literary magazine (Fall 1968). Collected in *Night Shift*.

"Harrison State Park '68." *Ubris*, University of Maine, Orono, literary magazine (Fall 1968).

"Night Surf." *Ubris*, University of Maine, Orono, literary magazine (Spring 1969). Collected in *Night Shift*.

"The Reaper's Image." *Startling Mystery Stories*, Vol. 2, No. 6 (Whole No. 12) (Spring 1969). Collected in *Skeleton Crew*.

"Stud City." *Ubris*, University of Maine, Orono, literary magazine (Fall 1969). Collected in" "The Body" in *Different Seasons*.

"The Dark Man." *Ubris*, University of Maine, Orono, literary magazine (Fall 1969).

"Slade." *The Summer Campus*, University of Maine, Orono, student newspaper. Chapter 1 (June 11, 1970), Chapter 2 (June 18, 1970), Chapter 3 (June 25, 1970), Chapter 4 (July 2, 1970), Chapter 5 (July 9, 1970), Chapter 6 (July 23, 1970), Chapter 7 (July 30, 1970), Chapter 8 (August 6, 1970).

"Graveyard Shift." *Cavalier* (October 1970). Collected in *Night Shift*.

"Donovan's Brain." *Moth*, University of Maine, Orono, literary magazine (1970).

"Silence." *Moth*, University of Maine, Orono, literary magazine (1970).

"The Blue Air Compressor." *Onan*, University of Maine, Orono, literary magazine (Spring [January] 1971).

Untitled ("In the Key-chords of Dawn."). *Onan*, University of Maine, Orono, literary magazine (Spring [January] 1971).

"I Am the Doorway." *Cavalier* (March 1971). Collected in *Night Shift*.

Untitled ("She has gone to sleep while..."). *Contraband*, No. 1, arranged and edited by Bruce Holsapple and Michael Barriault. Portland, ME: Contraband Press, 31 October 1971.

"Woman with Child." *Contraband*, No. 1, arranged and edited by Bruce Holsapple and Michael Barriault. Portland, ME: Contraband Press, 31 October 1971.

"The Hardcase Speaks." *Contraband*, No. 2, arranged and edited by Bruce Holsapple and Michael Barriault. Portland, ME: Contraband Press, 1 December 1971.

"Brooklyn August." *Io*, No. 10 ("Baseball Issue"), Cape Elizabeth, ME: Io Publications (1971). Collected in *Nightmares and Dreamscapes*.

"Suffer the Little Children." *Cavalier* (February 1972). Collected in *Nightmares and Dreamscapes*.

"The Fifth Quarter." *Cavalier* (April 1972). Collected in *Nightmares and Dreamscapes*.

"Battleground." *Cavalier* (September 1972). Collected in *Night Shift*.

"The Mangler." *Cavalier* (December 1972). Collected in *Night Shift*.

"The Boogeyman." *Cavalier* (March 1973). Collected in *Night Shift*.

"Trucks." *Cavalier* (June 1973). Collected in *Night Shift*.

"Gray Matter." *Cavalier* (October 1973). Collected in *Night Shift*.

"It Grows on You." *Marshroots*, Vol. Three, No. 1 (Fall 1973). Collected in *Nightmares and Dreamscapes*.

"Sometimes They Come Back." *Cavalier* (March 1974). Collected in *Night Shift*.

"The Lawnmower Man." *Cavalier* (May 1975). Collected in *Night Shift*.

"The Revenge of Lard Ass Hogan." *The Maine Review* (July 1975). Collected in *The Body* in *Different Seasons*.

"Weeds." *Cavalier* (May 1976). As" "The Lonesome Death of Jordy Verrill" in *Creepshow*.

"The Ledge." *Penthouse* (July 1976). Collected in *Night Shift*.

"I Know What You Need." *Cosmopolitan* (September 1976). Collected in *Night Shift*.

"The Cat from Hell." *Cavalier* (June 1977). Collected in *Just After Sunset*.

"Children of the Corn." *Penthouse* (March 1977). Collected in *Night Shift*.

"One for the Road." *Maine* (March–April 1977). Collected in *Night Shift*.

"The King Family and the Wicked Witch." *Flint*, newspaper, Manhattan, Kansas (August 25, 1977).

"The Man Who Loved Flowers." *Gallery* (August 1977). Collected in *Night Shift*.

"The Night of the Tiger." *The Magazine of Fantasy and Science Fiction*, Vol. 54, No. 2 (February 1978).

"The Gunslinger." *The Magazine of Fantasy and Science Fiction* Vol. 55, No. 4 (October 1978). *The Dark Tower: The Gunslinger.*

"Man with a Belly." *Cavalier* (December 1978).

"Jerusalem's Lot." *Night Shift*.

"The Last Rung on the Ladder." *Night Shift*.

"Quitters, Inc." *Night Shift*.

"The Woman in the Room." *Night Shift*.

"Nona." *Shadows*, edited by Charles L. Grant. Garden City, NY: Doubleday, 1978. Collected in *Skeleton Crew*.

"The Crate." *Gallery* (July 1979). Collected in *Creepshow*.

"The Way Station." *The Magazine of Fantasy and Science Fiction* Vol. 58, No. 4 (April 1980). *The Dark Tower: The Gunslinger*.

"The Mist." *Dark Forces: New Stories of Suspense and Supernatural Horror*, edited by Kirby McCauley. New York: Viking, 1980. Collected in *Skeleton Crew*.

"The Monkey." *Gallery* (November 1980). Collected in *Skeleton Crew*.

"The Wedding Gig." *Ellery Queen's Mystery Magazine*, Vol. 76, No. 6 (December 1, 1980). Collected in *Skeleton Crew*.

"Big Wheels: A Tale of the Laundry Game." *New Terrors*, edited by Ramsey Campbell. New York: Pocket Books, October 1982. Collected in *Skeleton Crew*.

"Crouch End." *New Tales of the Cthulhu Mythos*, edited by Ramsey Campbell. Sauk City, WI: Arkham House, 1980. Collected in *Nightmares and Dreamscapes*.

"The Oracle and the Mountains." *The Magazine of Fantasy and Science Fiction*, Vol. 60, No. 2 (February 1981). *The Dark Tower: The Gunslinger*.

"The Jaunt." *The Twilight Zone Magazine* (June 1981). Collected in *Skeleton Crew*.

"The Slow Mutants." *The Magazine of Fantasy and Science Fiction*, Vol. 61, No. 1 (July 1981). *The Dark Tower: The Gunslinger*.

"The Bird and the Album." *A Fantasy Reader: The Seventh World Fantasy Convention Program Book*, edited by Jeff Frane and Jack Rems. Berkeley, CA: Seventh World Fantasy Convention, October 30, 1981. *It*.

"The Monster in the Closet." *Ladies' Home Journal* (October 1981). *Cujo*.

"The Man Who Would Not Shake Hands." *Shadows 4*, edited by Charles L. Grant. Garden City, NY: Doubleday, 1981. Collected in *Skeleton Crew*.

"Do the Dead Sing?" *Yankee* (November 1981). As "The Reach" in *Skeleton Crew*.

"The Gunslinger and the Dark Man." *The Magazine of Fantasy and Science Fiction*, Vol. 61, No. 5 (November 1981). *The Dark Tower: The Gunslinger*.

"Survivor Type." *Terrors*, edited by Charles L. Grant. New York: Playboy Paperbacks, July 1982. Collected in *Skeleton Crew*.

"Father's Day." *Creepshow*.

"Something to Tide You Over." *Creepshow*.

"They're Creeping Up on You." *Creepshow*.

"Before the Play." *Whispers*, No. 17/18 (August 1982).

"Rita Hayworth and Shawshank Redemption: Hope Springs Eternal." *Different Seasons*.

"Apt Pupil: Summer of Corruption." *Different Seasons*.

"The Body: Fall from Innocence." *Different Seasons*.

"The Breathing Method: A Winter's Tale." *Different Seasons*.

"The Raft." *Gallery* (November 1982). Collected in *Skeleton Crew*.

"Skybar." *The Do-It-Yourself Bestseller: A Workbook*, edited by Tom Silberkleit and Jerry Biederman. New York: Dolphin, 1982.

"The Plant" (print version). Part One: Bangor, ME: Philtrum Press, 1982.

"The Word Processor." *Playboy* (January 1983). As "The Word Processor of the Gods" in *Skeleton Crew*.

"The Return of Timmy Baterman." *Satyricon II Program Book*, edited by Rusty Burke. Knoxville, TN: Satyricon II/DeepSouthCon XXI, June 1983. *Pet Sematary*.

"Uncle Otto's Truck." *Yankee* (October 1983). Collected in *Skeleton Crew*.

"The Plant" (print version). Part Two: Bangor, ME: Philtrum Press, 1983.

"Gramma." *Weirdbook*, No. 19 (Spring 1984). Collected in *Skeleton Crew*.

"Mrs. Todd's Shortcut." *Redbook* (May 1984). Collected in *Skeleton Crew*.

"The Ballad of the Flexible Bullet." *The Magazine of Fantasy and Science Fiction* Vol. 66, No. 6 (June 1984). Collected in *Skeleton Crew*.

"The Revelations of 'Becka Paulson." *Rolling Stone* (July 19–August 2, 1984).

"Beachworld." *Weird Tales* (Fall 1984). Collected in *Skeleton Crew*.

"Dolan's Cadillac." *Castle Rock: The Stephen King Newsletter*. Part 1 (February 1985). Part 2 (March 1985). Part 3 (April 1985). Part 4 (May 1985). Part 5 (June 1985). Collected in *Nightmares and Dreamscapes*.

"Morning Deliveries (Milkman No. 1)." *Skeleton Crew*.

"Paranoid: A Chant." *Skeleton Crew*.

"For Owen." *Skeleton Crew*.

"Heroes for Hope: Starring the X-Men." Comic book, Marvel Comics Group special X-Men issue (December 1, 1985).

"The Plant" (print version). Part Three: Bangor, ME: Philtrum Press, 1985.

"For the Birds." *Bred Any Good Rooks Lately?*, edited by James Charlton. Garden City, NY: Doubleday, 1986.

"The End of the Whole Mess." *Omni* (October 1986). Collected in *Nightmares and Dreamscapes*.

"The Doctor's Case." *The New Adventures of Sherlock Holmes: Original Stories by Eminent Mystery Writers*, edited by Martin Harry Greenberg and Carol-Lynn Rössel Waugh. New York: Carroll and Graf, 1987. Collected in *Nightmares and Dreamscapes*.

"Popsy." *Masques II: All-New Tales of Horror and the Supernatural*, edited by J.N. Williamson. Baltimore: Maclay, 1987. Collected in *Nightmares and Dreamscapes*.

"The Night Flier." *Prime Evil: New Stories by the Masters of Modern Horror*, edited by Douglas E. Winter. West Kingston, RI: Donald M. Grant, 1988. Collected in *Nightmares and Dreamscapes*.

"The Reploids." *Night Visions 5*, edited by Douglas E. Winter. Arlington Heights, IL: Dark Harvest, 1988.

"Sneakers." *Night Visions 5*, edited by Douglas E. Winter. Arlington Heights, IL: Dark Harvest, 1988. Collected in *Nightmares and Dreamscapes*.

"Dedication." *Night Visions 5*, edited by Douglas E. Winter. Arlington Heights, IL: Dark Harvest, 1988. Collected in *Nightmares and Dreamscapes*.

"Rainy Season." *Midnight Graffiti* (Spring 1989). Collected in *Nightmares and Dreamscapes*.

"Home Delivery." *Book of the Dead*, edited by John Skipp and Craig Spector. Willimantic, CT: Mark V. Ziesing, 1989. Collected in *Nightmares and Dreamscapes*.

"Secret Window, Secret Garden." *Four Past Midnight*.

"The Library Policeman." *Four Past Midnight*.

"The Sun Dog." *Four Past Midnight*.

"The Moving Finger." *The Magazine of Fantasy and Science Fiction*, Vol. 79, No. 6 (December 1990). Collected in *Nightmares and Dreamscapes*.

"The Bear." *The Magazine of Fantasy and Science Fiction*, Vol. 79, No. 6 (December 1990). *The Dark Tower III: The Waste Lands*.

"You Know They Got a Hell of a Band." *Shock Rock: The New Sound of Horror*, edited by Jeff Gelb and Claire Zion. New York: Pocket Books, 1992. Collected in *Nightmares and Dreamscapes*.

"Chattery Teeth." *Cemetery Dance*, No. 14 (Fall 1992). Collected in *Nightmares and Dreamscapes*.

"Umney's Last Case." *Nightmares and Dreamscapes*.

"The Ten O'clock People." *Nightmares and Dreamscapes*.

"The House on Maple Street." *Nightmares and Dreamscapes*.

"The Beggar and the Diamond." *Nightmares and Dreamscapes*.

"Jhonathan and the Witchs." *First Words: Earliest Writing from Favorite Contemporary Authors*, collected and edited by Paul Mandelbaum. Chapel Hill, NC: Algonquin, 1993.

"The Killer." *Famous Monsters of Filmland*, No. 202 (Spring 1994).

"Blind Willie." *Antaeus: The Final Issue*, edited by Daniel Halpern. Hopewell, NJ: Ecco Press, No. 75-76 (Autumn 1994). Collected in *Hearts in Atlantis*.

"Dino." *The Salt Hill Journal*, No. 1, edited by Michael Paul Thomas. Syracuse University, Syracuse, NY, Autumn 1994.

"The Man in the Black Suit." *The New Yorker* (October 31, 1994). Collected in *Everything's Eventual*.

"Luckey Quarter." *USA Weekend* (June 30-July 2, 1995). Collected in *Everything's Eventual*.

"Lunch at the Gotham Café." *Dark Love: Twenty-two All-original Tales of Lust and Obsession*, edited by Nancy A. Collins, Edward E. Kramer, and Martin Harry Greenberg. New York: Roc Book, 1995. Collected in *Everything's Eventual*.

"L.T.'s Theory of Pets." *Six Stories*. Also collected in *Everything's Eventual*.

"Autopsy Room Four." *Six Stories*. Also collected in *Everything's Eventual*.

"Everything's Eventual." *The Magazine of Fantasy and Science Fiction* Vol. 93, No. 4 and 5 (Whole No. 556) (October-November 1997). Collected in *Everything's Eventual*.

"That Feeling, You Can Only Say What It Is in French." *The New Yorker* (June 22-29, 1998). Collected in *Everything's Eventual*.

"The Little Sisters of Eluria." *Legends: Short Novels by the Masters of Modern Fantasy*, edited by Robert Silverberg. New York: Tor, 1998. Collected in *Everything's Eventual*.

"Low Men in Yellow Coats." *Hearts in Atlantis*.

"Hearts in Atlantis." *Hearts in Atlantis*.

"Why We're in Vietnam." *Hearts in Atlantis*.

"Heavenly Shades of Night Are Falling." *Hearts in Atlantis*.

"The Road Virus Heads North." *999: New Stories of Horror and Suspense*, edited by Al Sarrantonio. Baltimore: Hill House /Cemetery Dance, 1999. Collected in *Everything's Eventual*.

"1408." *Blood and Smoke*. Also collected in *Everything's Eventual*.

"In the Deathroom." *Blood and Smoke*. Also collected in *Everything's Eventual*.

"The Old Dude's Ticker." *Necon XX: Twentieth Anniversary Commemorative Volume*, edited by Bob Booth. Bristol, RI: The Necon (Northeastern Writers' Conference) Committee, July 2000.

"The Plant," Installment One. Bangor, ME: Philtrum Press, 2000 (electronic book only).

"The Plant," Installment Two. Bangor, ME: Philtrum Press, 2000 (electronic book only).

"The Plant," Installment Three. Bangor, ME: Philtrum Press, 2000 (electronic book only).

"The Plant," Installment Four. Bangor, ME: Philtrum Press, 2000 (electronic book only).

"The Plant" [Installment Five]. Bangor, ME: Philtrum Press, 2000 (electronic book only).

"The Plant," Installment Six. Bangor, ME: Philtrum Press, 2000 (electronic book only).

"All That You Love Will Be Carried Away." *The*

New Yorker (January 29, 2001). Collected in *Everything's Eventual.*

"Dark Tower V — Prologue: Calla Bryn Sturgis." Posted on King's official Internet site, www. stephenking.com (August 21, 2001). *The Dark Tower V: Wolves of the Calla.*

"The Death of Jack Hamilton." *The New Yorker* (December 24–31, 2001). Collected in *Everything's Eventual.*

"The Tale of Gray Dick." *McSweeney's Quarterly Concern*, No. 10 (January 2003), edited by Michael Chabon. Collected in *The Dark Tower V: Wolves of the Calla Harvey's Dream. The New Yorker* (June 30, 2003). Collected in *Just After Sunset.*

"Rest Stop." *Esquire* (December 2003). Collected in *Just After Sunset.*

"Stationary Bike." *Borderlands 5: An Anthology of Imaginative Fiction*, edited by Elizabeth E. Monteleone and Thomas F. Monteleone. Grantham, NH: Borderlands Press, 2003. Collected in *Just After Sunset.*

"Lisey and the Madman." *McSweeney's Enchanted Chamber of Astonishing Stories*, edited by Michael Chabon. New York: Vintage Books, 2004. *Lisey's Story.*

"The Things They Left Behind." *Transgressions*, edited by Ed McBain. New York: Forge Books, 2005. Collected in *Just After Sunset.*

"The Pulse." www.amazon.com (July 7, 2005). *Cell.*

"The Furnace." *Know Your World Extra*, magazine distributed to grade school students; published by The Weekly Reader Corporation. Vol. 39, No. 2 (September 23, 2005).

"Chapter 71— Sword in the Darkness." *Stephen King: Uncollected, Unpublished*, by Rocky Wood with David Rawsthorne and Norma Blackburn. Baltimore, MD: Cemetery Dance, 2005.

"Memory." *Tin House*, Vol. 7, No. 4 (Issue No. 28) (Summer 2006). *Duma Key.*

"Willa." *Playboy* (December 2006). Collected in *Just After Sunset.*

"Graduation Afternoon." *Postscripts*, No. 10, edited by Peter Crowther and Nick Gevers. Hornsea, United Kingdom: PS Publishing, Spring 2007. Collected in *Just After Sunset.*

"The Gingerbread Girl." *Esquire* (July 2007). Collected in *Just After Sunset.*

"Ayana." *The Paris Review*, No. 182 (Fall 2007). Collected in *Just After Sunset.*

"Mute." *Playboy* (December 2007). Collected in *Just After Sunset.*

"A Very Tight Place." *McSweeney's Quarterly Concern* No. 27 (May 2008). Collected in *Just After Sunset.*

"The *New York Times* at Special Bargain Rates." *The Magazine of Fantasy and Science Fiction.* Volume 115, No. 4 and 5 (October-November, 2008). Collected in *Just After Sunset.*

"N." *Just After Sunset.*

"Throttle." *He is Legend: An Anthology Celebrating Richard Matheson*, edited by Christopher Conlon. Colorado Springs, CO: Gauntlet Publications, 2009.

"Mostly Old Men." *Tin House*, Vol. 10, No. 4 (Issue No. 40) (Summer 2009).

"Morality." *Esquire* (July 2009). *Blockade Billy.*

"The Cannibals." (Part One) www.stephenking. com. September 15, 2009.

"The Cannibals." (Part Two) www.stephenking. com. October 4, 2009.

"Untitled" (excerpt from unpublished story" "Muffe"). *The Stephen King Illustrated Companion*, by Bev Vincent. New York, New York: Fall River Press, 2009.

"The Bone Church." *Playboy* (November 2009).

"Premium Harmony." *The New Yorker* (November 9, 2009).

"Black Ribbons." *Black Ribbons*, by Shooter Jennings and Hierophant. Black Rock Records/ Rocket Science Ventures, 2010.

"Tommy." *Playboy* (March 2010).

"American Vampire." *American Vampire.* New York: Vertigo. No. 1 (May 2010). No. 2 (June 2010). No. 3 (July 2010). No. 4 (August 2010). No. 5 (September 2010).

"1922." *Full Dark, No Stars.*

"Big Driver." *Full Dark, No Stars.*

"Fair Extension." *Full Dark, No Stars.*

"A Good Marriage." *Full Dark, No Stars.*

Further Reading

The following books will assist those interested in a broad survey of King's canon and the importance of his work. Readers should note that older books often contain outdated material and errors of fact. In compiling this book the author undertook original research to compile the vast majority of the material, facts and quotes included. In most cases this meant accessing and checking original published (and unpublished) material.

Beahm, George. *Stephen King Collectibles: An Illustrated Price Guide.* Williamsburg, VA: GB Books, 2000.

_____. *Stephen King from A to Z.* Kansas City, MO: Andrews McMeel, 1998.

_____. *The Stephen King Story.* London: Little, Brown, 1993.

Blue, Tyson. *The Unseen King.* Mercer Island, WA: Starmont, 1989.

Brooks, Justin. *Stephen King: A Primary Bibliography of the World's Most Popular Author.* Abingdon, MD: Cemetery Dance Publications, 2006.

Collings, Michael R. *Horror Plum'd: An International Stephen King Bibliography and Guide.* Woodstock, GA: Overlook Connection Press, 2002.

_____. *The Stephen King Phenomenon.* Mercer Island, WA: Starmont House, 1987.

Furth, Robin. *The Dark Tower: The Complete Concordance.* Baltimore: Cemetery Dance Publications, 2009.

Jones, Stephen. *Creepshows: The Illustrated Stephen King Movie Guide.* New York: Billboard Books, 2002.

Landa, Elaine. "I Am a Hick, and This is Where I Feel at Home." In *Feast of Fear.* Edited by Tim Underwood and Chuck Miller. New York: Carroll and Graf, 1989.

Spignesi, Stephen J. *The Essential Stephen King.* Williamsburg, VA: GB Books, 2001.

_____. *Lost Work of Stephen King: A Guide to Unpublished Manuscripts, Story Fragments, Alternative Versions, and Oddities.* Secaucus, NJ: Birch Lane Press, 1998.

_____. *The Shape Under the Sheet: The Complete Stephen King Encyclopedia.* Ann Arbor, MI: Popular Culture Ink, October 1991.

Terrell, Carroll F. *Stephen King: Man and Artist.* Orono, ME: Northern Lights, 1990.

Underwood, Tim, and Chuck Miller. *Feast of Fear: Conversations with Stephen King.* New York: Warner Books, 1993.

Vincent, Bev. *The Road to the Dark Tower: Exploring Stephen King's Magnum Opus.* New York, NY: New American Library, 2004.

_____. *The Stephen King Illustrated Companion.* New York, NY: Fall River Press, 2009.

Winter, Douglas. *Stephen King: The Art of Darkness.* New York, NY: New American Library, 1986.

Wood, Rocky, David Rawsthorne and Norma Blackburn. *The Complete Guide to the Works of Stephen King* (third edition). Melbourne, Australia: Kanrock Partners, 2004.

Wood, Rocky, and Justin Brooks. *Stephen King: The Non-Fiction.* Baltimore: Cemetery Dance Publications, 2008.

Wood, Rocky, with David Rawsthorne and Norma Blackburn. *Stephen King: Uncollected, Unpublished.* Baltimore: Cemetery Dance Publications, 2005.

Index